Living with Grief: Diversity and End-of-Life Care

Edited by
Kenneth J. Doka & Amy S. Tucci
Foreword by Richard Payne

**HOSPICE FOUNDATION
OF AMERICA**

This book is part of Hospice Foundation of America's *Living with Grief* ® series

This book is part of HFA's *Living with Grief®* series.

Ordering information:

Call Hospice Foundation of America: 800-854-3402

Or write:
Hospice Foundation of America
1621 Connecticut Avenue, NW #300
Washington, DC 20009

Or visit HFA's website:
www.hospicefoundation.org

Managing Editor: Keith Johnson
Typesetting and Design: The YGS Group

Publisher's Cataloging-in-Publication
(*Provided by Quality Books, Inc.*)

Living with grief : diversity and end-of-life care / edited
    by Kenneth J. Doka & Amy S. Tucci ; foreword by Richard
    Payne.
        p. cm.
    Includes bibliographical references and index.
    LCCN 2008943061
    ISBN-13: 978-1-893349-10-0
    ISBN-10: 1-893349-10-1

    1. Death--Social aspects--Cross-cultural studies.
    2. Grief--Cross-cultural studies. 3. Bereavement--
    Cross-cultural studies. 4. Terminal care--
    Cross-cultural studies. 5. Funeral rites and ceremonies
    --Cross-cultural studies.   I. Doka, Kenneth J.
    II. Tucci, Amy S.   III. Title: Diversity and end-of-life
    care.

HQ1073.L57 2009   306.9
                                QBI08-200016

Dedication

To my Godson, Keith
As he begins his post-college life

To my nephew, Dylan
As he begins college

And to my grandchildren, Kenny and Lucy
As they begin their educational journeys.

Kenneth J. Doka

To all of those who work to make the dying process an
experience in which a patient's and family's culture is treated
with the respect and reverence it deserves.

Kenneth J. Doka & Amy S. Tucci

Contents

Foreword

Richard Payne

The proverb that opens this book, "Every person is like all others, like some others, and like no others," makes three important points. It points to a great challenge for professional and family caregivers who wish to be present and supportive of the terminally ill and bereaved. It should be the guiding principle as we journey with each person through illness and loss. After all, death is one of the few things that every individual on the planet will experience. And, we will all feel its sting through the loss of family and loved ones. Thus, through experiencing illness and loss, we acknowledge our common humanity—that "every person is like all others." It has been said that "our confrontation with death lays bare the spiritual dimension of the human experience" (Ira Byock, personal communication). This spiritual dimension that becomes evident when facing our mortality involves a nearly universal yearning to understand our connection to other people, to wonder about creation (and perhaps a Creator), and to find meaning in the life that is about to end. When confronted with terminal illness, the imminent loss of self, or the loss of a loved one, important spiritual values (which transcend race, gender, class, and geography) are paramount: the desire to be in the company of family and loved ones; the desire to be free of physical pain; the desire to reconcile with, and say goodbye to, family and friends.

These values transcend the common social and political categorizations of human life. But the ways in which these needs and desires are voiced, and the way we understand them, demand that we also respond and attend to the nuances and characteristics that make up the rich diversity of our human species. The great common ground of human concern that makes us "like all others" is often confounded by the distinctive cultures of our communities and our individual personalities.

In this context, we are "like some others" in the common cultural patterns that bind us together in a particular community. But even here, there are important caveats. Culture and community often refer to groups of individuals who share a common language, lifestyle, and worldview. Community may be geographically defined or virtual, unencumbered by physical limitations of space and time. Adding to the complexity, notions of community and culture may override racial and ethnic categories and concerns, and make our conventional categorizations problematic and not at all predictive of how people are likely to respond to disease and loss. Examples of these complexities—for example, the Jewish, African-American, Native-American, deaf and hard-of-hearing, or gay, lesbian, bisexual, and transgender communities—are nicely illustrated in this book.

Of course, racial and ethnic characterizations are sharply influenced by socioeconomic considerations. For example, although, in aggregate, African-Americans are very underrepresented in the use of hospice in the United States, a recent study of highly insured individuals in California found that blacks and whites utilized hospice care, within the confines of a single health plan, at approximately equal rates (Keating, Herrinton, Zaslavsky, Liu, & Ayanian, 2006). This data is important in demonstrating that socioeconomic status might be a greater factor for preferences for hospice use than cultural differences stemming from race or ethnicity.

Finally, each individual and family experiencing death and bereavement is "like no other." For example, every spiritual tradition is uniquely interpreted and modified by each of its adherents. As Richard Fife astutely opines in his chapter on "Diversity and Access to Hospice Care," true respect and understanding of individual needs (including religious needs), leads one to acknowledge that current models of end-of-life care and grief and bereavement counseling may not fit all. This calls for better assessment and adaptation of current models of care. For example, more involvement of churches, mosques, and synagogues in hospice life could lead to improved utilization of hospice by underrepresented minorities.

Respect for diversity and individual preference raises questions that go beyond the considerable challenges of being aware and tolerant of different views. Just how far should we go in attempting to meet the individualized needs of the sick and the bereaved? One aspect of becoming culturally competent might involve being comfortable with some people who do not want to work with you. But are all individual preferences, intentions, and motivations legitimate? What about the individual who only feels comfortable with another member of their particular community because they are acting on racist emotions or assumptions about the inferiority of another group? What about the legal obligations of individuals and institutions to uphold non-discrimination laws? Questions such as these raise important challenges to notions of the primacy of personal autonomy and the appropriateness, or even legality, of responding to all individual preferences. As caregivers and professionals, we will be confronted with such challenges. One must carefully analyze the underlying circumstances, always proceeding with a motivation to do what is ethical, legal, and appropriate to facilitate meaning-making and healing for the sick and bereaved. What my death means to me is surely "like no other." It is always helpful to have an awareness of, and sensitivity to, input from diverse perspectives when coming to the best decision or way of responding to specific requests.

This book is about witnessing and appreciating individuality that is built on a foundation of common humanity. The distinctiveness of culture, language, social circumstance, religion, personality, and gender are key foundations by which individuals find meaning and purpose in their living and dying and come to terms with the loss and remembrance of family and loved ones. The authors provide important insights and timely data and information to help us navigate the nourishing yet turbulent waters that accompany death, dying, and bereavement. In the final analysis, it is only by tapping into the commonalities of our humanity and having the desire and skill to learn about and to come to understand another person that we can help our fellow brothers and sisters find meaning in illness, death, and loss.

REFERENCES

Keating, N. L., Herrinton, L. J., Zaslavsky, A. M., Liu, L., & Ayanian, J. Z. (2006). Variations in hospice use among cancer patients. *Journal of the National Cancer Institute, 98*(15), 1053–1090.

Acknowledgments

It is critical to acknowledge the personal and professional relationships that allow us to publish a companion book every year. This so much includes the staff of the Hospice Foundation of America. David Abrams, the now retired president of HFA, always uses his editorial hand to keep us focused. He will be missed. In a small staff, everyone makes an indirect or direct contribution. This includes Sophie Viteri Berman, Keith Johnson, Kristen Baker, Susan Belsinger, Marcia Eaker, Lisa Veglahn, Chester Velasco, and Marceline Bateky. We also acknowledge the authors of these chapters. They are valued for their willingness to share their expertise in such a timely manner.

As editors, there are some acknowledgments shared even as we remember our personal support:

I would like to acknowledge and thank my co-editor Amy Tucci. It continues to be so special to work with her. Her grounded knowledge of the field as well as her incredible journalistic instincts keeps this book, and her co-editor, clear and focused.

I also wish to thank my administrators and colleagues at The College of New Rochelle for maintaining a stimulating environment that allows me to write and edit. I need to thank so many there, including President Stephen Sweeny, Vice-President Dorothy Escribano, Dean Guy Lometti and Associate Dean Marie Ribarich. Diane Lewis and Vera Mezzaucella provide critical assistance. Colleagues at the College of New Rochelle as well as the Association of Death Education and Counseling (ADEC), and The International Work Group on Dying, Death, and Bereavement are always there to offer encouragement, inspiration, and friendship.

I, of course, need to acknowledge all those in my personal life who offer love and help me to balance my life. My son and daughter-in-law, Michael and Angelina, and my grandchildren, Kenny and Lucy, provide love and balance. Other members of my intimate network of family, friends, and neighbors include my godchildren and their families (James Rainbolt, Scott Carlson, and Keith Whitehead), Kathy Dillon, my sister, Dorothy and my brother, Franky, and all of their families as well as Eric Schwarz, Dylan Rieger, Larry Laterza, Ellie Andersen, Jim, Karen and Greg Cassa, Paul Kimbal, Don and Carol Ford,

Allen and Gail Greenstein, Jim and Mary Millar, Robert and Tracey Levy, Linda and Russell Tellier, Jill Boyer, Fred and Lisa Amore, Chris and Dorotta Fields, Lynn Miller, Tom and Lorraine Carlson, Matt Atkins, and Kurt Mulligan, who all offer support and frienship.

—Kenneth J. Doka

I, too, would like to acknowledge my co-editor, Ken Doka. During our five years of working together on the *Living with Grief*® series and *Journeys*, Ken has amazed me with his deep knowledge of the subject at hand and his limitless energy to produce quality products for so many audiences: families, professionals, and students of end-of-life care. Beyond the professional realm, however, he's a terrific person who I'm proud to call my friend.

One person on HFA's staff deserves special recognition for his role in this book. Keith Johnson, managing editor for *Cultural Diversity and End-of-Life Care*, oversaw the editing and production of the book. It is his first year at this daunting task, which involves everything from the business of contracts and deadlines to grammar and style sheets. This is a job that even large publishers run from; Keith is to be commended for his work.

Our printer, The YGS Group, was also instrumental in making this project a success. It is York's imaginative artwork, as well, developed by their graphic artists, which so creatively captures the message inherent in this book. It is as if all of the multi-colored hands are reaching out to be called on, to be recognized, and to share what is important to them, both as individuals and as members of cultural groups who have their own important identities.

I would also like to acknowledge EEI Communications, which provides editorial support to us; the company's copyeditors, proofreaders, and indexers are instrumental to our maintaining the quality standards that we insist upon.

Finally, I want to thank my family, Michael, Nicholas, and Rebecca for their love and support that I treasure each day.

—Amy S. Tucci

We continue to acknowledge the legacy of the late Jack Gordon, founder and former chair of Hospice Foundation of America and the continued assistance of his wife, Myra McPherson. This teleconference and book, we hope, are some of their many ongoing legacies.

Understanding and Responding to Cultural Diversity

There is a proverb that states, "Every person is like all others, like some others, and like no others." This paradoxical proverb recognizes three major truths. First, every human being shares some common human needs. It is also true that each person is like no other—this truism affirms the individuality of each of us. Yet, there is also validity in the statement that every person is like some others. This confirms that we share a variety of cultural identities with those around us and acknowledges the commonalities that emerge within our shared cultural identity.

Cultural diversity is more than simply a buzzword. Regulatory agencies now assess the way organizations like hospice address the needs of diverse populations. It is critical that they do so. Since the 1965 Immigration Act, the United States has become even more diverse as immigrants migrate not only from Europe, but also from Asia, Africa, South America, and the Middle East. As they have migrated, the United States has become increasingly diverse—ethnically, racially, and spiritually. Hospitals and hospices that wish to effectively serve these diverse populations and thrive in this new environment do well to increase their own sensitivities and skills in order to more effectively reach out to newer groups in their service areas.

In doing so, it is important to recognize that there are multiple sources of diversity. Race, ethnicity, and spirituality are three major sources. Yet, it is dangerous to characterize persons simply by their membership in one cultural group. Most individuals juggle multiple identities—race, religion, ethnicity, gender, social class—that wax and wane in personal importance as they navigate the various problems of everyday life. In the varied crises of end-of-life care, it is always important to assess what identities become the critical defining ones.

In this book, culture is defined as a *way of life*. Hence, cultural identities can be based on a number of variables or multiple sources of diversity. Section II considers race and ethnicity. Section III focuses on spirituality as a source of cultural diversity. A final section considers other sources of diversity such as sexual orientation, shared life experiences, or cultures of disability.

Yet, even this relatively wide-ranging list of topics does not give full service to the diversity of diversity itself. Social class—often implied and sometimes addressed in these chapters—remains a major source of diversity, affecting everything from a person's chance of being born healthy to the age and cause of his or her death. Sensitivity to social class is often neglected. For example, a photomontage, a staple activity in children's bereavement groups, may assume that a child has ample photos—an assumption that may be incorrect in lower-income populations.

Joel Garreau describes another source of diversity in his book, *The Nine Nations of North America* (1981). He divides North America into nine geographic cultural regions. Each region, Garreau notes, has its own distinct way of life and unique culture. Similarly, Strauss and Howe (1991) explore generational differences as a source of diversity. Gender is another identity by which individuals define themselves.

Five chapters in this section broadly explore the theme of diversity. Bert Hayslip and GiBaeg Han begin with an overview of cultural differences related to dying a "good death," end-of-life decision making, and grief. While acknowledging the distinct differences that exist *between* groups, the authors remind readers of the important differences *within* groups. Their chapter provides a basis for understanding core differences and values. Hayslip and Han reaffirm that cultural competence begins by asking the right questions rather than assuming to know the correct answer. Paul Rosenblatt's chapter echoes many of these themes as he focuses on the culturally competent counselor. Rosenblatt stresses that while knowledge and skill are critical components of cultural competence, it is also essential to have an open and accepting attitude—one that is constantly willing to learn and accept people, patients, and families on their own terms.

Bruce Jennings notes another aspect of diversity in end-of-life care. As Jennings discusses end-of-life ethics, he calls attention to the highly individualistic framework that has developed in Western bioethics—one that might not be shared by cultures with a more familial, communal, or collectivist ethos. Jennings notes that reliance on broad ethical principles alone is unlikely to bridge these gaps. The key lies in a respectful process of communication that acknowledges that even core bioethical principles may not translate well across diverse cultures.

Richard Fife offers a chapter on access to hospice care. While hospice has been one of the most successful social innovations of the past half-century, not all cultural groups have embraced it. Fife's chapter offers two great gifts. First, there is a careful analysis of why some groups have different levels of acceptance of hospice care. Second, Fife offers examples of successful programs to increase access to hospice even among resistant populations. The chapter offers another question relevant to diversity. Acceptance of diversity means that one may need to acknowledge that any form of care, including hospice and palliative care, may not always be a good fit with all cultural groups.

Stephen Mack and Sumner Waring's chapter on funeral rituals concludes this section. This chapter emphasizes that numerous sources of diversity, including religion, ethnicity, and age, are encouraging funeral directors to both understand and embrace diversity. Their practical suggestions for signage and materials in languages other than English, as well as for sensitivity to the way structures support diversity, has import for and beyond funeral service.

Together, these chapters remind readers of the need to look at practices through different lenses. Each cultural group has its own perceptions—a unique way to understand reality. However, even when one dons these lenses, one should remain sensitive to both common human needs and individual differences. The proverb holds true: "Every person is like all others, like some others, and like no others."

REFERENCES

Garreau, J. (1981). *The nine nations of North America.* Boston: Houghton Mifflin.

Strauss, W., & Howe, N. (1991). *Generations: The history of America's future* (pp. 1584–2069). New York: Quill.

Cultural Influences on Death, Dying, and Bereavement: An Overview

Bert Hayslip, Jr. and GiBaeg Han

Culture is central in preparing for a "good death," and clarity regarding culture is vital for end-of-life care workers. In a diverse society such as the United States, people nearing death and their families often must interact with representatives of hospitals, hospices, churches, and funeral homes. In this chapter, we will look at the impact of culture on attitudes toward dying, end-of-life care, and grief and bereavement. We will set aside the idea that the dying or grieving process can be described by any single theory of death (e.g., that of Kübler-Ross) or grief (e.g., stage-based models). Being aware of how cultural variations relate to different parameters of death (e.g., cause of death, relationship to the dying or deceased person, the death trajectory, or the dying person's age and gender) is very important—if not required—for understanding dying and grieving. In the United States, patterns of mourning vary according to different cultural heritages. And, mourning traditions can change, sometimes rapidly (Matsumoto, 2000).

Whether our expectations about grief are confirmed depends on how much grievers identify with culturally patterned expressions of mourning. Although there is some agreement that the core experience of grief is similar across cultures (see Corr, Nabe, & Corr, 2009), expressions of mourning may be subject to a particular culture's script (Long, 2004). Our assumptions regarding these issues may be inaccurate if we apply them to persons whose life experiences and cultural heritages are different from our own. Acknowledging the influence of culture on people's views and behaviors may enhance communication and improve services for those who do not speak English or who are from a different culture.

Culture shapes what is considered a "good" or a "bad" death (Seale & van der Geest, 2004), the value of autonomy, how pain is experienced, the role of the family in caring for the dying, end-of-life decisions, and the meaning attributed to death and suffering (Werth, Blevins, Toussaint, & Durham, 2002). Culture influences whether the patient should be told of a terminal illness; how quality of life is defined; and how, when, and how long mourners should grieve. Awareness of cultural differences can help the staffs of intensive care units, hospices, and nursing homes deliver more sensitive and compassionate care (allowing dying persons "to feel less isolated, more intimate in their relationships with others") and provide closure ("allowing those involved to seek understanding and meaning") (Bourgeois & Johnson, 2004, p. 100). Such care should be provided in a nonjudgmental way and should communicate respect for the dying person's cultural uniqueness. Long (2004) described several cultural scripts that help people "die well," including some that emphasize modern medicine and some that emphasize religion. Such scripts are chosen relative to the time and place of death as well as one's personhood in the context of dying.

A good death (at least in Western culture) involves being at peace, accepting the timeliness of the death, embracing one's family, being of little burden to loved ones, minimizing pain to self and to family members, and communicating final goodbyes (Hansson & Stroebe, 2007). In this context, Rosenblatt (2008) says that culture provides us with meaning (embedded in our own beliefs and religious systems), traditional scripts for caring for the dying and deceased, and for the capacity for continuing relationships between the deceased and surviving friends and family.

Central to our discussion is what Kastenbaum and Aisenberg (1972) have termed the *death system*—the "sociophysical network by which we mediate and express our relationship to mortality" (p. 310). The death system's expectations, norms, and mores can mediate or buffer our relationship with death, dying, and grieving. In some cases, it can protect us from the harshness of death and grief, as predicted in Terror Management Theory (e.g., McCoy, Pyszczynski, Solomon, & Greenberg, 2000). In other cases, the death system may exacerbate death's impact, as exemplified by Doka's (2002) notion of disenfranchised grief. Thus, one's culture is the medium through which basic emotions and behaviors that define dying and grieving are expressed (Cole, 1999).

DEFINING CULTURE

Culture can be described as the average, mainstream tendencies of a group of persons, but it does not accurately predict all aspects of behavior for all persons in the culture (Matsumoto, 2000). Rosenblatt (2008) characterizes cultures as social constructions that encompass "language, beliefs, practices, history, identity, something like a religion, and so on" (p. 208). Culture's influence must be inferred through our behavior—actions, rituals, and traditions. Culture is never static; rather, it is dynamic and changing in the context of such behaviors (Matsumoto, 2000; Rosenblatt, 2008). Because of differences in acculturation (Matsumoto, 2000), little can be learned from studies that compare dying or grieving among persons categorized solely by race or ethnicity. Understanding cultural diversity requires that one examine psychological variables (e.g., experienced culture, ethnic identity and its development, and acculturation). Matsumoto distinguishes "culture" from "race" (culture is learned behavior, while race is biological) and from "ethnicity" (which is characterized by a common nationality, geographic origin, or language). In a pluralistic society, we interact with many different kinds of people, which raises important questions for the end of life beyond those related to discrimination and stereotyping. For example, do we really understand one another? Do we respect one another?

CULTURAL SHIFTS IN END-OF-LIFE ISSUES AND GRIEVING

Because cultures change over time, attitudes toward dying and end-of-life issues have changed, creating dilemmas for people who must make decisions about the quality of their own or others' lives, manage their emotions after a death, and seek support from others for help through their grief. The dominance of the dual-process model of grief (Stroebe & Schut, 1999) over the stage-based approach (Worden, 1982) reflects a cultural shift in how grieving persons manage their feelings and influences the judgments they make about themselves as grievers.

The importance of cultural changes as they interact with race and ethnicity is highlighted by findings from a 30-year time-lag study of two heterogeneous groups of approximately 600 adults each (Hayslip & Peveto, 2005; Kalish & Reynolds, 1976). The groups' opinions regarding end-of-life issues and appropriate grieving were ascertained over time, and the results were stratified by race and ethnicity (African American, Hispanic American, Asian American, and Caucasian). In the 1976 sample, Caucasians and, to a lesser extent, African Americans, Japanese Americans, and Mexican Americans (in that order) were more likely to favor telling a person that he or she was dying, often citing the importance of preparing a will and determining the person's wishes regarding life-sustaining medical interventions. Mexican Americans were least likely to say that people hasten or slow their death by their own will. And, causing grief for others was a principal reason for not wanting to die for Mexican

Americans. In this study, persons in all cultures were equally likely to believe that it is the physician's role to inform patients of a terminal illness, and that people who are terminally ill (with cancer) know about their diagnosis before being told. Also, avoiding pain was mentioned equally often as a reason for not wanting to die. Generally speaking, African Americans' views on death were most different from those of other ethnic groups. Among the Japanese, death attitudes were dominated by themes of reciprocity and cohesiveness among family members. Mexican Americans' views were the most homogeneous.

In Hayslip and Peveto's 2005 study, Caucasians and Asian Americans were most likely to want to be told they were dying. The participants in this study (irrespective of ethnicity) were less likely to say they would tell someone that he or she was dying, and less likely to say they would accept death peacefully or would dramatically change their behavior if they knew they were dying. They were more likely to say that they would show concern for others if they themselves were dying and also more likely over time to say that reducing uncertainty about death was most important to them. More Asian Americans and African Americans indicated that they would accept death peacefully, while Hispanic Americans were most likely to say they would "fight" death. Caucasians were most ambivalent in this respect.

Hayslip and Peveto (2005) found that experience with dying people had increased most over time for Caucasians and African Americans, and that these groups also showed the greatest increase in concern for others regarding their own deaths. However, Hispanics' and Japanese Americans' experiences with dying people did not change since 1976. African Americans' and Hispanic Americans' concerns that their death would cause others to grieve increased most over time.

The Hayslip and Peveto (2005) findings suggest that, compared with 30 years ago, people are more attuned to matters surrounding their relationships with dying persons, as well as the quality of their own lives and the amount of control they want to have over the end of their lives. Feelings about these issues vary somewhat by ethnicity, signaling the need for more attention to both ethnic and cultural variations.

DYING, GRIEVING, AND CULTURE

Rosenblatt (2008) suggests that grief needs to be understood in a "culturally bound" manner and that culture influences "how, when, and possibly whether grief is expressed, felt, communicated, and understood" (p. 208). Whether and how grief is expressed is related to a person's tendency to be emotionally guarded in the presence of others (*emotional regulation* [Chapman & Hayslip, 2006]), which varies by culture.

Rosenblatt argues that cultural scripts define the context for grief and influence the meaning of death (i.e., whether one's death is good or not). Culture also influences whether a narrative is developed (how the death came about, whether the person suffered, etc.), the bereaved person's relationship with the deceased, and what happened as a result of the death. Cultures hold various beliefs about whether the spirit of the deceased continues to exist; how grief should be expressed (whether or not it is pathological to do so, how long one should grieve, whether grief is somaticized); whether the deceased should be remembered or forgotten; what language is used to define grief (as an emotion, as a blend of feelings and thoughts, as a social role); whether grief differs from mourning; whether and how bereaved persons are identified; and whether certain rituals must be performed to allow the soul of the deceased to move on (Rosenblatt, 2008). While grief itself may be universal, ignoring culture handicaps us in understanding a grieving individual.

Emerging literature speaks to views and customs surrounding dying and grieving among culturally diverse subgroups. For example, Corr, Nabe, and Corr (2009) describe differences among Hispanics, African Americans, Asian and Pacific Islanders, and American Indians/Native Americans. The differences revolve around the importance of family, the role of religion, the interrelatedness of life and death, whether grief is expressed openly, the nature of after-death rituals (e.g., Day of the Dead, storytelling, cleaning and preparing the body for burial within a specific period after death), and the griever's relationship to the deceased person.

Other sources address the death beliefs and behaviors of various cultural groups. Cox (2003) describes the deterministic nature of death and the ceremonial nature of dying, death, and grieving among Native Americans. Rambachan (2003) addresses the Hindu emphasis on the fulfillment of the physical body's purpose at death, which is considered the medium through which life is experienced. Sultan (2003) describes the Muslim stress on dying as a distinctly familial experience (although not including children) and the confession of faith when death is near. Suzuki (2003) addresses the attempted resuscitation of the dying person in Japan. Crowder (2003) describes the preparation of the body as the key to soul satisfaction in Chinese culture. Further, Schindler (2003) describes Jewish beliefs about reducing pain and suffering but not artificially extending life.

INFLUENCE OF CULTURE ON END-OF-LIFE CHOICES

Various ethnic groups have distinct attitudes toward end-of-life decisions. For example, Blackhall, Murphy, Frank, Michel, and Azen (1995) found that Korean Americans and Mexican Americans were more likely than European Americans and African Americans to favor a family-centered decision-making model over a patient-centered autonomy model. Hopp and Duffy (2000) and Torke, Garas, Sexson, and Branch (2005) found that African Americans, more than whites, favored the use of any type of medical care to prolong life. Smith (2004) found that African Americans favored the primacy of the family in concert with the dying person's wishes and their religious or spiritual beliefs to guide them. Seriously ill African Americans are more likely than seriously ill white patients to favor the use of cardiopulmonary resuscitation to extend life (Borum, Lynn, & Zhong, 2000), while Kiely, Mitchell, Marlow, Murphy, and Morris (2001) found that whites were more likely to have a living will or a do-not-resuscitate order.

Other research has explored end-of-life attitudes among native-born Chinese and Chinese Americans (Yick & Gupta, 2002); Greeks (Papadatou, Yfabtopoulos, & Kosmidis, 2001); Latinos (Sullivan, 2001); Bosnian immigrants (Searight & Gafford, 2005); Hawaiians and Filipinos (Braun, Onaka, & Horiuchi, 2001; Braun, Tanji, & Heck, 2001); and black Caribbeans (Koffman & Higginson, 2001). These studies uniformly suggest a rejection of the Western cultural emphasis on patient autonomy in decision making.

CULTURAL DIFFERENCES IN GRIEF AND MOURNING

Most participants in Kalish and Reynolds' 1976 study were reluctant to cry or publicly display their emotions. Less than half of the study participants in all ethnic groups (except Mexican Americans) would worry if they could not cry. Three-fourths of the Japanese, white, and black Americans reported that they would "try very hard" to control their emotions in public, but less than two-thirds of Mexican Americans agreed. Japanese Americans were most likely to control the expression of emotion.

Braun and Nichols (1997) found different responses to death and grief among four Asian-American groups: Chinese, Japanese, Vietnamese, and Filipino. Differences in religious affiliation might explain these findings.

In addition to variation among cultures, Hayslip and Peveto (2005) found a historical cultural shift in emotional control, indicating a substantial change over time, especially for Mexican Americans and Asian Americans. The finding suggests that Americans now try harder to control their emotions when they are grieving, in effect isolating them emotionally from others at a time when sharing such feelings might be beneficial. This historical shift may relate to increased encounters with dying persons, looser family ties, or the influence of technology on dying. For example, more participants in the Hayslip and Peveto survey knew dying people and had visited or talked with them than in the Kalish and Reynolds 1976 survey. Thus, the increased attempts to control grief may be due to changes in the frequency of interactions with dying and grieving persons. Dying persons, in turn, may receive less support from those who cannot know what they are feeling, wherein such persons may be less likely to express their feelings because they sense that others are not comfortable hearing them tell their story. This may lead to the disenfranchisement of their emotions and thoughts, in part as a consequence of others' efforts to control their emotions in the presence of dying persons. Regarding sources of comfort and support in bereavement, about 50% of all respondents in the Kalish and Reynolds study said they would turn to a family member, while about 25% cited clergy. In contrast, more than 50% of Caucasian, Hispanic, and Asian Americans in the Hayslip and Peveto study sought support from a family member, compared with only a third of African Americans. These results suggest that African Americans are more likely to seek support from the church; in fact, many cited their religious background as being most influential in their attitudes toward death (Kalish & Reynolds, 1976).

In the 1976 study, Caucasian participants were least likely to rely on their family in times of loss; in the 2005 study, African Americans were least likely to depend on their family. Such findings perhaps indicate a historical shift in individualism. Otherwise, we might expect African Americans to be more likely to depend on their families, which would otherwise be collectivistic in nature. Collectivistic cultures emphasize familial bonds, responsibility, and reciprocal expectations within families. In contrast, individualistic cultures stress independence and self-reliance. This trend toward individualism in handling grief may not bode well for some persons who need support to process their feelings related to death, and it underscores the importance of grief support groups and culturally sensitive individual therapy. A majority of persons in the Kalish and Reynolds study believed that a week or less was enough time to remain away from work and agreed that bereaved persons should wait for 6 months to 1 year after the loss of their spouse to begin dating. More Caucasians and African Americans than Mexican and Japanese Americans said that it was unimportant to wait for any specific period before dating. Similar racial or ethnic differences were found regarding getting married after a death. In the Hayslip and Peveto study, all ethnic groups agreed that bereaved persons should wait at least a year before remarrying, but more Caucasians and African Americans than Hispanics and Asian Americans considered it unimportant to wait. A majority of all ethnic groups agreed that the amount of time before dating and remarriage depends on the situation; the biggest change between the two surveys occurred among African Americans. These findings suggest a cultural shift toward less judgment of bereaved persons' behavior, with the effects of race and ethnicity most likely covarying with different experiences with death (particularly among African Americans).

A majority of Caucasians and African Americans in the Kalish and Reynolds 1976 study cited abnormal behavior (e.g., extreme withdrawal or apathy) as defining abnormal grieving. Mexican Americans said that abnormal grieving was most evident when there were no overt signs of grief. Most Japanese had no opinion, although they cited preoccupation with the death as a criterion for abnormal grief. In contrast, all ethnic groups in the Hayslip and Peveto 2005 study believed that extreme withdrawal or apathy, abnormal behavior, and no overt signs of grief signaled abnormal grieving. Such perceptions may contribute to the disenfranchisement of grief, stemming from a failure to empathize with the grieving person (Neimeyer & Jordan, 2002).

A common theme cuts across these studies: the influence of individualism versus collectivism. Cross-cultural researchers (e.g., Lalande & Bonanno, 2006) suggest that the Western European culture encourages bereaved persons to break bonds with the dead, creating new bonds that can serve them in the future. In contrast, collectivistic cultures with an Asian or Latin heritage emphasize familial bonds, interdependence, reciprocity, and harmony. In Japan, for instance, bereaved relatives regularly engage in ancestor worship at home (food is offered to the spirits of the deceased), which enhances a cohesive social identity and promotes a continuing bond between the living and the dead (Lalande & Bonanno, 2006). Many Latino families appreciate the spiritual and psychological continuity between the living and the dead, and the need to keep working on relationships, even after death (Shapiro, 1995). Catlin (2001) found that grieving persons in the United States were less negatively affected (e.g., in self-esteem or relationships with others) by death than persons in Spain, because of the latter group's greater interconnectedness. Interestingly, Pressman and Bonanno (2007) found that the avoidance of grief lacked clear psychological consequences in China compared with its negative impact in the United States, reinforcing the individualistic nature of grief in America. Support groups for grieving persons have become commonplace in the United States, perhaps to counter the effects of the individualistic nature of grief in American society.

Asai and Barnlund (1998) found that Americans showed more self-knowledge and self-disclosure than Japanese, because in American culture (a low-context culture with more diversity), individuals are encouraged to express their thoughts and feelings. In contrast, in the high-context Japanese culture, cultural homogeneity is emphasized and verbal expression is often suppressed. Thus, whether an individual's bereavement-related behavior is adaptive or not is contextually determined (Paletti, 2008).

Cultural differences abound, but there is also much variation within cultures, and perhaps within cultural types (i.e., collectivist versus individualistic), though the latter distinction has received considerably less attention than has the focus on cultural differences per se. For example, while both Japanese-American and Mexican-American cultures emphasize familial bonds and reciprocal expectations within the family in coping with death-related crisis and loss, Japanese Americans are most likely of all ethnic groups to control their expression of grief in public, while Mexican Americans are most expressive. Religious differences between the two cultures have an impact: Buddhism (the religion of most Japanese Americans) emphasizes acceptance of reality and emotional self-control, while Catholicism (the dominant religion among Mexican Americans) does not stress emotional self-control.

IMPLICATIONS FOR PROFESSIONALS

For white Americans and perhaps for those who are fully acculturated to American beliefs about death and grief, culturally based assumptions related to the death of a family member include beliefs that death severs bonds with the deceased, that people recover relatively quickly from the loss of a close family member and become free to form new attachments, and that feelings of grief can be handled privately (Kagawa-Singer, 1994). In light of these assumptions, we may misinterpret collectivistic cultural beliefs and behaviors (e.g., regular visits to parental graves) or disregard them as maladaptive. When professionals from an individualistic culture try to disassemble a client's cultural tapestry and analyze it according to the template of their own cultural perspective, miscommunication may occur (Kagawa-Singer, 1994). Helping professionals in a multicultural society must recognize the cultural diversity and uniqueness of their bereaved clients so they can provide culturally sensitive services for them. Professionals should understand that great variations exist in the dying and grieving processes even within a specific culture. Winkel (2001) suggested that modern mourning culture should focus on the individualization or "emotionalization" of mourning. Thus, the bereaved person in a particular culture may demonstrate a diversity of behaviors and feelings in grieving a loss (Kauffman, 2002). Indeed, persons whose belief system stresses independence and putting the death behind them, emotionally speaking, may be at a disadvantage relative to those whose beliefs stress reliance on others in the face of loss. This distinction has some parallels in the manner in which men (being instrumental) and women (being expressive) cope with loss (see Martin & Doka, 1996).

Helping professionals should be aware that grief may be disenfranchised by cultural expectations for what constitutes "good" grieving (Neimeyer & Jordan, 2002). Culture, race, and ethnicity can interfere with end-of-life choices, undermine communication, and disenfranchise grief if the diminished expression of emotions is culturally scripted. This might be especially true in the case of immigrants to a country whose cultural script is different from their own; dying and grieving may have different meanings and serve different functions for a person, depending on the degree of acculturation and identification with the dominant culture.

CONCLUSION

Professionals need to recognize the importance of cultural diversity and minority group preferences—as well as individual differences—related to dying, end-of-life decision making, and grieving. Waddell (1997) warned of the "stereotypical fallacy" of treating all persons in a given culture as similar to one another, based on a comparison of the beliefs of Anglos and Chinese Australians about impending death. Waddell suggested that there is no such thing as a "pure" cultural belief; beliefs must be understood in terms of the broader sociohistorical context in which they occur. He said, "[C]ulture can be misunderstood; it should not be used to perpetuate the stereotypical fallacy" (p. 156). A lack of understanding about the multiple influences on each person can create barriers to the open communication that is so important for both dying persons and their families (Glaser & Strauss, 1968).

Western cultural values that emphasize patient/personal autonomy may not be understood or shared—and, in fact, may be rejected—by persons whose cultural heritage or individual life experiences emphasize respect for authority, collectivistic decision making, or peace at life's end (Barrett & Heller, 2002). One proposed solution is to conduct a *cultural ethnography* with dying persons to explore their understanding of the illness and of suffering, and their values and goals given the limited time they have left to live (see Krakauer, Crenner, & Fox, 2002). Kagawa-Singer and Blackhall (2001) recommend that professionals ask culturally sensitive questions to understand the patient's attitudes toward frankness about the impending death, religious or spiritual beliefs, languages spoken, experience with poverty and discrimination, degree of integration into the ethnic community, whether decisions are patient-centered or family-centered, and what resources are available to understand this person's cultural heritage and beliefs (see Werth, Blevins, Toussaint, & Durham, 2002).

While Hallenbeck and Goldstein (1999) argue that cultural competence is crucial to understanding preferences for end-of-life care, sensitivity to individual differences is equally important to understanding and supporting both dying and grieving persons. We believe it is important to acknowledge diversity within and across race and ethnicity as well as within and across generations, where cultural change is likely to create cohort differences among dying persons, family members, and younger physicians. Just as a culture may influence grieving rituals (Laungani, 2005), different generations may view these rituals differently (Hayslip, Servaty, & Guarnaccia, 1999).

Bert Hayslip, Jr., *received a doctorate in experimental developmental psychology from the University of Akron in 1975. After teaching at Hood College in Frederick, MD, for 3 years, he joined the faculty at the University of North Texas, where he is Regents Professor of Psychology. He is a Fellow of the American Psychological Association, the Gerontological Society of America, and the Association for Gerontology in Higher Education. He is currently associate editor of* Experimental Aging Research *and editor of the* International Journal of Aging and Human Development, *and is on the editorial board of* Developmental Psychology. *His research deals with cognitive processes in aging, interventions to enhance cognitive functioning in later life, grief and bereavement, hospice care, death anxiety, grandparents raising grandchildren, and mental health and aging.*

GiBaeg Han *is a South Korean doctoral student in the Counseling Psychology Program in the University of North Texas Psychology Department. His research and clinical interests are cross-cultural counseling processes and outcomes, trauma and attachment, positive psychology, life span development, psychotherapy* *supervision, and interracial relationships. His dissertation examines the mechanism through which traumatic and positive life experiences mediate the relationship between childhood attachment/family relationship and adulthood attachment/mental health. He plans to gather data from a longitudinal perspective and analyze them from both quantitative and qualitative perspectives.*

REFERENCES

Asai, A., & Barnlund, D. C. (1998). Boundaries of the unconscious, private, and public self in Japanese and Americans: A cross-cultural comparison. *International Journal of Intercultural Relations, 22*(4), 431–452.

Barrett, R., & Heller, K. (2002). Death and dying in the black experience. *Journal of Palliative Medicine, 5,* 795–799.

Blackhall, L., Murphy, S., Frank, G., Michel, V., & Azen, S. (1995). Ethnicity and attitudes toward patient autonomy. *Journal of the American Medical Association, 274,* 820–826.

Borum, M., Lynn, J., & Zhong, Z. (2000). The effects of patient race on outcomes in seriously ill patients in SUPPORT: An overview of economic impact, medical intervention, and end-of-life decisions. *Journal of the American Geriatrics Society, 48,* S194–S198.

Bourgeois, S., & Johnson, A. (2004). Preparing for dying: Meaningful practices in palliative care. *Omega: Journal of Death and Dying, 49,* 99–107.

Braun, K., & Nichols, R. (1997). Death and dying in four Asian-American cultures: A descriptive study. *Death Studies, 21,* 327–359.

Braun, K., Onaka, A., & Horiuchi, B. (2001). Advance directive completion rates and end-of-life preferences in Hawaii. *Journal of the American Geriatrics Society, 49,* 1708–1713.

Braun, K., Tanji, V., & Heck, R. (2001). Support for physician-assisted suicide: Exploring the impact of ethnicity and attitudes toward planning for death. *The Gerontologist, 41,* 51–60.

Catlin, G. (2001). The role of culture in grief. *Journal of Social Psychology, 133,* 173–184.

Chapman, B., & Hayslip, B. (2006). Emotional intelligence in young and middle adulthood: A cross-sectional analysis of latent structure and means. *Psychology and Aging, 21,* 411–418.

Cole, M. (1999). Culture in development. In M. Bornstein & M. Lamb (Eds.), *Developmental psychology: An advanced textbook* (pp. 73–124). Mahwah, NJ: Lawrence Erlbaum.

Corr, C., Nabe, C., & Corr, D. (2009). *Death and dying: Life and living.* Belmont, CA: Thomson.

Cox, G. R. (2003). The Native American way of death. In C. Bryant (Ed.), *The handbook of death and dying: Volume 2* (pp. 631–639). Thousand Oaks, CA: Sage.

Crowder, L. S. (2003). The Taoist (Chinese) way of death. In C. Bryant (Ed.), *The handbook of death and dying: Volume 2* (pp. 673–686). Thousand Oaks, CA: Sage.

Doka, K. J. (2002). Introduction. In K. J. Doka (Ed.), *Disenfranchised grief: New directions, challenges, and strategies for practice* (pp. 5–22). Champaign, IL: Research Press.

Glaser, B., & Strauss, A. (1968). *Time for dying.* Chicago: Aldine.

Hallenbeck, J., & Goldstein, M. (1999). Decisions at the end of life: Cultural considerations beyond medical ethics. *Generations, 23,* 24–29.

Hansson, R. O., & Stroebe, M. S. (2007). *Bereavement in late life: Coping, adaptation, and developmental influences.* Washington, DC: American Psychological Association.

Hayslip, B., & Peveto, C. (2005). *Cultural changes in attitudes toward death, dying, and bereavement.* New York: Springer.

Hayslip, B., Servaty, H. L., & Guarnaccia, C. (1999). Age cohort differences in perceptions of funerals. In B. de Vries (Ed.), *End-of-life issues: Interdisciplinary and multidimensional perspectives* (pp. 23–36). New York: Springer.

Hopp, F., & Duffy, S. (2000). Racial variations in end-of-life care. *Journal of the American Geriatrics Society, 48,* 658–663.

Kagawa-Singer, M. (1994). Diverse cultural beliefs and practices about death and dying in the elderly. *Gerontology and Geriatrics Education, 5*(1), 101–116.

Kagawa-Singer, M., & Blackhall, L. (2001). Negotiating cross-cultural issues at the end of life. *Journal of the American Medical Association, 286,* 2993–3001.

Kalish, R. A., & Reynolds, D. K. (1976). *Death and ethnicity: A psychocultural study.* Los Angeles: University of Southern California Press.

Kastenbaum, R. J., & Aisenberg, R. (1972). *The psychology of death.* New York: Springer.

Kauffman, C. (2002). The psychology of disenfranchised grief: Liberation, shame, and self-disenfranchisement. In K. J. Doka (Ed.), *Disenfranchised grief: New directions, challenges, and strategies for practice* (pp. 61–78). Champaign, IL: Research Press.

Kiely, D., Mitchell, S., Marlow, A., Murphy, K., & Morris, J. (2001). Racial and state differences in the designation of advanced directives in nursing home patients. *Journal of the American Geriatrics Society, 49,* 1346–1352.

Klass, D. (2001). Continuing bonds in the resolution of grief in Japan and North America. *American Behavioral Scientist, 44*(5), 742–763.

Koffman, J., & Higginson, I. (2001). Accounts of carers' satisfaction with health care at the end of life: A comparison of first-generation black Caribbean and white patients with advanced disease. *Palliative Medicine, 15,* 337–345.

Krakauer, E., Crenner, C., & Fox, K. (2002). Barriers to optimum end-of-life care for minority patients. *Journal of the American Geriatrics Society, 50,* 182–190.

Lalande, K. M., & Bonanno, G. A. (2006). Culture and continuing bonds: A prospective comparison of bereavement in the United States and the People's Republic of China. *Death Studies, 30,* 303–324.

Laungani, P. (2005). Cultural considerations in Hindu funerals in India and England. In J. Morgan & P. Laungani (Eds.), *Death and bereavement around the world, 4* (pp. 39–63). Amityville, NY: Baywood.

Long, S. (2004). Cultural scripts for a good death in Japan and the United States: Similarities and differences. *Social Science and Medicine, 58,* 913–928.

Martin, T., & Doka, K. (1996). Masculine grief. In K. J. Doka (Ed.), *Living with grief after sudden loss: Suicide, homicide, accident, heart attack, stroke* (pp. 161–172). Bristol, PA: Taylor & Francis.

Matsumoto, D. (2000). *Culture and psychology* (2nd ed.). Belmont, CA: Wadsworth/Thomson.

McCoy, S., Pyszczynski, T., Solomon, S., & Greenberg, J. (2000). Transcending the self: A terror management perspective on successful aging. In A. Tomer (Ed.), *Death attitudes and the older adult* (pp. 37–63). Philadelphia: Brunner-Rutledge.

Neimeyer, R. A., & Jordan, J. R. (2002). Disenfranchisement as empathic failure: Grief therapy and the co-construction of meaning. In K. J. Doka (Ed.), *Disenfranchised grief: New directions, challenges, and strategies for practice* (pp. 95–117). Champaign, IL: Research Press.

Paletti, R. (2008). Recovery in context: Bereavement, culture, and the transformation of the therapeutic self. *Death Studies, 32,* 17–26.

Papadatou, D., Yfabtopoulos, J., & Kosmidis, H. (2001). Death of a child at home and in hospital: Experiences of Greek mothers. *Death Studies, 20,* 215–235.

Pressman, D. L., & Bonanno, G. A. (2007). With whom do we grieve? Social and cultural determinants of grief processing in the United States and China. *Journal of Social and Personal Relationships, 24*(5), 729–746.

Rambachan, A. (2003). The Hindu way of death. In C. Bryant (Ed.), *The handbook of death and dying: Volume 2* (pp. 640–648). Thousand Oaks, CA: Sage.

Rosenblatt, P. C. (2008). Grief across cultures: A review and research agenda. In M. S. Stroebe, R. O. Hansson, H. Schut, & W. Stroebe (Eds.), *Handbook of bereavement research and practice: 21st century perspectives* (pp. 207–222). Washington, DC: American Psychological Association.

Schindler, R. (2003). The Jewish way of death. In C. Bryant (Ed.), *The handbook of death and dying: Volume 2* (pp. 687–693). Thousand Oaks, CA: Sage.

Seale, C., & van der Geest, S. (2004). Good and bad death: Introduction. *Social Science and Medicine, 58,* 883–885.

Searight, H., & Gafford, J. (2005). It's like playing with your destiny: Bosnian immigrants' views of advanced directives and end-of-life-care decision making. *Journal of Immigrant Health, 7,* 195–203.

Shapiro, E. R. (1995). Grief in family and cultural context: Learning from Latino families. *Cultural Diversity and Mental Health, 1,* 159–176.

Smith, S. (2004). End-of-life decision-making processes of African-American families: Implications for culturally sensitive social work practice. *Journal of Ethnic and Cultural Diversity, 13,* 1–23.

Stroebe, M., & Schut, H. (1999). The dual-process model of coping with bereavement: Rationale and description. *Death Studies, 23,* 197–224.

Sullivan, M. C. (2001). Lost in translation: How Latinos view end-of-life care. *Plastic Surgical Nursing, 21,* 90–91.

Sultan, D. H. (2003). The Muslim way of death. In C. Bryant (Ed.), *The handbook of death and dying: Volume 2* (pp. 649–655). Thousand Oaks, CA: Sage.

Suzuki, H. (2003). The Japanese way of death. In C. Bryant (Ed.), *The handbook of death and dying: Volume 2* (pp. 656–672). Thousand Oaks, CA: Sage.

Torke, A., Garas, N., Sexson, W., & Branch, W. (2005). Medical care at the end of life: Views of African-American patients in an urban hospital. *Journal of Palliative Medicine, 8,* 593–602.

Waddell, C. (1997). The stereotypical fallacy: A comparison of Anglo and Chinese Australians' thoughts about facing death. *Mortality, 2,* 149–161.

Werth, J. L., Blevins, D., Toussaint, K., & Durham, M. (2002). The influence of cultural diversity on end-of-life care decisions. *American Behavioral Scientist, 46,* 204–219.

Winkel, H. (2001). A postmodern culture of grief? On individualism of mourning in Germany. *Mortality, 6,* 65–79.

Worden, W. (1982). *Grief counseling and grief therapy: A handbook for the mental health practitioner.* New York: Springer.

Yick, A., & Gupta, R. (2002). Chinese cultural dimensions of death, dying, and bereavement: Focus group findings. *Journal of Cultural Diversity, 9,* 32–42.

The Culturally Competent Practitioner

Paul C. Rosenblatt

The culturally competent practitioner is one who works well with clients from cultures other than his or her own. Cultural competence implies an ability to understand the realities of other cultures and deal respectfully with them. It suggests a sense of openness to other cultures and enables the practitioner to help people from other cultures. Culturally competent caregivers should be aware of their own attitudes, practices, beliefs, knowledge, and assumptions, and should see them as aspects of culture rather than eternal truths. One must be neither judgmental nor defensive about the cultural realities of others. Rather, one should be knowledgeable about the culture of the other and able to learn quickly what one does not yet know. Skills in relating to people of other cultures—including the ability to modify behavior to align with etiquette and propriety of other cultures—are also necessary.

Assessing outcomes after helping a person from another culture is not a simple matter. Assessment can be challenging, because what might be considered help in one culture might not be help in another, and cultures differ in how, if at all, people express gratitude and satisfaction.

Although cultural competence might seem like something anyone can learn, it is not that simple. Some people are not likely to become culturally competent. Perhaps they cannot put aside their own cultural values and standards or get past their own prejudiced attitudes. Perhaps they cannot tune in to their own attitudes at all. Also, a person who is culturally competent in one interaction might not be competent in another, even when interacting with the same culture, because individuals from another culture and their situations can differ markedly, and what clicks with them or offends them may also differ.

There are traps in the concept of cultural competence. In focusing on cultural competence, you may be dealing with personal and institutional anxieties rather than engaging the ethical, existential, cultural, or political issues connected to death (see Gunaratnam, 2008, for an interesting discussion on this topic). Another trap is that the concept of cultural competence implies that you can achieve expertise, while the reality is that we are always beginners. However many bereaved people from other cultures you have worked with, you are starting over with each new person. From that perspective, perhaps the label of cultural competence should be declined or worn with great modesty.

From a relationship systems perspective, the barriers to cultural competence are not just in the service provider, but also in the relationship itself. Many cultures have no concept of therapy, counseling, or support services, so people from these cultures would not seek such services and would not know what to make of them if they were offered. Something may have to happen before such services make sense to the potential recipient. Also, in many cultures, people typically distrust outsiders, so an outsider who hopes to provide bereavement services must first get past the distrust.

Among people who are open to the possibility of professional help, many would prefer to have help from someone with whom they share a culture. For example, in research I co-authored (Rosenblatt & Wallace, 2005), an African-American woman talked about how assertive she had to be with her HMO to get a referral to an African-American therapist. The HMO staff initially said that they had no idea which providers were African American, but she insisted that they could find that information and that they had to do it to help her. So they did. Thus, one aspect of becoming a culturally competent helper might involve being comfortable with the fact that some people do not want to work with you. Perhaps you can build a trusting and productive relationship with some of those people, but perhaps not.

Part of becoming a helper for bereaved people is learning your limits of energy, comfort, tolerance of imperfect communication, tolerance of being reminded of your own past and future losses and your own mortality, tolerance of pain and tears, and tolerance of stories that make you uncomfortable. In working with those who are culturally different, there are more limits to learn. For example, can I work in a situation in which someone else speaks for the bereaved person; where family members angrily blame each other for a death that no one seems to have caused; where a widow is ostracized because of the death of her husband; where a widow is remarried within days of her husband's death; or where death rituals include animal sacrifice?

CULTURAL DIVERSITY IN GRIEF AND BEREAVEMENT

One might assume that the same basic psychological and social processes operate in bereavement, regardless of a person's culture. But that assumption can create problems in working with someone from a culture other than one's own (Rosenblatt, 2007). Dying and death set off emotions, social relationship processes, and rituals in one culture that are unlike those in another culture and that may even be incomprehensible to most people from another culture. We cannot assume, for example, that the English-language words for grief apply to people in another culture or that a translator can translate feeling terms from another language into English. We cannot assume that a translation exists for the character or meaning of crucial social relationships in another culture, or that descriptions and cultural meanings for rituals can be translated into English. Having a competent translator can be helpful when working across cultures, but it may not be enough. We may need considerable help to understand, for example, bereavement terms such as *fago* and *lalomweiu*, which are used among the Ifaluk, a Pacific Island culture (Lutz, 1985). We may need considerable help to understand South African Zulu beliefs about the pollution and dangers of widows and the extensive, yearlong ritual expressions of grief that are imposed on them (Rosenblatt & Nkosi, 2007). Even with considerable help, we may need to stretch mightily to understand and deal respectfully with emotion terms, relationship terms, and rituals that are outside our experience and that seem very strange.

BASIC SKILLS AND SENSITIVITIES

What does one need in order to be helpful to a bereaved person from another culture? There is no formula, no set of lesson plans, no training program, no set of adages, no advice that will guarantee competence in working across cultures. However, below are suggestions for achieving greater expertise.

Know Yourself

It may seem paradoxical that a good starting place for helping culturally different others is to know yourself. It helps enormously if you know your attitudes, areas of ignorance, prejudices, assumptions, and cultural biases. Do you assume that people who will not talk about a loss are in serious trouble? Do you assume that your own experience of loss is key to understanding the experiences of others? Can you deal respectfully with someone who believes a loved one is dying because of sorcery? If your assumptions do not allow someone from a different culture to have his or her own ideas about death, you may not be helpful as a practitioner. If you assume that your own experiences are like those of others, will you be able to deal with people whose experiences are significantly different? If you are shocked, horrified, or upset by how a person from another culture understands the cause of death, can you provide respectful support to that person?

Knowing yourself is a lifelong project. There is always more to learn. There are always new situations and new relationships that can teach you about yourself. If you are like me, you are always making new mistakes from which to learn. You may learn a lot about yourself in helping others; in fact, that can be a genuine (if secondary) benefit of helping. It is also useful to be open to the possibility that you cannot help someone from another culture or that, at best, you are a beginner whose help might be clumsy and limited.

Assuming Cultural Similarity and Difference

As a cultural outsider, it is useful to assume that each person is somewhat similar to you and to others you have worked with—and also very different. As you work with the person, you should be prepared to doubt each of these assumed similarities and assumed differences. It can be useful to assume that there are similarities, because that may be correct. Arguably, a core set of reactions and ways of dealing with death translate to some extent from culture to culture. Assuming similarity may also make it easier to draw on your wellsprings of empathy and understanding. Assuming similarity makes it easier for us to be "real" with others, and that honesty may be appreciated even if in our realness we violate their etiquette, beliefs about reality, or standards of emotional expression. But it is always equally helpful to assume that this person and this situation are different, and that whatever you know, feel, believe, or have experienced may not be applicable.

Experience

The more you have dealt with grieving people from a specific culture other than your own or with grieving people from various cultures, the more you may be able to understand and help. Even indirect experience can be very helpful—for example, reading about another culture or speaking with someone from another culture who is not bereaved but from whom you can learn background information.

Learning another language is a major investment of time and effort, but language is key to the realities, feelings, relationships, and understandings of people of another culture. If you interact with people only in your own language, you may miss or misunderstand a great deal about them and your help may be limited. Acquiring even a small vocabulary in another person's language can be valuable to connect with the person and establish trust. For example, acquiring an understanding of the cultural meanings imbued in terms that do not translate well into English but are central to the processes of dying and grieving can be quite helpful.

It takes courage to try to help someone from another culture or to accumulate experiences that can enhance your capacity to help. Many people would rather not be beginners or do not feel comfortable in a different cultural milieu. Many people do not want to risk doing harm by trying to help outside their area of competence. But each experience has the potential to help us do better with the next person.

Specialist or Generalist?

One issue that may come up is whether to become a specialist in dealing with one culture or a generalist in dealing with diverse cultures. There is a lot to be said for becoming a specialist. There is much to learn and understand about any culture. If being helpful requires you to make good connections in the community of that culture, it may take a lifetime to establish trust and build connections. Specialization is not uncommon. I know, for example, Anglo workers who have become fluent in Spanish and do their work primarily in the local Mexican-American community.

On the other hand, there is a great need for generalists. I live in a metropolitan area that includes people from several hundred different cultures. No institution can employ hundreds of specialists. No patient and family can wait several years for someone to acquire expertise in their culture. Generalists can provide help across cultural lines.

Don't Pathologize, Judge, or Condemn

It's easy to see the grief of people from a culture other than your own as pathological, to judge them as deficient or dysfunctional, or to condemn their actions as not moral, normal, or healthy. However, the realities of those people are their realities; their feelings are their feelings. Thinking and behaving in accordance with the standards of their culture is totally appropriate. It is not helpful to see your own culture as superior to another culture. On the other hand, you may have legitimate cultural bottom lines that you do not want to abandon. For example, I would have a difficult time working with bereaved people from a culture where children who have lost a parent are mutilated as part of mourning rituals, or where all deaths are assumed to be caused by someone, so that a death often leads to someone's taking revenge on someone else.

If you can be open to and accepting of how people in another culture grieve, the next step is to be open about the kind of help you provide. Among English-speaking people in the United States, those of us who help the bereaved often do so by listening and sometimes giving advice. But a person in another culture might need something quite different; for example, help buying a sacrificial goat, help feeding the crowd at the death rituals, help paying for long-distance telephone calls, or help sewing mourning clothing. The challenge for a would-be helper is not just to tolerate what others say and do but also to feel okay about helping them in ways that do not fit the common North American pattern.

Some of the greatest challenges in dealing with dying and death issues across cultures come when the standards of a culture clash with one's ethics. Sometimes the clash is not after a death but before a death. The dying person may come from a culture in which people never say that someone is dying or in which a senior family member speaks for a dying person who is quite capable of speaking. You might have to decide whether to go along with what seems like dishonesty and whether to deny a patient informed consent or a chance to speak for himself or herself about palliation and other issues. If you violate your personal ethics to work in ways that support cultural standards, you might later find it challenging to provide grief support if you feel bad about what you have done. Similarly, if you insisted on doing something that family members of a dying person did not want done, it may later be hard to provide them grief support.

Cross-Cultural Writings and Cultural Insiders

Literature exists in English about almost every culture. So if you are working with, say, a grieving Chinese person from Taiwan, you will be able to find a number of published works about the Chinese of Taiwan. However, sometimes the literature is misleading. For example, there is more than one Chinese culture in Taiwan, and social class, religion, and age differences might be very important. And if you are trying to help a Taiwanese person living in North America, that person may be in some ways quite different from a person who lives in Taiwan. For example, the person may have a North American partner, may have left Taiwan to get away from certain aspects of Taiwanese culture, or may have loss issues that are compounded by not being able to go home.

So read the literature and take to heart what it offers, but remain open to the possibility that the persons you work with do not fit that literature.

The literature on grief in other cultures is often written by people from those cultures. Thus, it is subliminally suggested that only people from that culture have had sufficient experience dealing with bereavement in that culture and only they can be considered experts. As a cultural outsider, you might find that message dispiriting. But cultural insiders are not necessarily best at helping or understanding bereaved persons from their culture, and you might be able to be of real help despite having no insider knowledge.

You may have access to a nonbereaved cultural insider. For example, you might want to work with a grieving Nigerian and have the good fortune to have a friend, neighbor, or colleague who is Nigerian. This cultural insider can provide you with insights and advice. But, again, the cultural insider's help may be misleading. He or she may be from a different Nigerian culture than the person you want to help. Even if the two are from the same culture, the insider's knowledge may be off base because of gender, class, education, religion, or another difference. The insider might have left Nigeria 30 years ago and may be offering stale information. Or your friend might withhold certain information from you because it is precious insider information, because she fears your reaction, because she thinks you would not be interested, or because she thinks it is obvious or trivial. So, just as with reading cross-cultural literature, remember that a cultural insider may be wonderfully helpful, but you should be open to the possibility that what the insider offers does not apply to the person you want to help.

Other Issues Attached to Grief

Grief can be attached to many other issues. For example, a white therapist who offers help to a bereaved African American may hear accounts of racism in the life of the bereaved person and the life of the deceased (Rosenblatt & Wallace, 2005). People who have come to the United States from other countries may need sympathetic understanding of the political and economic situations that motivated them to leave their homes and that block them from returning to grieve with family members. They may need support and understanding regarding the many losses involved in leaving home and coping with life in the United States.

SKILLED INSIGHTS AND INTERVENTIONS

How should you try to help a grieving person from another culture? Experts do not necessarily agree on what standards to use, and, in fact, the standards of another person's culture may call for a process and outcome that seem very strange by the standards of one's own culture and professional peers (Rosenblatt, 2008).

Ester R. Shapiro (1996, 2002) provides excellent overviews of approaches to grief therapy across cultures, and others offer overviews of cross-cultural counseling and therapy—for example, Pedersen, Lonner, Draguns, and Trimble (2007) and Constantine and Sue (2005). But I know of no literature that goes into fine detail about how to do grief therapy across cultures. Zebracki and Stancin (2007) provide a case example with many details, but even that work does not get into the specifics of therapist-client interaction. However, I have relatively concrete advice to offer about working with clients from other cultures. First, I will suggest some questions that might be useful in cross-cultural grief therapy. Then I will describe my own experience of providing grief support in long-term, nontherapeutic, cross-cultural relationships. And finally, I will offer a perspective on helping in a single grief therapy encounter.

Useful Questions

Sometimes the best way to help is to ask good questions. The answers to these questions can help build trust, understanding, and a basis for further help. In the spirit of Kleinman, Eisenberg, and Good (1978) and Fadiman (1997, p. 260), who wrote about cross-cultural medical practice, I suggest the following questions to ask in a cross-cultural bereavement helping situation:

1. What is happening (has happened) to your family member?
2. What do you think caused this to happen?
3. How have you been affected by what is happening (has happened)?
4. How have others in your family been affected?
5. In your culture, how do family members grieve? What, if anything, would be expected from you?
6. Please teach me the terms in your language for feelings people are likely to have when they grieve.
7. Tell me about your family member who is dying (has died)—the person's life and what he or she is (was) like.
8. In your culture, what kinds of help would people try to provide for someone whose family member is dying (has died)?
9. Tell me what else I would need to know to understand you and possibly help you.

However, these questions are only good if they are culturally appropriate. You have to be alert to the possibility that some or all of them might be inappropriate in a particular culture. They may be inappropriate or rude if one is a stranger, a cultural outsider, a woman talking to a man, a man talking to a woman, a young person talking to an older person, or anyone talking to someone who is bereaved.

Asking questions takes a certain amount of cultural sensitivity and luck, and it also may take skill at recovering from mistakes. For example, if you ask a question that makes the wrong assumption about someone's culture or relationship with the dying person, you may need to apologize, atone in some way, and go back to the beginning in trying to build trust. On the other hand, people are inclined to be lenient with a cultural outsider who is trying to help. They may have had enough experience themselves as cultural outsiders to be sympathetic. They may be grateful for any offer of help. They may even prefer to talk to a cultural outsider, because they can say things to an outsider that would not be appropriate to say to insiders. Even if the questions I suggest do not work, it may still be helpful to the people you are trying to help, and to you in learning how to help, if you continue to be curious.

Grief Support in Long-Term Cross-Cultural Relationships
The ideal relationship for cross-cultural support is a relationship that was of long standing before the death and that will continue for a long time after the death. I am not a grief therapist, but I have had a number of cross-cultural relationships in this manner. This, however, is rare for grief support practitioners.

I work with international and ethnically diverse U.S. students and find that my work teaching, advising, and supervising them sometimes leads to providing grief support. The student may have taken classes with me in which we built mutual trust, knowledge of one another, and a shared vocabulary about relationships, culture, and communicating across cultures. Often I have been the advisor, supervisor, or research collaborator with a student for several years, building a strong relationship. Then somebody in the student's life dies. The long-term relationship we have built greatly facilitates my ability to provide grief support. The student has already taught me much about his or her culture—the etiquette of communication, ways of viewing my culture, cultural terms and standards for emotional expression, and cultural issues in relating across our differences (not only in culture but also, often, in gender, age, and relative power). A student whose first language is not English might teach me the words I should say as part of bereavement support. With ethnically diverse American students whose cultural history includes a long struggle with white racism, we will have had conversations about the barrier my whiteness might create between us. Foreign students will have given me a sense of their home culture and their allegiance to that culture and the people in it. Often I know something about the student's family members—not only their roles, but their names and a fair amount of information about them. Almost always we have become comfortable with a pattern of my asking naïve questions and learning from the student. All of this is a wonderful foundation for bereavement support.

The support I give always involves offering my condolences and listening to what the student has to say. Because we have an ongoing relationship that entails interactions about topics other than the loss, we may have many opportunities to interact about the loss. Sometimes it is a matter of a few words about the loss before we get on to other issues, but sometimes it is much more. The long-term nature of the relationship, the fact that it is based on grounds other than bereavement, and the flexibility of the relationship with regard to grief matters may in some ways be ideal. There is room for grief support, but only as needed and appropriate. Furthermore, because we have built a relationship that processes our cultural differences, the student's interactions with me about grief are likely to include cultural commentary and the translation of relevant terms. That enables me to have some understanding of the cultural issues, and some students have said that it enables them to feel more culturally grounded in their grief. Students have told me that my questions were helpful to them, that my listening enabled them to figure things out, that they found peace by talking with me and explaining themselves and their culture to me, and that they felt understood and known.

One-Time Encounters

To be effective, cross-cultural help may require more time than within-culture help—time for connecting and learning about one another's culture, understanding, and clearing up cultural misunderstandings. But sometimes you have only a single brief encounter to try to make a difference. What can you do? There is no formula that guarantees success. Your own intuition and spontaneity may work well. The questions suggested earlier may help. Here are five additional suggestions:

1. Always offer condolences in your own way.
2. It is better for them to do most of the talking. What you have to offer most of all is listening.

3. Be comfortable with silence. Being with people in silence may be supportive, and many cultures include silence as part of interactions to a greater extent than we do in many cultures in the United States.

4. Use your cultural differences to try to move the encounter forward. For example, it might be helpful to ask questions such as "In my culture, we don't have many rituals to support people who are grieving. Is that true in yours?"

5. Always leave the door open to more interaction. Make sure that your goodbye includes an invitation to call or visit again.

Paul C. Rosenblatt has a PhD in psychology and is Morse-Alumni Distinguished Teaching Professor of Family Social Science at the University of Minnesota. His recent books include Two in a Bed: The Social System of Couple Bed Sharing, African-American Grief *(with Beverly R. Wallace),* Parental Grief: Narratives of Loss and Relationship, *and* Help Your Marriage Survive the Death of a Child. *He is completing work on a book tentatively titled* Shared Obliviousness in Family Systems *and is also working on a book about how African-American novelists have characterized the effects of white racism on African-American families. Among his current research projects are a study (with John R. Barner) of how couple relationships are influenced by the death of a parent of one of the partners and a study (with Liz Wieling) of how people experience and understand intimacy in a close relationship.*

REFERENCES

Constantine, M. G., & Sue, D. W. (2005). *Strategies for building multicultural competence in mental health and educational settings.* Hoboken, NJ: Wiley.

Fadiman, A. (1997). *The spirit catches you and you fall down.* New York: Farrar, Straus and Giroux.

Gunaratnam, Y. (2008). From competence to vulnerability: Care, ethics, and elders from racialized minorities. *Mortality, 13,* 24–41.

Kleinman, A., Eisenberg, L., & Good, B. (1978). Culture, illness, and care: Clinical lessons from anthropologic and cross-cultural research. *Annals of Internal Medicine, 88,* 251–258.

Lutz, C. (1985). Depression and the translation of emotional worlds. In A. Kleinman & B. Good (Eds.), *Culture and depression* (pp. 63–100). Berkeley, CA: University of California Press.

Pedersen, P. B., Lonner, W. J., Draguns, J. G., & Trimble, J. E. (2007). *Counseling across cultures* (6th ed). Thousand Oaks, CA: Sage.

Rosenblatt, P. C. (2007). Grief: What we have learned from cross-cultural studies. In K. Doka (Ed.), *Living with grief: Before and after the death* (pp. 123–136). Washington, DC: Hospice Foundation of America.

Rosenblatt, P. C. (2008). Recovery following bereavement: Metaphor, phenomenology, and culture. *Death Studies, 32,* 6–16.

Rosenblatt, P. C., & Nkosi, B. C. (2007). South African Zulu widows in a time of poverty and social change. *Death Studies, 31,* 67–85.

Rosenblatt, P. C., & Wallace, B. R. (2005). *African-American grief.* New York: Brunner-Routledge.

Shapiro, E. R. (1996). Family bereavement and cultural diversity: A social developmental perspective. *Family Process, 35,* 313–332.

Shapiro, E. R. (2002). Family bereavement after collective trauma: Private suffering, public meanings, and cultural contexts. *Journal of Systemic Therapies, 21*(3), 81–92.

Zebracki, K., & Stancin, T. (2007). Cultural considerations in facilitating coping to a father's illness and bereavement in a Latino child. *Clinical Case Studies, 6,* 3–16.

Characteristics of Culturally Effective Counselors

Kenneth J. Doka

- **SKILLED AND KNOWLEDGEABLE.** Effective counselors serving diverse populations can readily employ a range of theories and techniques, and their practice is evidence-based in that they stay current with research in the field. Because cultural groups can vary so widely, effective counselors must be eclectic, using diverse strategies with different populations.

- **ALWAYS OPEN TO LEARNING.** Counselors who work with culturally diverse populations should be intellectually curious, always seeking more information. They attempt to learn about the populations they serve from research, careful observation, and cultural informants. Ethnic or cultural newspapers, magazines, or other media are often good sources of information—windows to the issues and perceptions of a particular group. While effective counselors are knowledgeable about the groups they work with, they are also careful not to make assumptions about individual clients. Instead, they are ready to observe, listen, and ask. Effective counselors recognize the value of mutual learning.

- **SENSITIVE.** Culturally proficient counselors operate with deep sensitivity. They recognize that identity is more often an issue for those in nondominant groups. Culturally proficient counselors listen for or ask about cultural affiliation and identification rather than assume them. They maintain an open, nonjudgmental attitude. Questions are open-ended and carefully crafted, employing neutral language (such as "partner" rather than "spouse," "boyfriend," or "girlfriend").

- **SELF-AWARE.** Counselors should be aware of their own biases and monitor the potential effects of these biases on their practice. They should be aware of the "culture of counseling"—employing an individualistic emphasis, a future orientation, a bias toward self-disclosure and emotional and verbal expressiveness, a linear orientation toward cause and effect, an assumption of activity and internal locus of control, a belief in the value of insight, a view of the counselor as facilitator, and, often, a nondirective style (Sue & Sue, 2008). Effective counselors are sensitive to the fact that the values and beliefs of the counseling culture are not always congruent with the orientations of clients.

- **WORK AS A CULTURAL BROKER.** Culturally sensitive counselors understand that they sometimes function as "cultural brokers." This means that, in a nonjudgmental manner, they help clients explore the differences between their cultural practices and those of the dominant society. Such counselors serve as advocates in the larger society, helping clients meet their needs.

REFERENCE

Sue, D. W., & Sue, D. (2008). *Counseling the culturally diverse: Theory and practice* (5th ed.). New York: John Wiley and Sons.

Ethical Aspects of Cultural Diversity

Bruce Jennings

America is a culturally diverse society. This diversity has several dimensions, including religion, ethnicity, culture, race, and socioeconomic class. Assimilation and the deliberate suppression of background, tradition, and special identity were once the rule, but no longer. Instead, difference and diversity are expressed and embraced as a norm. People find these aspects of their identity meaningful and important, and increasingly they expect that such differences will be recognized and respected by others. A new social ethic has emerged in recent years—an ethic of plurality and difference rather than one of assimilation and universality. The mosaic has replaced the melting pot as a metaphor for America.

This change in American life has important implications for health care. And it has important ethical implications for the education and attitudes of healthcare providers, as well as for the practical dilemmas that arise in healthcare decision making. Understanding the culturally mediated beliefs, values, and expectations of patients is crucial for the effective, ethical practice of medicine. It is as crucial as understanding the biochemistry and physiology of patients' bodies.[1]

---

1 It is useful to distinguish the issue of recognition and respect for cultural diversity in healthcare relationships and decisions, on the one hand, from the issue of racial, ethnic, and cultural disparities in healthcare access and health status, on the other. The empirical pattern of health disparities is undeniable; its causes and explanation are less certain. To what extent disparities in outcomes are linked to failures of recognition and respect is also an open question. Intuitively, it seems that some link exists, but improving respect and recognition of cultural identity alone will not necessarily get at the root cause of disparities (Institute of Medicine, 2003). From an ethical point of view, these two phenomena pose parallel problems for an account of social justice: disparities seem to pose the challenge of redistribution, while respect poses the challenge of just recognition. On the relationship between these two dimensions of justice, see Fraser and Honneth, 2003.

The purpose of this chapter is to explore the implications of cultural diversity for the ethical dimensions of health care, especially in the end-of-life care setting. How might the principle of autonomy be understood in light of cultural diversity, and how might we change our approach to end-of-life care if we were to value and accommodate cultural diversity as a fact of life for patients and families?

My aim and approach are more conceptual than social-scientific. I do not attempt to document the nature and extent of cultural diversity in health care, nor do I review specific ethnographic differences. Rather, I address the concept of diversity as such and what follows from it for ethics.

CULTURE AND SELF-IDENTITY

It is foolhardy to begin with a general definition of the concept of culture because it has been so strongly debated in the field of anthropology for so long (Sahlins, 1978; Shweder, 1991). For our purposes, the following characterization will provide the necessary orientation.

Human beings possess a degree and a kind of consciousness that is unique in the animal world; they have primary sensation and experience that evokes behavioral response, as well as secondary or symbolic perceptions and experiences that they interpret as meaningful and communicate about socially (Harré, 1998; Metzinger, 2003; Tugendhat, 1986). The human capacity for language and other modes of complex symbolic thought makes these secondary experiences possible (Aronson, 2008). Moreover, human beings are not fully developed at birth; they rely on the plastic capacity for learning through experience in social interaction far more than other species, whose mental world and behavioral repertoire are more closely linked to genetic adaptation and instinctual response (Harré & Gillett, 1994).

This accounts for diversity in various groups of human beings because, unlike basic biological mechanisms, culture and linguistic patterns vary widely in different parts of the world. The great dependency of human thought, feeling, and behavior on such variable patterns leads to diversity of human behavior.

But cultures or patterns of meaning are not static, no more than social structures or personality structures are. The notion of cultural determinism is not correct, because cultures are not fixed molds that shape individuals. The appropriate outlook is not deterministic but dynamic and relational.[2] It

---

2 For a rich and suggestive account of the general perspective sketched briefly here, see Mithen, 2006.

might be called a "perspective of recognition" that contrasts sharply with the perspective of autonomy.

People are shaped by culture and society, by symbolic patterns of meaning and institutional patterns of interaction. But in all cultures and societies that we know about so far, these powerful shaping cultural patterns are the media of change as well as conformity. The same cultural patterns can empower people and make it possible for a human being to be culturally creative as well as culturally created (Harré, 1998).

People internalize meanings and values from their cultural environment—forming what George Herbert Mead called the "me"—and then individuate those meanings and norms to form a unique personal identity, which he called the "I" (Honneth, 1996; Mead, 1934; Tugendhat, 1986). There follows from this a kind of universal "tension of recognition" wherein the unique identity of the individual interacts with the general patterns of the culture. When these tensions coalesce over a long period and in a large enough number of people, the traditional cultural and social structures themselves undergo change (Honneth, 1996).

The cultural patterns and social institutions that shape individuals are rearticulated and rebuilt by those same individuals. Thus, human beings are both social members and social critics, both cultural creatures and culture creators. They follow rules and reinterpret (occasionally rewrite) them. Their minds and brains are engines of both continuity and innovation. Their behavior is remarkably plastic and diverse, but it is not incomprehensible, random, or chaotic.

To this basic point about innovation and continuity, a second must be added about universal and situational experience. The fact of cultural diversity does not mean that people from different backgrounds must be complete strangers to one another; behind the diversity lies a set of meanings and behaviors that are so widely shared that they comprise an overlapping human zone of understanding. No culture values human experiences such as fear, pain, or suffering for their own sakes; these are conditions that all human beings everywhere generally try to avoid. Nonetheless, different languages, cultures, and traditions interpret these concepts in varying ways and offer differing evaluations of their *situational* meaning, however much they may agree on their abstract meaning. In a particular culturally interpreted situation (such as adolescent rites of passage), these experiences may be created or deliberately sought out rather than avoided. The same may be said for positive experiences such as security, love, caring, friendship, and respect. They are generally sought out by everyone everywhere, but they are sometimes eschewed in situations with special cultural meaning.

The domain of ethics involves reasoning about how best to respond to universal human needs and to the diverse, culturally mediated interpretations and applications of those needs. If the relationship between the individual and the culture is a process of reciprocal constitution, what capabilities and rights must the individual have? This question has both psychological and political dimensions.

I suggest that the following conditions are necessary if the ideal possibilities of human development and flourishing are to be realized. These are norms of social justice and equality, cultural plurality, and mutual esteem and respect in interpersonal relations (Honneth, 1996; Nussbaum, 2001; Powers & Faden, 2008):

- Basic security and an environment in which children can develop and flourish appropriately
- Equal access to education and to the resources of the symbolic order of a culture, as well as equality of opportunity and access to the various roles and institutional positions that the society affords
- A pattern of thought and feeling in the culture as a whole that negatively sanctions ethnic prejudice and discrimination, that not only tolerates but affirms diversity and individuality, and that provides the social and cultural bases for individual self-esteem and respect

On these bases, group membership can be affirmed without political fragmentation, and social spaces can be created that allow for both the continuity of cultural and ethnic tradition and the freedom of self-expression. A pluralistic society is not only a society with a diversity of cultures and affiliations, it is also a society with a plurality of ways of finding and making meaning—a society open to individual experiments in living (Appiah, 2005).

With regard to diversity in health care, in some situations it is possible for physicians to assume a continuity between their personal intuition and outlook—their own cultural experience—and what their patients perceive and want. These assumed connections are often implicit; they make up the tacit dimension of professional knowledge, what has been called the "silent world of doctor and patient" (Katz, 2002). Increasingly, however—especially in urban areas and areas with a substantial population of recent immigrants—the risk of misunderstanding and miscommunication is high. In these areas, the silent world must become vocal, and it is no longer appropriate for physicians to assume evaluative continuity between themselves and their patients.

This situation significantly complicates clinical encounters and requires time-consuming mitigation. Time is a resource in extremely short supply in clinical settings today, largely for economic and managerial reasons. Still, more explicit, direct communication is necessary, and the "ethnographic" knowledge of physicians and other health professionals must be much richer and more sophisticated than it ever has been before. In other words, physicians must understand a good deal about the traditions and belief systems with which their patients and the patients' families identify. They must be adept at modes of communication that are culturally and psychologically appropriate to those backgrounds.

RESPECT FOR PERSONS

If one ethical tenet has come to the fore in the past 50 years and has been embraced throughout health care, it is respect for the human individual, the person. Behind this norm of respect for persons stands the doctrine of informed consent, the right to forgo life-sustaining treatment, the right to privacy and confidentiality, and many similar values that are enshrined in medical ethics and the law.

Some in medicine, bioethics, and law are beginning to question how effectively this norm is being put into practice and institutionalized in various healthcare settings, from end-of-life care to human subject research, experimental treatment, and everything in between (Jennings & Murray, 2005). But the norm itself remains strong as a goal and an end, no matter how difficult it is to achieve.

Two different mistakes violate the norm of respect for persons. One is characteristic of medical science; the other has been characteristic of medical ethics and bioethics. The first is to reduce the uniqueness and individuality of the patient as a person to the universality of scientific regularities governing the functioning of the patient's body. This mistake makes a physician focus so much on the patient as a body with a disease that he or she loses sight of the patient as a person. Bioethics has been attacking this form of misprision for a long time (Ramsey, 1970).

The mistake characteristic of bioethics is not overlooking the norm of respect for persons, but misinterpreting it. This mistake views the person in overly atomistic and individualistic terms. Medical ethics and law have set up standards and guidelines that assume that the patient stands alone, with rights and interests, preferences and values autonomously defined. Many safeguards and protections have been put in place to support and defend the patient in that socially unencumbered state: to defend the patient against the automatic use of powerful but burdensome technology, to protect against well-meaning but insolent physician paternalism, and even to safeguard against the possible malevolence of the patient's own family.

This abstract individualism is most apparent in the paradigm of ethical guidelines and legal regulations concerning decision making near the end of life (Meisel & Jennings, 2005). In this paradigm, as elsewhere, medical ethics bumps up against the fact of diversity.[3]

AUTONOMY VERSUS RECOGNITION

Taking the concept of culture and the fact of diversity seriously raises fundamental questions about an individualistic understanding of respect for persons. In order to examine this issue more fully, I suggest we distinguish two different perspectives on the norm of respect for persons: (1) an individualistic *perspective of autonomy*, and (2) a relational *perspective of recognition*.

The concept of autonomy is not synonymous with the principle of respect for persons, although it is often used that way in the bioethical literature (Beauchamp & Childress, 2008; President's Commission, 1983). To be precise, autonomy is a particular, individualistic way of understanding the notion of a person and interpreting what is required for a human being to be respected as a person. Seen through the lens of autonomy, to be a person is (a) to be free from outside coercion or constraint; and (b) to have the mental capacity to make decisions and choices freely, including the choice of values, lifestyles, and life plans (Jennings, 2007; O'Neill, 2002; Schneider, 1998).

Notice how this conception views the relationship between the individual and his or her cultural context, or the internal psychological relationship between the *I* and the *me*. The autonomous self is somehow detached from the culture, much as a shopper is detached from the commodities on display in a store. The meanings, beliefs, values, roles, statuses, bodies of information, tools, and all the other resources a culture and a society offer to individuals are there to be selectively appropriated or rejected by the freely choosing self or person.

---

3 Medical science has also collided with cultural diversity, with interesting, disturbing results; for a full consideration of that side of the issue, see Fadiman, 1998.

The autonomous *I* looks at the social *me* in much the same way: Identities are to be constructed by the self in a selective process of appropriation from the cultural stock.

This view raises a difficult philosophical question—namely, where does this autonomous self, this I, come from in the first place (Metzinger, 2003)? It must logically preexist or stand apart from the cultural milieu from which it constructs its own identity. But, if so, then the concept of autonomy does not simply mean free choice by a self; it means the spontaneous creation of the self *ex nihilo*. The concept of autonomy in bioethics gives us an understanding of the relationship between culture and self-identity that centers on what we might call "revelation"—that is, the unveiling of the already complete person, or the manifestation of a person's being through the process of selecting and appropriating cultural resources.

The concept of autonomy is one way of defining the ethical tenet of respect for persons. The much less individualistic and more relational, interactionist perspective of recognition provides another way to define respect for persons. In contrast to revelation, *recognition* is the ongoing, dynamic becoming of the person through the social, communicative action of making cultural meaning. Recognition is an account of the relationship between culture and self-identity that posits a dialectic of self and culture, shaping and being shaped, the production and reproduction of meaning and identity (Taylor, 1992).

I believe that this perspective of recognition is the best way to understand the principal ethical implications of cultural diversity for health care. In the next stage of work on bioethics and the ethics of health care—prompted in no small measure by the demands of a culturally diverse society and patient population—it will be necessary to move beyond the perspective of autonomy and to rethink the basic conception of the person, the human individual, on which our ethical traditions are so fundamentally based. Persons need support in their struggle for recognition, but that support is not best provided to them if we assume that they are culturally generic autonomous selves. Reform that would institutionalize respect for the *individuality* and the distinct identity of each person has been undermined by the philosophical *individualism* that has dominated bioethics.

This, I submit, is precisely what has happened in American end-of-life care in mainstream medicine, but not (or at least to a much lesser degree) in hospice. Consider the apparatus of patient autonomy that has been built in the end-of-life care setting since the mid-1970s (Field & Cassel, 1997). It includes living wills, durable powers of attorney for health care (proxies), do-not-resuscitate (DNR) orders, the legal concept of substituted judgment for surrogate decision making, the creation of the Medicare hospice benefit, and the medical information and privacy provisions of the Health Insurance Portability and Accountability Act (HIPAA). Each of these policy tools has caused conflict, uncertainty, and considerable stress in hospitals and nursing homes throughout the country; none has worked quite as its architects anticipated or hoped.

One reason for that has been the negative reaction, or confusion, of patients and families for whom the notions of autonomy, privacy, advance planning, and individual decision making are not familiar and do not feel intuitively comfortable. These rules and procedures designed to protect the separate individual often seem constraining rather than protective; they often go against the grain of family practice and cultural tradition; they do not comport with the right way to be sick or the right way to relate to doctors and family members when one is sick.

This is the collision between the autonomy ethic in end-of-life care and cultural diversity. The paradox is that an alienating personal and cultural experience lacking in respect has been created for many people at the end of their lives, precisely because a massive social and legal effort has been made to create the conditions for respect for persons in the medical setting, which is so often reductionistic, technocratic, and dehumanizing.

THE LESSONS OF DIVERSITY FOR END-OF-LIFE CARE

The topic of cultural diversity was not much discussed in bioethics (with the exception of special cases, such as the refusal of blood transfusions by members of the Jehovah's Witnesses) until the mid-1990s (Blackhall, Murphy, Frank, Michel, & Azen, 1995; Carrese & Rhodes, 1995; Dula, 1994; Jonsen, 1986). The initial reaction was something like the creation of checklists of culturally distinctive beliefs, attitudes, and practices that clinicians should learn and refer to when they encountered a patient who fell within a certain cultural or ethnic classification (Koenig & Gates-Williams, 1995). This was exactly the wrong lesson to be drawn, of course; but it was an understandable reaction of a profession in a clinical setting that is committed to the development of rule-governed protocols to guide decision making and practice.

Four main ethical issues are directly associated with cultural diversity in end-of-life care.

The first is the issue of cultural values versus professional values and institutional interests. This has to do with the possible conflicts, just mentioned, between the goal of providing culturally appropriate and flexible systems of care, on the one hand, and the priorities of the medical profession and medical institutions, on the other. Physicians rely on certain protocols and have difficulty when called upon to deviate from them. Medical technologies and medical-scientific knowledge have their own ways of framing reality and decision making, and they impose a certain structure on the caregiving process. And medical institutions—especially hospitals, but also long-term care facilities and even hospice programs—have their own institutional and economic imperatives (Kaufman, 2005).

The second issue involves cultural values versus individual rights. This often takes the form of a conflict between seemingly incommensurable values, particularly when some of those values are institutionalized in mainstream medical ethics and law. An example of this type of problem would be the situation in which a family member or a person of significance in a given cultural group insists that the rights of a patient be superseded in favor of other values important to that cultural group. Here, cases often focus on the right of an adult with decision-making capacity to refuse medical treatment or to be given the opportunity to give informed consent to treatment (Manson & O'Neill, 2007).

The third issue is autonomy versus beneficence. It arises when there is a conflict between what a specific cultural context or tradition directs a patient or family to decide and what is in the patient's objective best interest. If the patient himself or herself is making such a choice, this problem can be construed as a conflict between the principles of autonomy and beneficence—respecting what the patient wants and values versus doing what is beneficial for the health of the patient.

Finally, there is the definition of reason. In the context of cultural diversity, this dilemma can become quite complex, because questions about the rationality and validity of the patient's own choices are sometimes raised. From a mainstream American perspective, some medical choices are rational and some are not. Does autonomy require that health professionals honor and support irrational choices? Arguably not. But the factor of cultural diversity raises the prior question of whether a health professional is in any position to make a judgment about the rationality of any decision made by someone with a background and worldview that the health professional may not understand or be able to sympathize with.

Each of these ethical problems is important, and the resolution of each should be a part of the assessment that any hospice or other healthcare facility makes of its capacity to provide culturally appropriate care. However, it is likely that there will be no clear-cut solution to cases that present ethical dilemmas of these four kinds. Consider the following example:

> A physician is faced with an ethical dilemma when an eldest Korean son refuses to allow the doctor to tell an elderly Korean woman (his mother)—a recent immigrant who speaks no English—that she has cancer. The son announces that he will be making all medical decisions for his mother and that she would be unduly burdened by knowledge of her condition. The physician approaches the patient and asks her if he has her permission to consult with her son and to have him make decisions about her care. The doctor is hoping for an autonomous waiving of autonomy and believes that would be ethically acceptable. However, the ploy backfires. The patient (through an interpreter) expresses outrage that the doctor would question her about what her son is doing, and she refuses to speak with the doctor further. This also estranges the physician from the patient's son and puts a chill on their interactions.

Turning to autonomy to resolve a dilemma involving autonomy will not work unless the value of autonomy has a foothold with the patient and family in the first place (Freedman, 1993). The ethical dilemma remains because the concept of autonomy gives one interpretation of the reality of the situation, while the patient's cultural value orientation gives another (Orona, Koenig, & Davis, 1994).

There is no principle-based resolution here. What is needed is a process through which the terms are redefined on both sides and the conflicting interpretations gradually give way to an overlapping interpretation. In this case, indirect and nonverbal means were found to communicate information to the patient about her condition, and this was culturally and personally acceptable to both mother and son.

If process and communication are the keys to handling cultural diversity appropriately, what are some important elements of that process? What does a postautonomy perspective on relationality and recognition imply for specific steps that can be taken by healthcare organizations? The following points, while certainly not comprehensive, seem to be in keeping with the perspective of recognition and respect for persons in a culturally diverse environment:

- Establish adequate means of communication and overcome language barriers with appropriate translation and linguistic interpretation resources (Solomon, 1997).
- Regularly assess routine institutional patterns of communication; they may not be functioning in a culturally appropriate way.
- Trust is fundamental to successful communication and decision making (Dula, 1994).
- Avoid stereotyping or default approaches to individuals or groups.
- Develop culturally knowledgeable mediation skills in house or ensure that they are readily available (Dubler & Liebman, 1994).
- Establish good relations with the broader cultural communities the health facility serves.

CONCLUSION

Cultures give people a language within which to comprehend and communicate their experience, a lens through which to perceive themselves and the world, and a repertoire of meanings and symbols with which to organize their experiences and make them cohere into some kind of whole. These cultural lenses and traditions vary greatly on the surface, but at a deeper level they tend to converge on some similar themes and core meanings. The subjects of death, dying, pain, suffering, care, dignity, and peace at the end of life may, in fact, lead one to that terrain where our diverse humanness recedes and our common humanity comes to the fore.

Bruce Jennings is director of the Center for Humans and Nature, a private foundation that supports work on environmental and public health policy and planning. He is also senior consultant to the Hastings Center and teaches at the Yale School of Public Health. He has written or edited 20 books and has published more than 150 articles on bioethics and public policy issues. He is currently working on new ethical guidelines on end-of-life care under development at the Hastings Center.

REFERENCES

Appiah, K. A. (2005). *The ethics of identity.* Princeton, NJ: Princeton University Press.

Aronson, E. (2008). *The social animal* (10th ed.). New York: Worth Publishers.

Beauchamp, T., & Childress, J. (2008). *Principles of biomedical ethics* (6th ed.). New York: Oxford University Press.

Blackhall, L. J., Murphy, S. T., Frank, G., Michel, V., & Azen, S. (1995). Ethnicity and attitudes toward patient autonomy. *Journal of the American Medical Association, 274*(10), 820–825.

Carrese, J. A., & Rhodes, L. A. (1995). Western bioethics on the Navajo reservation. *Journal of the American Medical Association, 274*(10), 826–829.

Dubler, N. N., & Liebman, C. B. (1994). *Bioethics mediation: A guide to shaping shared solutions.* New York: United Hospital Fund.

Dula, A. (1994). African American suspicion of the healthcare system is justified: What do we do about it? *Cambridge Quarterly of Healthcare Ethics, 3*(3), 347–357.

Fadiman, A. (1998). *The Spirit catches you and you fall down.* New York: Farrar, Straus and Giroux.

Field, M. J., & Cassel, C. K. (Eds.). (1997). *Approaching death: Improving care at the end of life.* Washington, DC: National Academy Press.

Fraser, N., & Honneth, A. (2003). *Redistribution or recognition: A political-philosophical exchange.* London: Verso Press.

Freedman, B. (1993). Offering truth: One ethical approach to the uninformed cancer patient. *Archives of Internal Medicine, 153*(5), 572–576.

Harré, R. (1998). *The singular self.* London: Sage Publications.

Harré, R., & Gillett, G. (1994). *The discursive mind.* Thousand Oaks, CA: Sage Publications.

Honneth, A. (1996). *The struggle for recognition: The moral grammar of social conflicts.* Cambridge, MA: MIT Press.

Institute of Medicine. (2003). *Unequal treatment: Confronting racial and ethnic disparities in health care.* Washington, DC: National Academy Press.

Jennings, B. (2007). Autonomy. In B. Steinbock (Ed.), *The Oxford handbook of bioethics* (pp. 72–89). New York: Oxford University Press.

Jennings, B., & Murray, T. H. (2005). The quest to reform end-of-life care: Rethinking assumptions and setting new directions. In B. Jennings, G. Kaebnick, & T. H. Murray (Eds.), *Improving end-of-life care: Why has it been so difficult? Hastings Center special report 35*(6), S-52–S-57.

Jonsen, A. R. (1986). Blood transfusions and Jehovah's Witnesses: The impact of the patient's unusual beliefs in critical care. *Critical Care Clinics, 2*(1), 91–100.

Katz, J. (2002). *The silent world of doctor and patient.* Baltimore: Johns Hopkins University Press.

Kaufman, S. R. (2005). *And a time to die: How American hospitals shape the end of life.* New York: Scribner.

Koenig, B. A., & Gates-Williams, J. (1995). Understanding cultural difference in caring for dying patients. *Western Journal of Medicine, 163*(3), 244–249.

Manson, N. C., & O'Neill, O. (2007). *Rethinking informed consent in bioethics.* Cambridge, MA: Cambridge University Press.

Mead, G. H. (1934). *Mind, self, and society.* Chicago: University of Chicago Press.

Meisel, A., & Jennings, B. (2005). Ethics, end-of-life care and the law: Overview and recent trends. In K. J. Doka, B. Jennings, & C. Corr, (Eds.), *Ethical dilemmas at the end of life* (pp. 63–80). Washington, DC: Hospice Foundation of America.

Metzinger, T. (2003). *Being no one: The self-model theory of subjectivity.* Cambridge, MA: MIT Press.

Mithen, S. (2006). *The Singing Neanderthals: The origins of music, language, mind and body.* Cambridge, MA: Harvard University Press.

Nussbaum, M. C. (2001). *Women and human development.* Cambridge: Cambridge University Press.

O'Neill, O. (2002). *Autonomy and trust in bioethics.* Cambridge: Cambridge University Press.

Orona, C. J., Koenig, B. A., & Davis, A. J. (1994). Cultural aspects of nondisclosure. *Cambridge Quarterly of Healthcare Ethics, (3)*3, 338–346.

Powers, M., & Faden, R. (2008). *Social justice: The moral foundations of public health and health policy.* New York: Oxford University Press.

President's Commission on Ethical Problems in Medicine and Biomedical and Behavioral Research (1983). *Deciding to forego life-sustaining treatment.* Washington, DC: Government Printing Office.

Ramsey, P. (1970). *The patient as person.* New Haven: Yale University Press.

Sahlins, M. (1978). *Culture and practical reason.* Chicago: University of Chicago Press.

Schneider, C. E. (1998). *The practice of autonomy: Patients, doctors, and medical decisions.* New York: Oxford University Press.

Shweder, R. A. (1991). *Thinking through cultures: Expeditions in cultural psychology.* Cambridge, MA: Harvard University Press.

Solomon, M. Z. (1997). From what's neutral to what's meaningful: Reflections on a study of medical interpreters. *Journal of Clinical Ethics, 8*(1), 88–93.

Taylor, C. (1992). *Multiculturalism and "the politics of recognition."* Princeton: Princeton University Press.

Tugendhat, E. (1986). *Self-consciousness and self-determination.* Cambridge, MA: MIT Press.

Diversity and Access to Hospice Care

Richard B. Fife

T he modern hospice movement, which had its roots in the work of Cicely Saunders and others in the United Kingdom, began in the United States a little over 30 years ago in a hospice created in Connecticut. The primary purpose of hospice was to provide comfort care and emotional support for those who are terminally ill. Although it would eventually include a wide range of life-threatening illnesses, at the beginning hospice focused on patients dying from cancer, and cancer remains the main focus of hospice in general. According to the statistics of the National Hospice and Palliative Care Organization (NHPCO), America's minorities face significantly higher rates of death from cancer (as well as many other life-threatening diseases). If hospice is truly appropriate for all persons, it would seem to follow that minority patients would be admitted to hospice in numbers at least comparable to their percentage of the population. However, according to the NHPCO's *Facts and Figures* released in October 2008, a great disparity continues to exist in hospice care.

In 2007, 1.4 million patients were being cared for by more than 4,700 hospices in the United States. While only two-thirds of the U.S. population was non-Hispanic white, a full 81% of hospice patients were non-Hispanic white. Although Hispanics are the largest minority in the United States, representing 15% of the population in 2007, only 5.1% of hospice patients were of Hispanic or Latino origin. In 2003, that percentage was 4%. So, although hospice use among Hispanics has increased slightly, it still falls far short of their percentage of the population. In 2007, the percentage of black American residents using hospice care was 9%. The figure was 7.5% in 2003. Both numbers fall far short of the estimated 13.5% of the U.S. population identifying as black. These are the two largest minorities in the United States, and both are greatly underserved by hospice. The disparity is even more striking for Asian Americans, who represent only 1.6% of hospice patients (5% of the population), and Native Americans, who make up only 0.3% while representing 1.5% of the population (National Hospice and Palliative Care Organization [NHPCO], 2008; U.S. Census Bureau, 2008).

These numbers suggest a question: Is hospice care appropriate for all minority groups? If the answer is yes, the question becomes "What are the barriers to hospice access and how can they be overcome?"

BARRIERS TO ACCESS FOR AFRICAN AMERICANS

For several years, I chaired the corporate ethics committee for VITAS Healthcare. In 2003, I asked a member of the committee—Dr. Richard Payne, director of the Duke Institute on Care at the End of Life—to give a thorough and firsthand report on barriers to hospice care for African Americans. Payne began by telling a story of his experience at M. D. Anderson Research Hospital in Houston, where, at the time, he was one of two African-American physicians on staff. He suggested palliative care to a black man dying of cancer, who responded by asking him if he talked with all of his patients about this. Payne went on to say that this patient, like most African Americans, was extremely resistant to hospice and to what Payne considered to be a painless and dignified death. He said that blacks were twice as likely to request life-sustaining treatment as whites and much more resistant to making advance directives. He said hospice was seen by African Americans as giving up hope. One of the reasons his black patient would not listen to him was a widespread mistrust of the medical establishment by African Americans. Payne cited statistics illustrating that many African Americans do not have access to good medical care and that years of neglect, abuse, and discrimination by the medical establishment have taken their toll. According to Dr. Payne, "The medical community's long, sorry history of racism and unethical behavior toward African Americans must be acknowledged and corrected" (Payne, 2000).

In a presentation to an NHPCO conference in 2005, titled "Ethical Barriers to End-of-Life Care for African Americans," I listed three reasons that black Americans may mistrust the medical establishment:

- Vestiges of slavery
- History of abuse of minorities in research
- Ongoing disparities in access and treatment, including treatment of pain

A brief discussion of these three points sheds some light on a major barrier to hospice care for African Americans. Earl Ofari Hutchinson (2007) writes, "The ugly truth is that a mainstay of America's continuing racial divide is its harsh and continuing mistreatment of poor blacks. This can be directly traced to the persistent and pernicious legacy of slavery." Slavery in the United States was not a fleeting phenomenon. Rather, it lasted for hundreds of years and placed an almost indelible mark on one racial group. And although slavery ended in 1865, discrimination and segregation endured. Not until 1954 did the Supreme Court strike down segregation in the school system; not until 1965 was a sweeping civil rights bill passed in Congress; and not until 2008 did the American Medical Association apologize to black doctors for years of discrimination (Associated Press, 2008).

Slavery's legacy was the creation of institutionalized racism. It reproduced itself through stereotypes, underserviced public schools, drugs, guns, prisons, violence, powerlessness, AIDS, and poverty. The civil rights legislation and affirmative action of the past 45 years have not been enough to correct hundreds of years of mistreatment and racism.

The history of abuse of minorities in research can be illustrated by two medical experiments, only one of which is relatively well known. The lesser known experiment is the theory of eugenics, or "good breeding," which moved from theory to practice in the early 1900s in the United States. Elements of this racist theory became policy, for example, in the forced sterilization laws enacted in 27 states, through which more than 60,000 people were sterilized (Black, 2003). Eugenics was directed primarily at the poor and at minorities. In one state, North Carolina, more than 60% of those affected were black.

The more well known medical experiment was the Tuskegee Syphilis Study carried out in Macon, Alabama, from 1932 through 1972. This study has been described as "the longest nontherapeutic experiment on human beings in medical history" (Sanford, Hartnett, & Jolly, 1999). The study involved 600 black men—399 who had syphilis and 201 who did not. The men were told that they were being treated for "bad blood," but they received no treatment at all for their disease. During the course of the study, perhaps as many as 100 men died of complications of the disease. In 1997, President Bill Clinton apologized for this deception.

Slavery, medical experiments, and mistrust of the medical establishment may not seem so important today, but these issues still resonate in the black community. As late as March 2008, Dr. Jeremiah Wright, former pastor of Trinity United Church of Christ in Chicago and an influential spokesperson in the black community, blamed the government for "inventing the HIV virus as a means of genocide against people of color" (Lapidos, 2008).

Ongoing disparities in health care have been pointed out in many scholarly articles. The *New England Journal of Medicine* has reported on studies showing that inequality in health care remains pervasive; for example, African Americans are less likely to be referred for cardiac catheterization than whites, and pain is widely undertreated in blacks (Freeman & Payne, 2000). Only 25% of pharmacies in predominantly nonwhite neighborhoods carry opiates to treat pain, compared with 72% of pharmacies in white neighborhoods (Morrison, Wallenstein, Natale, Senzel, & Huang, 2000). When one considers barriers to hospice care for African Americans, one cannot overstate the issue of mistrust of the medical establishment. As the Duke Institute states, "Providers must be willing to understand that the mistrust of the healthcare system evidenced in the African-American community is based on a history of malfeasance, neglect, and inequality in health care" (Burrs, Ervin, & Harper, 2006).

Another barrier for African Americans to hospice care is cultural differences. Some aspects of black culture are seemingly in conflict with the hospice philosophy. For example, spirituality and the church have always been extremely important parts of African-American culture. Spirituality was vital during the period of slavery. Many blacks survived by believing that there is nobility in suffering. What does that part of the culture say to hospice's philosophy of pain management? Moreover, life is seen as sacred regardless of its condition. Shouldn't every effort be made to preserve life? What does that say to palliation? If God is responsible for health and miracles do occur, should one be limiting life-sustaining treatments? Does the church come into conflict at this point with palliation?

In addition to spiritual concerns, some preferences in the culture may be at odds with hospice. There is a long-standing tradition in the black community of the family and the community taking care of those who suffer from serious illness. To allow a group such as hospice to enter into the situation alters some of the traditional balance. Additionally, in spite of the tradition of family care at home in the black community, there is a cultural reluctance to allow a person to die at home. Often, near the end, the dying patient will be taken to the hospital setting and the family will insist that everything be done for the patient. In the black community, there is a much greater insistence on heroic measures than in the community at large. Another obstacle to hospice care lies in the fact that there is often not a primary caregiver in the home itself. This seems to be a contradiction to the cultural tradition of family care in the black community.

However, such care is often performed by extended family members, friends, church members, and neighbors, rather than primary caregivers in the home.

Providing care to a patient in the black community may require alterations in the typical hospice approach. The hospice team must recognize the importance of family and extended family in the patient's care, as many blacks prefer to divulge preferences and wishes to family members, so these people must, in effect, be incorporated into the hospice care team of doctor, nurse, social worker, and other usual players (Harris & Phipps, 2001).

Finally, there is little understanding about hospice in the African-American community. Few marketing or education efforts have targeted this community.

Part of the author's personal history in overcoming barriers to hospice in the African-American community involved the access program of VITAS Healthcare Corporation, one of the largest hospice providers in the country. One of the more successful VITAS access programs began almost 10 years ago on the Chicago South Side. VITAS made a long-term commitment to the African-American community that dominates that part of Chicago and took a number of steps to break down barriers to hospice access.

First, VITAS hired management and interdisciplinary team members who represented the community. To do this, it developed and implemented a culturally specific recruitment plan, provided diversity education, and fostered a philosophy of diversity. It evaluated the care delivery model and modified it as needed. VITAS conducted focus groups with the staff to identify prospective needs in the community. Externally, VITAS conducted focus groups to determine geographically and culturally specific needs. It implemented a community outreach program focused on recruiting religious leaders throughout the community. VITAS held a series of breakfast and dinner meetings and initiated open discussions. It provided educational materials to inform the community about hospice and evaluated these materials to ensure that they reflected cultural diversity.

VITAS directly addressed the issues of trust and cultural concerns by developing programs designed specifically for the community. One of these programs, developed at the Duke Institute for Care at the End of Life, was titled "Crossing over Jordan." It was presented three times in the community by Payne, Dr. Karla Holloway of Duke University, and local religious leaders who were incorporated into the program. Recognizing the importance of the church in the African-American community, VITAS collaborated with Jesse

Jackson's Rainbow Project on the Thousand Churches initiative. VITAS hired an African-American liaison to work with the community and placed a staff member on the Thousand Churches project.

Over time, VITAS developed specific marketing programs that greatly raised its profile with the African-American community. VITAS worked to find common goals of care, looking at the role of spiritual beliefs and practices in decision making and at the role of family and extended family in the community. In a recent report, Sharon R. Latson, senior director of access initiatives for VITAS, said that the organization has accessed the African-American media to create stronger visibility for hospice in the community; conducted educational workshops on "What Is Hospice?" at village halls, libraries, town halls, and senior centers; and implemented hospice education in community clinics serving mostly African-American clients. From 2004 to 2008, VITAS saw a 14% increase in the total black average daily census (Latson, 2008).

Breaking down barriers to access for African Americans requires frank, open discussions of trust issues, education in the community, an early and continuous emphasis on spirituality, hiring of African-American staff and volunteers, a focused involvement in the community, and flexibility of care and caregiving options. To return to the original question about appropriateness, in some ways, with some adjustments, the African-American community is the most appropriate of the various minorities and cultures for hospice.

BARRIERS TO ACCESS FOR HISPANICS

The word *Hispanic* refers to a broad group of various populations and diverse cultures. A Hispanic person in the United States may be from Spain or another European country but is more likely to be from Cuba, Mexico, the Dominican Republic, Puerto Rico, or South America. The category includes a variety of people who are proud of their cultures and their traditions, which may be vastly different, for example, for Hispanics in southern Florida compared with those in Texas or southern California.

With Hispanics, there is no history of slavery to consider, but discrimination in health care is widespread. Many Hispanics believe that the long history of discrimination reflects negligence on the part of the medical establishment. For example, one woman said that her husband lost a limb because of this negligence: "They didn't give him any care. It's because we are Mexicans. It happens a lot. They don't respect you" (Sullivan, 2001, p. 5). Discrimination in health care for Hispanics is compounded by language barriers in many hospital settings. Actual or perceived discrimination causes Hispanic patients and their families to seek alternative means of healing. Often this means the use of prayer and faith, but it may also involve traditional faith healers or homemade remedies.

Not only do Hispanics feel discriminated against by the healthcare system, they may actually fear it. In a 2-year study of Hispanic patients in southern Florida, a VITAS hospice medical director found that many had questions such as "Will they report me to the authorities?" "What will it cost?" and "Why are they invading my privacy?" (Policzer, 2004, slide 2).

The barriers to hospice care for Hispanics generally include the following:

- Discrimination in health care.
- Fear of the medical establishment.
- Language barriers.
- Belief that patients must pay for hospice. Very few potential Hispanic patients are aware that Medicare will pay for hospice care.
- Misunderstandings about hospice, such as the belief that loved ones will be taken away from the family.
- What Joel Policzer (2004) calls "a conspiracy of silence." Patients know they are dying and choose not to speak about it; families know the patient is dying and choose not to speak about it. I remember two cases from my hospice team in Miami. VITAS usually sent Spanish-speaking nurses and aides to Hispanic homes, because many elderly Hispanics in Miami do not speak English. One Hispanic family asked the hospice team not to send a Hispanic nurse or aide to the home, because they did not want them speaking with the mother about her condition. In another case, Maria, a Hispanic home health aide, was taking care of Isabel, an 84-year-old Colombian woman with pancreatic cancer. Maria would often sing to Isabel in Spanish as she bathed her. Isabel expressed her gratitude to Maria for caring for her during her illness. She said that her son had told her that she had a very bad ulcer but would be better soon.
- The responsibility of the family to care for the patient, rather than bringing in outsiders. As one Hispanic hospice chaplain put it:

    In the Latino community, as is true in the African-American community, taking care of your own [is important]. There is a certain level of distrust with people coming in, because there's a fear of what they are going to do. You have to establish the level of trust first, then they will allow you to provide care to their loved ones (Franey, 2008).

- The sacredness of life. Many Hispanics believe that life support or heroic measures must be continued. The family needs to see that something is being done besides just "waiting for the patient to die." They readily agree to percutaneous endoscopic gastrostomies and are generally in favor of IV nutrients.
- Culturally sensitive care. Policzer says competent patients should be "allowed to be as informed as they choose to be," with the understanding that such patients "will often require children to make decisions for them." He notes that "the use of Spanish is vital" (Policzer, 2004, slides 12–13).

In 2003, I invited the members of the corporate ethics committee of VITAS Healthcare to take a field trip to the hospice inpatient unit at Hialeah Hospital in Miami-Dade County. Hialeah is a predominantly Hispanic city, and the patients in the inpatient unit are almost all Hispanic. As the committee members went from room to room in the unit, Dr. Robert Fine—a palliative care physician and chairman of the ethics committee at Baylor Hospital in Dallas—asked, "Why are so many of the patients hooked up to IVs?" The hospice medical director explained that the IVs contained only a saline solution with a very slow drip. He explained that many family members, extended family members, and friends who came to be with the patients wanted to see that something was actively being done for them. The immediate families and the unit had agreed on the use of the IVs, which were essentially just for show. Fine asked, "Isn't that being a little ethically compromised?" The medical director replied, "No, it's being culturally sensitive."

Although their rate of participation in hospice is far below their percentage of the population, Hispanics are appropriate candidates for hospice. How, then, do you overcome the barriers to access? A program undertaken by a Florida hospice with a grant from the Robert Wood Johnson Foundation (RWJF) is instructive. In 2001, the Hospice by the Sea in Boca Raton was serving almost 4,000 patients. Only 1.5% were Hispanic, although the Hispanic population was 15% and growing. With a grant from RWJF, the Hospice by the Sea created a Hispanic team tailored to meet the needs of Hispanic patients. The hospice trained the team and all staff in a culturally competent learning program, hired two outreach coordinators and a liaison to work in the Hispanic community and with the hospice staff, and developed culturally sensitive educational materials and Spanish-language marketing materials for the community. The project increased the percentage of Hispanic patients from 1.5% to 5.78% over a 3-year period (Robert Wood Johnson Foundation [RWJF], 2006).

This project—and similar ones conducted by VITAS Healthcare in southern Florida, Texas, and California—offers some guidance for overcoming barriers to access for Hispanics:

- Develop an interdisciplinary Hispanic team with Spanish-speaking members.
- Hire staff and volunteers from the community to be served.
- Hire a liaison or find a volunteer who is a member of the community.
- Develop culturally sensitive Spanish-language educational and marketing materials.
- Train the Hispanic team and the entire hospice staff in the basics of Hispanic culture.
- Educate the Hispanic community about hospice.
- Develop flexibility with hospice services. In the admissions process, this may mean speaking with the family before you speak with the patient. Perhaps it will mean not using the word *hospice* with the patient or spouse. Perhaps it will mean putting more emphasis on the extended family. It will always mean being culturally sensitive.

BARRIERS TO ACCESS FOR OTHER MINORITY GROUPS

In its *Facts and Figures,* NHPCO shows hospice use by race. Almost 98% of users are white, African American, Hispanic, and multiracial. Of the remaining 2%, only two groups are mentioned: (1) Asian Americans, Hawaiian, or other Pacific Islander with 1.6%; and (2) American Indian or Alaskan Native with 0.3%. Although these percentages are not statistically insignificant, they constitute a very small part of the hospice picture. Of 1.3 million hospice patients, only about 27,000 were Asian Americans or Native Americans (NHPCO, 2008). What are the barriers to access, and what does this say about appropriateness for hospice care?

It is hard to speak in general terms about the Native American population. Although there are large concentrations of certain tribes throughout the southwestern and western parts of the country, there are also many smaller tribes in Florida, North Carolina, and other parts of the country. And Alaska has its own native population. Some beliefs are common to a number of tribes. One of these beliefs relates to speaking about death and dying. Once a negative word is spoken, it is feared that the words will become self-fulfilling (Jenko & Moffitt, 2006). Hospice values autonomy and believes that the patient should give informed consent. This concept is reflected in the Patient's Self-Determination Act of 1991. But perhaps patients should be asked how much they want to know about their illness. Would this compromise the hospice approach? Another belief among many Native Americans involves the power of healing touch. Many Native Americans believe that touch can reverse an evil spirit. How does this square with the hospice concept of palliative care? Native Americans also tend to place a high value on traditional treatments for illness, including the use of herbs, rituals, and traditional spiritual healing persons or medicine men.

The question is whether any of these beliefs make Native Americans inappropriate for hospice care, and the answer is no. Medicine men and spiritual healers could be part of the care team, and alternative therapies could be part of the care plan. However, a more significant problem is the question of appropriateness, especially with regard to available essential health services for the terminally ill and a person's desire not to be placed in a facility away from home, even if that is the only source of quality end-of-life services. Because of limited healthcare resources, only 6.5% of American Indian elders receive quality end-of-life care (Gorospe, 2006). The Indian Health Service is unprepared to take care of Native Americans who are living longer and facing life-threatening illnesses. Hospice and long-term care facilities are usually far from families and tribal communities. In 2002, the National Indian Council on Aging identified only 12 Indian nursing homes in the entire United States and estimated that 60% to 70% of Native Americans living in long-term care facilities have no access to palliative care services with the expertise to take care of their special needs (Gorospe, 2006). Think of the vast regions of Alaska or the rugged Southwest and the difficulty of bringing end-of-life services into these areas. Then consider the poverty level of most Native Americans, their meager resources, and the lack of sustainable funding for local healthcare systems. Looking at the overall picture, it is obvious that hospice will be appropriate only if funding is available to "establish a local Indian healthcare system that integrates culturally appropriate palliative care systems" (p. 3). Until such community-based palliative care systems can be developed, perhaps with the use of volunteers providing end-of-life services, the percentage of Native American hospice patients will remain small.

According to the *Asian Week Staff Report* of May 1, 2008, the Asian American and Pacific Islander population has surpassed 15.2 million in the United States—5% of the population. Asian Americans are the second fastest growing minority after Hispanics. They tend to have a lower utilization rate for hospice and other healthcare services "due to numerous cultural barriers, language barriers, and inadequate health insurance coverage" (Wang, Miler, Hufstader, & Bian, 2008, p. 15).

In addition to these barriers, there are matters of belief. As in many Native American tribes, speaking openly and truthfully about death and dying to persons from certain Asian cultures—especially many in Korea, China, and India—is believed to hasten the patient's death (Fife, 2005). In a recent presentation about Chinese and Japanese grief processes, Stella Kwong-Wirth, director of the Asian Home Care Program of the National Association of Social Workers in New York, made the following statement: "In the Asian family, death is not discussed. It is a common superstition that talking about death may lead to it" (pp. 217–218).

Another barrier is similar to one found in many Hispanic cultures: Discussions of death and dying often involve family members rather than the patient, and family elders may make decisions without consulting the patient. The hospice commitment to open discussion of the disease and of death is alien to this family dynamic (Tung, 1990).

These beliefs might seem to make the Asian-American patient an inappropriate candidate for traditional hospice care. However, as with the Hispanic culture, the hospice team should use flexibility and cultural sensitivity to work with the patient, the family, and their belief system.

CONCLUSION

In this chapter, I have considered the four primary minority groups receiving hospice care in the United States, diversity and access issues related to these groups, and the main barriers and how to overcome them and improve access to hospice care. In each case, I have raised the question of appropriateness. If one were to scale the groups for appropriateness for hospice care, they would fall in roughly the same order as their percentage of patients receiving hospice care. African Americans are easily the most appropriate. The barriers to their access to hospice can largely be overcome by education, frank discussions, hiring procedures, and cultural training. Hispanics follow in second place, with some belief barriers to be overcome. Then come Asian Americans and Native Americans.

For the last three groups to be considered appropriate, hospice caregivers will have to demonstrate real cultural understanding and a degree of flexibility. The same kind of flexibility is evident in the way hospice workers deal with Romanies, who believe that the locus of decision is in the grandparents, and with Orthodox Jews, who believe that no one should remove life-sustaining equipment or do anything that could be seen as hastening death. It is the same kind of flexibility that allows a wider understanding of the concept of family for the gay or lesbian patient and recognizes that questions of autonomy do not fit well in discussions with Buddhist or Hindu patients. The final question might be whether this flexibility is simply part of the growing dynamic of hospice or whether it actually alters the fundamentals of hospice, which began in this country as a primarily white, middle-class movement more than 30 years ago.

Richard B. Fife is a United Methodist minister, president/CEO of the Foundation for End-of-Life Care, and a founding and sustaining member of the Duke Institute for Care at the End of Life. An activist minister, he participated in civil rights marches beginning in the 1960s; demonstrated against nuclear power plants with William Sloane Coffin, Jr., in the 1970s; and led peace demonstrations in the Soviet Union, China, and Cuba during the 1980s. He has been involved with VITAS Healthcare for more than 20 years and was vice president of bioethics and pastoral care. In that position, he helped develop the first national hospice clinical pastoral education program, organized the first national hospice ethics committee, and served as an ethics consultant for 30 hospices. He participated on the panel for Hospice Foundation of America's 2005 teleconference on ethics and wrote the chapter "Ethical Dilemmas in Hospice Care" for the accompanying book.

REFERENCES

Associated Press. (2008, July 10). AMA apologizes to black doctors for racism. *MSNBC*. Retrieved August 10, 2008, from http://www.msnbc.msn.com/id/25614966/

Black, E. (2003, November 24). The horrifying American roots of Nazi eugenics. *San Francisco Chronicle*.

Burrs, F. A., Ervin, M. G., & Harper, B. C. (2006). The future of hospice care for African Americans: Clinical, policy, and caregiver perspectives. In Duke Institute on Care at the End of Life, *Key topics on end-of-life care for African Americans*. Retrieved August 19, 2008, from http://www.iceol.duke.edu/resources/lastmiles/papers/08.html

Fife, R. (2005). Ethical dilemmas in hospice care. In K. Doka, B. Jennings, & C. A. Corr (Eds.), *Living with grief: Ethical dilemmas at the end of life* (pp. 207–220). Washington, DC: Hospice Foundation of America.

Franey, L. (2008, January 2). Hospices reaching out to the Hispanic community. *Kansas City Star,* p. B1.

Freeman, H. P., & Payne, R. (2000). Racial injustice in health care. *New England Journal of Medicine, 342*(14), 1045–1047.

Gorospe, E. (2006). Establishing palliative care for American Indians as a public health agenda. *Internet Journal of Pain, Symptom Control and Palliative Care, 4(2).* Available from http://www.ispub.com

Harris, D., & Phipps, E. (2001, May–June). Study examines concerns in Philadelphia African-American community. Americans for Better Care of Dying Exchange. Retrieved August 10, 2008, from http://www.mywhatever.com/cifwriter/content/19/abcd1594.html

Hutchinson, E. O. (2007, February 26). Virginia apologizes for slavery, now it's Congress's turn. *The Huffington Post.* Retrieved August 10, 2008, from http://www.huffingtonpost.com/earl-ofari-hutchinson/virginia-apologizes-for-s_b_42179.html

Jenko, M., & Moffitt, S. R. (2006). Transcultural nursing principles: An application to hospice care. *Journal of Hospice and Palliative Nursing, 8*(3), 172–180.

Lapidos, J. (2008, March 19). The AIDS conspiracy handbook. *Slate.* Retrieved August 19, 2008, from http://www.slate.com/id/2186860/

Latson, S. R. (2008, May 6). Comparative analysis of pre- and post-access initiatives: Patient admissions and ADC within underserved populations. Private report.

Morrison, R. S., Wallenstein, S., Natale, D. K., Senzel, R. S., & Huang, L. L. (2000). We don't carry that: Failure of pharmacies in predominantly nonwhite neighborhoods to stock opioid analgesics. *New England Journal of Medicine, 342*(14), 1023–1026.

National Hospice and Palliative Care Organization (NHPCO). (2008, October). NHPCO facts and figures: Hospice care in America. Retrieved November 1, 2008, from http://www.nhpco.org/files/public/Statistics_Research/NHPCO_facts-and-figures_2008.pdf

Payne, R. (2000, February 15). At the end of life, color still divides. *Washington Post,* p. 15.

Policzer, J. (2004). You've got to go where he lives [PowerPoint slides]. Retrieved August 15, 2008, from www.amsa.org/dd/CulturallySensitive.ppt

Robert Wood Johnson Foundation (RWJF). (2006). Florida hospice uses grant to improve outreach, services to Hispanics. Retrieved August 19, 2008, from http://www.rwjf.org/reports/grr/046134.htm

Sanford, S. M., Hartnett, T., & Jolly, B. T. (1999, Summer). Lessons from the past: The roots of the informed consent process. *The Monitor.*

Sullivan, M. C. (2001, Winter) Lost in translation: How Latinos view end-of-life care. Last Acts. Available from http://www.lastacts.org

Tung, T. M. (1990). Death, dying and hospice: An Asian-American view. *American Journal of Hospice and Palliative Care,* (7)5, 23–25.

U.S. Census Bureau. (2008, May). *Table 3:* Annual estimates of the population by sex, race, and Hispanic origin for the United States: April 1, 2000 to July 1, 2007. NC-EST2007-03. Retrieved October 1, 2008, from http://www.census.gov/popest/national/asrh/NC-EST2007/NC-EST2007-03.xls

Wang, J., Miler, N. A., Hufstader, M. A., & Bian, Y. (2008, May 1). The health status of Asian Americans and Pacific Islanders and their access to health services. *Social Work in Public Health, 23*(1), 15–43.

Training for Diversity

Richard B. Fife

The 10 steps below can help a hospice develop a better program, with outreach to diverse and underserved communities. Five steps relate to the hospice program itself; five relate to the training of hospice staff.

HOSPICE PROGRAM

1. Make a long-term commitment.
Minority patients participate in hospice programs at rates well below their percentage in the population. After 30 years of the hospice movement, 81% of patients are Caucasian, and outreach to minority groups has been consistently slow and uneven. A long-term commitment is required to make a difference in these underserved communities.

2. Hold focus groups and community meetings.
Work with leaders in the targeted community to educate and promote hospice. In African-American and Hispanic communities, this may mean working with ministers and religious leaders. Educating the community is vital. Hold meetings in churches, synagogues, and other places where the community meets. Enlist community leaders to help lead these meetings. Be honest and forthcoming in discussions about issues of trust and discrimination in health care.

3. Hire a community liaison person.
If your budget allows, hire a liaison to work with community leaders. If not, try to find a volunteer in the African-American, Asian-American, or Hispanic community. Beginning in 2001, VITAS Healthcare placed community liaisons in five of its programs located in communities with large African-American or Hispanic populations. In May 2008, Sharon R. Latson, senior director of

access initiatives for VITAS, reported on a comparison of programs with community liaisons and similar programs that did not have community liaisons. In each case where there was a community liaison, increase in participation among the targeted underserved population exceeded overall program growth in both admissions and average daily census. In the programs without a community liaison, overall program growth greatly outpaced participation by underserved populations. The community liaison can be invaluable in breaking down the barriers that inhibit participation by diverse populations.

4. Recruit staff and volunteers from the community.

If you open a hospice program on the South Side of Chicago and want to reach out to the large underserved African-American population in that community, it is essential that you secure staff and volunteers who reflect the community. If you are reaching out to a Hispanic community, you must have staff who are fluent Spanish speakers. The best way to reach out to an underserved community is to involve the community in the process through hiring procedures and recruitment of volunteers.

5. Secure training materials, and develop focused programs and marketing materials.

The Duke Institute on Care at the End of Life and VITAS Healthcare have prepared a number of materials on African-American culture. These include "Key Topics on End-of-Life Care for African Americans," which can be downloaded from the Duke Institute website (www.iceol.duke.edu). The Duke Institute and VITAS have also prepared APPEAL (A Progressive Palliative Care Educational Curriculum for the Care of African Americans at Life's End) modules and training symposiums such as "Crossing over Jordan." For the Jewish culture, the Duke Institute has developed a symposium on "Jewish Ritual, Reality, and Response at the End of Life," also available on the website. In August 2008, the National Hospice and

Palliative Care Organization (NHPCO) held a 3-day conference on diversity, including a session on "Overcoming Barriers to End-of-Life Care in the Hispanic Community." Materials and sessions from that conference are available on the NHPCO website (www .nhpco.org). Each hospice needs to develop programs and marketing materials targeted to its underserved communities and groups.

TRAINING THE STAFF

6. Train for cultural awareness.
The first step in understanding another culture is to understand your own. Train the staff in self-reflection. What is positive or negative about your culture? What is your bias? How do you see yourself? How do others see you? What is peculiar about your culture? Encourage staff members to place themselves in another person's culture and ask similar questions. Do you understand how language affects the culture? How about issues of trust and discrimination in health? Customs in eating and dress? Rituals? How does the culture view death and speaking about death? How do people in another culture view advance directives?

7. Train in communication skills.
Communication is vital and is a paramount reason to hire staff members who represent the community. In the Hispanic community, it is extremely important that staff are fluent Spanish speakers. If you must use a translator, use a professional; a family member may tend to interpret rather than translate. In all minority communities, it is important that staff understand and communicate with the culture. Building a knowledge base and instilling respect and sensitivity for the distinctive culture of the minority group is essential to increase access for that population.

8. Train in flexibility.
Staff will need training to be flexible in working with the minority community. For example, in the Hispanic community, there is a

strong philosophy of "don't ask, don't tell." Patients know they are dying and choose not to speak about it; families know the patients are dying but do not discuss it. Some cultures believe that talking about death actually hastens the event. Hospice personnel are trained to speak with a competent patient, but some cultures insist that elders, grandparents, or other relatives be consulted first. This is especially true of Hispanics and Asians. Competent patients should be as informed as they want to be. Also, many cultures are very resistant to advance directives, and a do-not-resuscitate order may be seen as the pathway to second-rate care. Flexibility and an understanding of the particular culture are essential.

9. Take advantage of outside workshops and resources.
It is usually not sufficient for a program to secure training materials and try to train its own staff in cultural competence. Some staff members will need to be trained in settings where there is a fuller knowledge of the targeted cultural group.

10. Train to monitor and assess.
Staff should be trained to constantly monitor and assess cultural appropriateness, and to look for signs of unequal or insensitive treatment. Staff members should continually examine their own culture and beliefs, and assess their reactions to other cultures and beliefs.

CHAPTER 5

Cultural Diversity: Implications for Funeral Traditions

Stephen M. Mack and Sumner J. Waring, III

CHANGING DEMOGRAPHICS

Changing demographics and a more multicultural society are altering the traditional view of funeral service. Today's consumers have different, often highly individual, expectations and needs compared with those of consumers just 10 or 15 years ago. While a traditional religious funeral is still chosen by many families, demand for a wider range of options is rising. The funeral profession finds itself responding to a growing trend toward nontraditional, more secular ceremonies, while at the same time developing new services and facilities to meet the needs of emergent religious and ethnic communities.

A number of interrelated factors are shaping an increasingly diverse society. An examination of these factors reveals both the changing landscape of American society and implications for funeral traditions.

The Baby Boomer Influence

Baby boomers—the 78 million Americans born between 1946 and 1964—represent perhaps the single greatest social influence in the United States. Members of this generation have changed almost everything they have touched, preferring to forge their own trails rather than following those left by their parents.

Baby boomers tend to emphasize personal needs and personal expression, valuing the ability to be in charge of their own lives (Irion, 2007). Just as they have redefined other social conventions, baby boomers are likely to look outside long-standing funeral traditions for different kinds of ceremonies that offer greater personal expression.

In recent years, in fact, funeral professionals have seen an increase in the number of nontraditional services and a growing demand for different, more personally meaningful rituals. Families have strong opinions about what they want, and many are taking a more active role in planning for and participating in the service.

This trend seems likely to continue. Baby boomers are growing older themselves and many are caring for elderly parents. A survey by Campbell-Ewald Health (2005) found that some 13 million baby boomers are caregivers for sick or elderly parents. Just as they influence health care for their parents, these baby boomers are also making funeral decisions when their parents die. In addition, as baby boomers age and confront their own end-of-life decisions, they can be expected to influence funeral traditions in even more dramatic ways.

Growing Ethnic Diversity

Immigration patterns in recent decades are altering the nation's racial and ethnic mix. In 1960, the U.S. population was nearly 87% white and approximately 10% African American. Other races accounted for less than 1% of the population. By the year 2000, however, the United States was 75% white and 12.3% African American, with other races representing 12.5% of the population (Hobbs & Stoops, 2002). In 2005, whites accounted for 67% of the U.S. population; while African Americans represented 13%, Hispanics 14%, and Asians 5% (Passel & Cohn, 2008).

According to projections, the trend toward greater diversity will continue, and the nation will have a much different face by 2050. The percentage of whites will drop to 47%. The African-American segment of the population will remain relatively stable, while Hispanics (currently the fastest growing ethnic group) will represent 29% of the total population. The Asian-American population is expected to triple in size by 2050, accounting for 9% of the population (Passel & Cohn, 2008).

Ethnic populations are already predominant in some metropolitan areas. According to the U.S. Census Bureau (2006), Hispanics represent 49% of the population of Los Angeles and 42% of the population of Houston. Asians account for almost 12% of New York City's population and 10% of the population in Los Angeles.

Immigration is the major factor driving increased ethnic diversity. Immigrants and their descendants born in the United States will account for 82% of projected population growth by 2050 (Passel & Cohn, 2008).

Immigration can significantly influence funeral traditions, because new groups of immigrants bring with them the customs and traditions of their homelands. Immigrants, especially those in less acculturated groups, seek to continue observing familiar rituals after they enter the United States. Funeral professionals, especially those in ethnic communities, are increasingly aware of the need to provide for families who want to carry out funeral traditions with which we have little familiarity in the United States.

Religious Diversity

With changing demographics and the influx of new immigrant groups, the variety of religious traditions in the United States is also on the rise. Protestants remain the majority by 51%; however, Protestantism has become increasingly diverse, comprising hundreds of different mainline, evangelical, and historically black denominations. Roman Catholics today represent 24% of the population, and Jews 1.7%. Smaller religious segments include Mormons, Jehovah's Witnesses, Buddhists, Muslims, and Hindus (Pew Forum on Religion and Public Life, 2008).

The fastest growing segment is the 16% of Americans who have no formal religious affiliation. This unaffiliated group, while not primarily secular, is relatively young. Thirty-one percent of unaffiliated Americans are under 30 years old, and 71% are under 50 (Pew Forum on Religion and Public Life, 2008).

Greater religious diversity means greater diversity in funeral traditions. The funeral profession faces the need to accommodate the requirements of a greater variety of religions than ever before, including traditionally Eastern religions. At the same time, more families are seeking nonreligious alternatives to the traditional funeral. Religiously unaffiliated families may prefer a gathering of friends and family, a dinner, or another form of private remembrance, occasionally held outside the funeral home or place of worship. Given the increasing number of religiously unaffiliated persons and the age of this group, the need for nonreligious rituals seems likely to increase.

An Aging Population

Advances in medical technology are allowing people to live longer. The 2000 census identified 35 million Americans over the age of 65. Of that group, 12% were 85 years or older (Gist & Hetzel, 2004). The elderly population is growing faster than the general population and is expected to number 81 million by 2050. Fueling this growth is the huge baby boomer generation, which will add to the elderly population over the next several decades (Passel & Cohn, 2008).

The aging population is influencing funeral choices. The very elderly, especially those older than 85, may have outlived many of their contemporaries and perhaps even members of their own families. If they are living far from their families and original communities when they die, surviving family members may opt for direct cremation or direct burial. Some families choose a graveside service rather than a full funeral, because the community that once surrounded the deceased loved one is gone or greatly diminished. In fact, those who attend services for the very elderly often come primarily to support the surviving family.

A Changing View of Death and Dying

Two recent trends are influencing the general view of death and dying. One is the greater understanding of dying and grief (Irion, 2007). A view that death is a natural part of life is more common, perhaps in part because of the many books on death and dying available to the general public and helping professionals.

Hospice care is also changing the experience of death for many people. According to estimates by the National Hospice and Palliative Care Organization (2007), the number of patients receiving hospice services increased 162% between 1997 and 2006. More than one-third of all U.S. deaths in 2006 occurred in a hospice program.

Hospice care provides for the needs of the dying person while preparing survivors for the death. Through this extended process, survivors have the opportunity to say goodbye and begin coping with the loss (Corr, 2007). They may also begin to achieve a sense of closure that the funeral traditionally was thought to provide.

As a result of these trends, many families now seem to approach funeral services with a different set of expectations. Depending on their religious beliefs, more families prefer a ceremony that celebrates the life lived and reflects the individuality of the deceased loved one. The Roman Catholic, Orthodox Jewish, and Muslim faiths still require strict adherence to traditional rituals, focusing on the death itself and the promise of eternal peace. Among nonorthodox faiths, however, even traditional funeral services are more likely to emphasize a celebration of life. The growing number of religiously unaffiliated families also tend to desire ceremonies that honor the life and achievements of the deceased person.

CHANGING TRADITIONS IN A DIVERSE SOCIETY

Greater social and cultural diversity is influencing funeral customs and traditions. Many changes are evident, along with a greater variety of options for families to choose from when planning a funeral.

Personalization

One of the most visible new traditions is the trend toward personalized funeral services. Personalization—designing a service that reflects the individuality of the deceased person—is increasingly important to families.

Personalization may be expressed in a variety of ways. Some families opt for nontraditional ceremonies outside the funeral home or place of worship, such as a barbeque in the backyard or a memorial service at the beach. Props are frequently incorporated into services held in the funeral home. Families may choose to display possessions or hobbies that were important to their loved one, such as fishing poles, artwork, golf clubs, or a motorcycle. Pets may be included, as in the case of a hunting dog who sat next to his master's casket throughout the visitation. The family of one man who was known for his love of blue martinis chose to serve this unique drink at the visitation.

Friends and family are more likely to participate in services by offering tributes or sharing their memories of the deceased. The choice of pallbearers and participants in the procession may also reflect an individual's life and interests. After the service for an avid cyclist, for example, members of his cycling club joined the procession on bicycles.

The wider range of music used in funeral services today, including more nonreligious music, reflects the personal taste of families and their deceased loved ones. For example, the family of a woman who loved dancing asked the funeral home to arrange for music and a dance floor so that guests at the visitation could honor her memory by dancing.

Technology in the funeral home is still in its infancy, but nevertheless, it plays a role in personalization. Some funeral service providers can produce customized movies and slide shows using family photos. Internet memorials are becoming popular. Families can create an individual tribute that can be shared with others through the Internet. These products enable families to create a lasting legacy for future generations, while allowing friends and relatives from anywhere in the world to take part in memorializing the loved one. However, not all families are aware of this option. Funeral professionals have an opportunity to offer this service and educate families about the benefits and value of an Internet memorial.

The trend toward personalization is likely to continue as aging baby boomers enter the market for funeral services. Early indicators suggest that these consumers will want something different, not something less, in a funeral. The challenge for the funeral profession is to anticipate the next wave of consumer expectations and provide options to meet those needs.

Expanded Service Options

Today, the funeral profession and consumers alike have a greater understanding of grief, viewing the funeral as a milestone rather than an end point in the mourning process (Irion, 2007). This understanding, combined with increasing commoditization of funeral products such as caskets, has led to the development of value-added service options that benefit families before and after the funeral, as well as on the day of the service.

One funeral provider created bereavement travel services in response to the increased need for travel to a funeral. Many families are geographically scattered and can benefit from travel assistance. New funeral home facilities are designed to accommodate a wider range of needs. Large chapels, while still important, need the flexibility of configurable spaces that can be rearranged for many different types of personalized services. Funeral homes may offer hospitality rooms and special areas for young children. Even the appearance of some funeral homes is changing, from a traditional somber and formal character to a more contemporary, uplifting décor that reflects a focus on celebrating life.

Some funeral providers have added event coordination and catering services to help families organize and conduct a service held outside the funeral home. Funeral homes also combine event coordination and catering services with onsite reception centers that can accommodate large gatherings. These facilities meet the needs of families who want to have a gathering or meal after the service, especially when relatives have traveled long distances to attend the funeral. In addition, families may use such facilities for a service or observance on the anniversary of a death.

To address the need for grief support and recovery after the death, some funeral providers have developed specialized aftercare services. For example, grief helplines provide support and bereavement counseling by telephone 24 hours a day. To assist families with practical matters such as estate settlement, some funeral providers offer legal services packages and kits that guide families through the business transactions that are necessary after a death.

Many families expect funeral professionals to respond to the full range of their needs before, during, and after the funeral. Yet, as consumers, they may not know what to ask for and may be unaware of all the options available to them. The funeral profession is challenged to change in response to consumer expectations. The next generation of funeral professionals will have to combine compassion, empathy, and deep listening skills with an entrepreneurial spirit that can design creative solutions to meet families' needs.

Ethnic Traditions

The United States is becoming more ethnically diverse as large groups of immigrants enter the country. The current wave of mostly non-European immigrants is bringing new customs and traditions, often strikingly different from those of mainstream American culture. The two fastest growing ethnic groups, Hispanics and Asians, have begun to influence funeral traditions in numerous ways.

Some funeral service providers in Hispanic communities are creating facilities and specialized service options expressly for Hispanic families. For example, the funeral homes feature signage in Spanish, as well as architectural features and interior design that appeal to Hispanic consumers. The facilities are staffed with bilingual professionals who can easily communicate with families. Arrangement areas are more spacious to accommodate the large extended family groups that tend to be involved in planning the service. Funeral homes may be open around the clock to accommodate all-night visitation, an important tradition for certain recent immigrants from Latin America. When permitted by state law, the funeral service provider may coordinate in-home visitations, which are sometimes preferred by Hispanic families.

The Asian population, which encompasses multiple countries of origin and several different religions, is bringing a diversity of new funeral traditions. In many cases, Asian visitations and funeral services last longer than a typical Western funeral, sometimes 3 days or even longer. Some funeral service providers have designed custom chapel spaces to accommodate these longer services, as well as providing specialized altars, banners, decorations, and ventilation for burning incense during the service. Specific products may also be required, such as ceremonial paper, burial clothing, money envelopes, and longevity blankets that are placed in the casket with the deceased or used to wrap cremated remains. Cemeteries preferred by Asian families have dedicated specific sections of the grounds for burials, in some cases even developing specialized Asian gardens based on feng shui principles. Some cemeteries have begun to host Ching Ming festivals—annual observances in which Chinese families honor their ancestors by cleaning the graves and making offerings of flowers and food.

As American society becomes increasingly multicultural, funeral traditions will continue to diversify. Funeral professionals need flexibility and an open mind to effectively serve all families in a diverse society. In addition, serving consumers of multiple ethnic backgrounds requires the right facilities—from configurable spaces to specially designed chapels—and the right people, such as multilingual staff members.

New Religious Traditions

The Protestant, Catholic, and Jewish faiths have been the major religious influences in the United States for many years; however, our nation's religious landscape is becoming more diverse. Of particular significance to the funeral services profession is the growth of Eastern religions, such as Buddhism and Hinduism, as well as the growth of Islam and Orthodox Judaism. Although these religious groups are still quite small relative to the overall population, they may represent 30% to 40% of the client base for some funeral homes. For this reason, funeral providers are developing appropriate service offerings and facilities to accommodate families' religious needs.

Some religious observances require great flexibility and understanding on the part of funeral providers as these practices are carried out in a Westernized culture. For example, both the Orthodox Jewish and Islamic faiths require ritual washing and preparation of the deceased person. To allow observance of this tradition without violating health regulations, some funeral homes have set up rooms separate from the normal preparation area where families can perform these rites. Orthodox Jews may observe *shmeerah* (watching over the deceased person until burial takes place). The funeral home must be open and staffed 24 hours a day to allow it to take place. A Muslim service must not be delayed, because burial is required within 24 hours of the death. Orthodox Judaism also requires that burial take place without undue delay.

Buddhist services may be elaborate and require a great deal of coordination with the monk or temple. The monk may perform an initial service soon after death, before the deceased person is brought to the funeral home. The monk may also specify the most favorable time for burial. When cremation is chosen, the family may want the monk to stay near the deceased person, praying and chanting as the remains are placed in the crematory. Some funeral homes provide a special observation area for the monk to carry out this ritual.

Funeral directors have traditionally worked closely with clergy to arrange religiously compliant services. The funeral professional's role in helping families meet religious requirements has not changed. Serving a more diverse group of consumers, however, requires broader knowledge on the part of funeral professionals, as well as nimbleness and flexibility to meet the need for a greater variety of religious observances.

CONCLUSION

Funeral rituals serve the needs of survivors to receive the love and support of family and community after a death occurs. This fundamental purpose of the funeral profession has not changed and probably never will. The process of grieving and remembering a life lived is a very healthy one. While funeral traditions will continue to evolve with our changing society, the need for rituals that help survivors grieve is a human one, transcending culture and custom.

Stephen M. Mack is senior vice president, middle market operations, at Service Corporation International (SCI). He began working for a local funeral home in Lindenhurst, Long Island while still in his teens and joined SCI as an apprentice director in 1973. Over the next decade, he advanced through management positions at SCI funeral homes in New York City and Miami Beach, and served in several regional management roles before being elected a corporate vice president in 1998. Mack graduated from Farmingdale State University of New York in 1973; he has been a licensed funeral director since 1974. In his current role, he manages 571 Dignity Memorial® Funeral, Cremation and Cemetery providers throughout the United States.

Sumner J. Waring, III, is senior vice president, major market operations, at Service Corporation International (SCI). A fifth-generation funeral professional, he began his career with his family's funeral services firm in Fall River, Massachusetts. He has been a licensed funeral director since 1992. Waring joined SCI as area vice president of operations when SCI acquired his family's funeral business in 1996. Over the last 12 years, he has served in several management positions at SCI. He holds a bachelor's degree in business administration from Stetson University, a degree in mortuary science from Mount Ida College, and an MBA from the University of Massachusetts, Dartmouth. In his current role, he manages 494 Dignity Memorial® Funeral, Cremation and Cemetery providers throughout the United States and Canada.

REFERENCES

Campbell-Ewald Health. (2005). Thirteen million baby boomers care for ailing parents, 25% live with parents. *SeniorJournal.com*. Retrieved July 26, 2008 from http://seniorjournal.com/NEWS/Boomers/5-10-19BoomersCare4Parents.htm

Corr, C. A. (2007). Anticipatory grief and mourning: An overview. In K. J. Doka (Ed.), *Living with grief: Before and after death* (pp. 5–18). Washington, DC: Hospice Foundation of America.

Gist, Y. J., & Hetzel, L. I. (2004*). We the people: Aging in the United States*. U.S. Census Bureau. Retrieved June 26, 2008, from http://www.census.gov/prod/2004pubs/censr-19.pdf

Hobbs, F., & Stoops, N. (2002). *Demographic trends in the 20th century*. U.S. Census Bureau. Retrieved July 26, 2008, from http://www.census.gov/prod/2002/pubs/censr-4.pdf

Irion, P. E. (2007). The role of the funeral as survivors cope with death. In K. J. Doka (Ed.*), Living with grief: Before and after death* (pp. 65–81). Washington, DC: Hospice Foundation of America.

National Hospice and Palliative Care Organization. (2007). *NHPCO facts and figures: Hospice care in America*. Retrieved June 28, 2008 from http://www.nhpco.org/research

Passel, J. S., & Cohn, D. (2008*). U.S. population projections: 2005–2050*. Pew Research Center. Retrieved June 26, 2008, from http://pewhispanic.org/files/reports/85.pdf

Pew Forum on Religion and Public Life. (2008*). U.S. religious landscape survey*. Pew Research Center. Retrieved June 30, 2008, from http://religions.pewforum.org/pdf/report2-religious-landscap-study-full.pdf

U.S. Census Bureau. (2006). *American community survey*. Retrieved July 26, 2008, from http://factfinder.census.gov

Ethnicity and Race as Sources of Diversity

T wo major sources of diversity in the United States are ethnicity and race. This section's opening chapter by Ronald Barrett discusses the black experience of grief and loss. Barrett uses the term *black* because of the wide diversity within the black community. He uses *black* as a racial equivalent of *white*, noting the varied cultures within the black race, such as Kenyan-American, Jamaican-American, and Nigerian-American. He reserves the term *African-American* for those persons of the black race that trace their American ancestry back to the time of enslavement. Barrett also acknowledges the considerable diversity within the African-American and black communities, recognizing class, geographical region, and spirituality. He goes on to remind us that the African-American experience was shaped by several influences, including cultural vestiges from Africa, the long-standing interrelationship of blacks in American culture, as well as the unique historical black experience. Barrett then explores the special sensitivities and practices that caregivers should be aware of when offering end-of-life care and grief support.

Penelope Moore's chapter further explores that diversity as she views the cultures of more recent immigrants from both Africa and the Caribbean. Moore recognizes the roles that indigenous beliefs and practices have in these communities' responses to dying, death, and grief. She offers an excellent paradigmatic approach to groups, noting how cultural strengths can facilitate coping and acknowledging how the stresses of the immigrant experience can complicate grief.

Gerry Cox adds a chapter on Native Americans. Cox's chapter begins with two points. First, like all other cultural groups, Native Americans are diverse. Aspects of this diversity include tribal culture and residence in a traditional reservation. Second, Cox critically points out that Native-American culture, again like other groups, is constantly evolving. Cox describes critical values that frame Native-American responses to the end of life—a strong sense of spirituality, respect for others (especially elders), communal responsibility, the importance of relationships, the need for reciprocity, the value of silence, and respect for personal autonomy. Cox offers sage suggestions for sensitive practice with Native Americans that can help bridge historical mistrust.

Continuing the theme of diversity within cultures, Carlos Sandoval-Cros reminds readers of the extensive diversity in the Hispanic/Latino community. This diversity includes race, ethnicity, spirituality, region, acculturation, age, and class. Nonetheless, Sandoval-Cros asserts that there are values common to Hispanics and Latinos, including *personalismo* (trusted relationships developed by personal ties and self-disclosure), *presentismo* (emphasis on the present), *espiritismo* (belief in good and evil spirits that can affect health and well-being), *fatalismo* (the belief that fate determines life outcomes and that fate is basically predestined), and *familismo* (the importance of family and the value of familial consensus). Sandoval-Cros then describes how these values can influence the end of life and grief, and suggests ways to utilize them in care and support.

These chapters are representative rather than inclusive. While not claiming to describe all racial and ethnic groups, together they make three critical points. They first reaffirm the danger of defining someone solely by race and ethnicity. There is considerable variation within each group. Second, they remind readers to understand the values of each group and how these values may conflict with professional and counseling norms. Sue and Sue (2007), for example, note that the culture of counseling places value on individualism, self-disclosure, verbal expressiveness, insight, cause and effect, an internal locus of control, and adherence to clock time. Many of these values may not be fully compatible with the values of the groups that clinicians and healthcare professionals seek to serve. There is need then for dialogue that acknowledges these cultural differences. Finally, there is a need to view each culture through a prism that acknowledges how cultural practices can both facilitate and complicate end-of-life care and grief support—encompassing and affirming the strengths inherent in each culture.

REFERENCE

Sue, D. W., & Sue, D. (2007). *Counseling the culturally diverse: Theory and practice* (5th ed.). New York: John Wiley & Sons.

Sociocultural Considerations: African Americans, Grief, and Loss

Ronald Barrett

It is a central premise of this book that race and ethnicity are important, although they are not the only sources of social diversity. The experiences of various races and ethnic groups will influence their experience of dying, death, and grief (Irish, Lundquist, & Nelson, 1993; Parry & Ryan, 1995). This is certainly true of the African-American experience, in which three factors converge to create a unique cultural perspective. First, African Americans have a long history in the United States and have been influenced by their interaction with the larger American culture. Second, despite attempts to eliminate older African culture, vestiges remain and influence contemporary African-American perspectives on dying, death, and grief. Third, the struggle for equality and the history of discrimination and prejudice have had significant effects on African-American perspectives and practices (Barrett, 1993, 1994, 1995; Holloway, 2002; Perry, 1993; Prograis & Pellegrino, 2007; Rosenblatt & Wallace, 2005; Sullivan, 1995).

The primary goal of this chapter is to examine the unique cultural attitudes and beliefs of African Americans regarding death, dying, and funeral practices. While many African Americans share common sociocultural influences, this chapter attempts to call attention to the need for more careful study of critical distinctions among African Americans. To that end, this chapter offers an inferential model for breaking down some of the complexity of working with African Americans experiencing death and grief. A second goal is to call attention to the differences in the rate of death and dying among African Americans in the United States compared with whites, and to examine the causes of premature death among African Americans. A third goal is to explore the ways that the unique experiences of African Americans contribute to a sense of mistrust that might affect caregiving and counseling processes.

Finally, this chapter attempts to offer practical and useful considerations for caregivers who work with African Americans experiencing loss and grief.

SELF-REFERENCE AND SOCIOCULTURAL INFLUENCES

While many people may regard all blacks as the same, blacks themselves make important distinctions among cultural subgroups. In this chapter, I refer to all persons of African descent as *blacks*. This is an inclusive term that includes all subgroups of persons of African descent, including African Americans. Blacks have similar physical characteristics common to persons of sub-Saharan African descent. While there is great heterogeneity in the physical traits that characterize blacks (e.g., skin color, facial features, hair color and texture), some common characteristics are visible.

It is very important to note that while it is reasonable to refer to all persons of African descent as black, many subcultural groups have unique sociocultural variations and distinctions. For example, while most persons of African descent may share a similar physical appearance, African Americans are distinct from other subgroups of blacks (e.g., persons from Jamaica, Guyana, Trinidad, Barbados) in that they define themselves as being socialized primarily through values inculcated in the United States. Hence *black* is used—much as the term *white*—to designate racial identification. Ethnic identity among blacks is as diverse as among whites. For example, the term *black* might include Jamaican Americans, Kenyan Americans, and Haitian Americans as well as African Americans. The latter term then applies to blacks who were enslaved and transported to America between the 17th and 19th centuries.

To acknowledge a person's unique cultural heritage and identity is an important way of affirming his or her identity. One might offend and alienate a black person by making assumptions based on incorrect identification of his or her cultural or subcultural background. The use of terms varies extensively, even within a given group. Caregivers are always advised to listen for cues or to ask clients what terms they use to define themselves.

Various subcultural groups of blacks have unique approaches to death, dying, and funerals. For example, while most blacks might prefer ground burials, Jamaicans traditionally assist with the burial of their loved ones and insist on closing the grave. Caribbean blacks prefer immediate funeralization and burial of their dead.

Because of the conspicuous lack of detailed documentation on the unique cultural traditions, practices, and customs of many black subcultures, there is a need for more systematic study and research. Cultural sensitivity to the unique characteristics of subgroups is a significant first step in acknowledging the role of cultural identity in a black person's attitudes toward death and dying (Barrett, 1995, 1997b; Rosenblatt & Wallace, 2005).

RACE, ETHNICITY, AND HEALTH: COLLECTIVE IDENTITY AND COMMON FATE

The black and African-American experience of death and dying in the United States is fundamentally different from the white experience. While recognizing and acknowledging discrete subgroups among blacks is an important consideration regarding death and dying, the relationship of race and ethnicity to the quality of health among *all* blacks is noteworthy. The overwhelming evidence suggests that most blacks share a common fate of less robust health and wellness than whites and others who are more advantaged. This negatively affects their quality of life and contributes to premature death. Race and ethnicity, along with social class, are significantly correlated with health, wellness, and premature death (Dixon, 1994; Prograis & Pellegrino, 2007).

In addition to race and ethnicity, a number of other factors influence health and quality of life among blacks. While blacks are estimated to represent 13% of the U.S. population, approximately 33% of blacks fall below the federal poverty level. As a result of poverty, they tend to have less education than whites and less access to health insurance (Holsendolph, 1997), transportation, childcare, and time off work, and, thus, less access to health care, even when taking into account health status, age, and gender (Prograis & Pellegrino, 2007; Rosenblatt & Wallace, 2005; Washington, 1997).

The scarcity of doctors in the black community also contributes to a lower quality of life, less healthcare, and premature death. Washington (1997) reports that the national average is 150 doctors per 100,000 people. Yet the rate in New York City's Bedford-Stuyvesant area, for example, is below 75 per 100,000; while across town, affluent Manhattanites have access to 1,136 doctors per 100,000 people. The relationship of race and ethnicity to health suggests a pronounced trend of racism and classism. And the fundamental differences between blacks and whites in quality of life, wellness, and premature death contribute to significant additional losses (e.g., loss of health and wellness, loss of role functions, and related financial hardships) (Barrett, 1997a).

Cultural Mistrust

While many factors contribute to differences in quality of life and premature death in the United States, the role of cultural mistrust is often overlooked. In an important early study of trust dispositions among blacks and whites, Terrell and Barrett (1979) found that blacks, women, and the poor—politically disadvantaged groups that have experienced long-standing discrimination and prejudice—tended to mistrust medical systems identified with their oppressors (Prograis & Pellegrino, 2007; Rosenblatt & Wallace, 2005; Terrell & Terrell, 1983). Cultural mistrust is one reason African Americans tend to underutilize health services and are more likely than whites to drop out of institutionalized heathcare systems (Barrett, 1997b, Washington, 1997). This higher attrition rate is observed in institutional providers of both physical and mental health care (Sue & Sue, 1990).

In addition to cultural mistrust, the fear of medicine (iatrophobia) contributes to the tendency of many African Americans to avoid doctors and to seek care only at the last minute. In a 1989 survey, the Harvard School of Public Health found that—considering income, health status, age, and gender—African Americans had a significantly lower number of annual medical visits than whites. Not incidentally, African Americans also express greater dissatisfaction with the way they are treated in medical interactions (Prograis & Pellegrino, 2007; Washington, 1997).

African Americans who mistrust the system often experience alienation from care providers and are thus likely to be revictimized by insensitivity to their lack of trust (Barrett, 1986). The tendency to judge the mistrustful person's alienation from social establishments can lead caregivers to blame the victims. As a group, African Americans have a historical pattern of mistreatment, betrayal, and victimization by institutions. Many African Americans share the perception that white physicians in institutional settings are slow to treat and quick to experiment on blacks. A 1991 *American Journal of Public Health* study reported that blacks tend to avoid AIDS clinical trials because of the painful legacy of the Tuskegee Syphilis Study, in which treatment was withheld from approximately 400 black sharecroppers between 1932 and 1972 (Prograis & Pellegrino, 2007; Washington, 1997). African-American consumers of health care often report that they believe they receive less assiduous treatment than whites; that they are patronized in the doctor's office; that doctors don't communicate effectively with them; and that they are more likely to leave the doctor's office unsure of their diagnosis and the options for treatment (Washington, 1997).

UNDERSTANDING BLACKS, DEATH, AND DYING: THE BARRETT INFERENTIAL MODEL

While certain aspects of the human response to grief and loss are universal, a growing body of research documents ethnic and cultural differences in attitudes, beliefs, and funeral customs (Irish, Lundquist, & Nelson, 1993; Kalish & Reynolds, 1981; Parry & Ryan, 1995). Significant variations within ethnic and cultural groups have also been observed, suggesting that race, ethnicity, and culture may not be definitive conceptual tools for understanding the distinctive features in any group (Barrett, 1995). The significant heterogeneity among blacks suggests that racial, ethnic, and cultural grouping is not enough to provide insight into their attitudes toward death, dying, and funeralization.

The tremendous heterogeneity among blacks requires that one take into account more than race or ethnicity to understand and appropriately respond to loss in the black experience. A clear sense of the person's cultural and subcultural identification is important. It is important to note how strongly the person identifies with his or her respective cultural heritage. Blacks of all subgroups who identify as being Africentric reflect values, beliefs, and attitudes derived from African traditions. West Africa was the point of deportation of slaves during the diaspora to the North American continent. Barrett (1993) documents the sociocultural origins of attitudes, beliefs, and funeral practices of African Americans, suggesting a strong link with and influence of West Africa. Nichols (1989) also supports the thesis that West African culture influences African-American funeral practices. Striking similarities in attitudes, beliefs, and funeralization practices support this thesis (Barrett, 1993; Holloway, 2002; Rosenblatt & Wallace, 2005).

While distinct identities and traditions may exist among blacks, evolving research on death and dying among African Americans suggests that most African Americans share a number of characteristic attitudes toward death, dying, and funeral rites. For example, most African Americans can be characterized as being inclined toward the following:

- To be "death accepting"—that is, perceiving death as part of the natural rhythm of life
- To oppose active euthanasia
- To regard death, dying, and the dead with great reverence and respect
- To regard funerals as primary rituals—that is, to invest greatly in the execution of the ritual and closely follow tradition and protocol
- To believe that attendance at and participation in funerals is an important social obligation

- To prefer ground burial for final disposition
- To believe in life after death and the notion that a person transitions to the spirit world
- To acknowledge the presence of dead ancestors' spirits in the community
- To engage in rituals and traditions to honor the dead, e.g., naming a baby after a deceased person, passing babies over the caskets of loved ones, and acknowledging the presence of the dead at family gatherings

Most African Americans share common African sociocultural traditions blended with Western customs and practices (Barrett, 1993, 1995; Holloway, 2002; Rosenblatt & Wallace, 2005). Consequently, most blacks tend to view death as a part of the continuum of life as opposed to the end of life and believe in the existence of an afterlife—that one transitions from the physical world to the spirit world. Consistent with this view is the belief in an indistinguishable separation between the physical world and the spirit world.

Most African Americans view life and death with reverence, and great care is paid to the funeralization of the dead. In other words, funerals are regarded as primary rituals (Barrett, 1993; Holloway, 2002; Rosenblatt & Wallace, 2005) with great social significance (Barrett, 1995; Holloway, 2002; Rosenblatt & Wallace, 2005). African Americans as a demographic group are inclined to invest considerably more discretionary income than whites in funerals (Barrett, 1995), and to value attendance at and participation in the final rites of a loved one as a significant gesture of support and condolence. Close relatives are expected to be present and participate; not to honor this social obligation can be perceived as being disrespectful.

SOCIOECONOMIC STATUS AND SOCIAL CLASS

Socioeconomic status is an important influence on attitudes, beliefs, and funeral practices. African Americans of lower socioeconomic status tend to be keepers of tradition and are more conservative in their attitudes, beliefs, and funeral practices (Barrett, 1997b). As African Americans move up in socioeconomic status, they have increased exposure to alternative lifestyles and increased opportunities for educational influences. With wealth and upward socioeconomic status, African Americans literally move away from their traditional communities and are exposed to other value systems that influence their attitudes, beliefs, and practices (Holloway, 2002).

For example, lower-class African Americans are more likely to have funeral services characterized as traditional, emotional "homegoing" services. On the other hand, middle-class and affluent African Americans are more inclined to have funeral services similar to those of the white middle class, which tend to be significantly less emotional, more stoic, and more formal. African American funerals in general tend to have a longer planning stage, with the funeral occurring an average of 1 week after the death. Traditionally, this delay served a pragmatic purpose: It allowed family members to travel from afar and gave survivors more time to gather financial resources for the funeral.

The traditional African-American funeral is a social event; it does not start until all significant persons have gathered. The more esteemed the deceased loved one, the greater the investment in time, resources, and participation in the service. In the black experience, presence at a funeral is a significant gesture of respect and esteem. Traditional black funeral services are also longer than white funerals, sometimes lasting for hours, and usually include more spontaneity and musical participation. The traditional funeral might be a full-day affair, including the service, the committal, and the family gathering and repast afterward.

As African Americans have become more acculturated to dominant American society and have achieved greater socioeconomic status, observation of some traditional practices has declined. Consequently, an upper-class African American funeral service might now more closely resemble a white funeral—shorter, less emotional, and more formal, with no wake or social gathering afterward.

SPIRITUALITY AND RELIGION

An African-American person's spirituality or religious orientation can have a significant influence on his or her attitudes, beliefs, and funeral practices. The religious orientation of blacks varies from liberal to conservative on matters related to death, dying, and funeralization (e.g., baptism, anointing, postmortem examinations, tissue donations, organ transplants, blood transfusions, euthanasia, and final disposition). Barrett (1995) postulated that the conservative or liberal religious orientation of an African-American person can play a more influential role in his or her disposition toward death, dying, and funeral practices than race alone. For example, in a medical emergency, blacks who are Jehovah's Witnesses, Christian Scientists, or Rastafarians might make choices consistent with their religion—for example, to refuse blood transfusions. Similarly, blacks who follow Christian Science, Afro-Caribbean blacks, and Rastafarians may be opposed to postmortem examinations. Thus, religion may be a stronger determining factor than race alone. More empirical research is needed on the relative influence of one's formative versus current religious orientation on attitudes, beliefs, and practices regarding dying, death, and funeral rites.

EXPRESSIONS OF CONDOLENCE

While funerals in the Western cultural tradition signify the end of a life, in the African-American experience, they also honor the great worth of the deceased in the community. The funeral is a critical moment in the life cycle and is handled with great reverence and attention to detail. Traditionally, African Americans invest heavily in funeral societies and burial policies to ensure a decent and proper funeral. For the average African American—who may have been denied much in life, including any significant measure of human dignity—a grand funeral may represent a final triumph and one last attempt to be regarded as somebody. The contemporary value of the funeral as a primary ritual is an extension of the traditional African view of funerals, reflecting the value of the individual to the community.

Death is a defining moment in the African-American experience, and there is an implicit social obligation to gather to express support and condolence. Unsolicited expressions of condolence and support are expected and greatly valued. It is generally believed that the greater and more personal one's investment in expressing condolence, the greater the value and regard for the survivors (Barrett, 1995). For example, on hearing of a death in the community, African Americans may immediately gather without solicitation at the home or place of death to provide support and express condolences. While modes of notification have evolved with technological advancements, African Americans still tend to prefer the more personal word of mouth.

One of the most highly valued expressions of condolence is the personal sacrifice of being present during the time of loss (e.g., going to the home upon notification of a death, attending the wake, the funeral, the burial service, and the repast afterward). It is the social norm among blacks to offer money, resources, and food to survivors. While immediate family members are expected to be present, participate, and make contributions as needed, others who provide personal assistance are held in high regard by survivors. The more personal the sacrifice, the higher the regard for the offering. For example, while the donation of uncooked or store-bought food is appreciated, it is considered less personal and regarded less highly than the sacrifice of a person who prepares food (Barrett, 1995).

For most African Americans, gestures of condolence are valued expressions of respect to the deceased and the survivors during a time of loss and bereavement. As one elderly African-American widow commented, "During your time of sorrow, you learn who your true friends are." This statement reflects the traditional expectation that friends and relatives should be present and available to the bereaved.

Because of the cultural reverence for death as a critical moment in the life cycle, the appropriateness of one's response often has significant consequences for familial and social relations. Family ties and relationships can be dramatically redefined as a result of a person's participation and conduct during a time of loss and grief. Those who respond appropriately are gathered closer and regarded highly; those who fail to respond appropriately are often regarded as additional losses to mourn and grieve.

THE ROLE OF CLERGY AS CAREGIVERS

During illness, dying, and death, African Americans tend to have high expectations of clergy and can be unforgiving of clergy who do not live up to those expectations. Because African Americans have a very reverent regard for death and believe in the spiritual transition of the deceased, the active participation of their spiritual leaders during serious illness and death is very meaningful to members of the deceased's family and community. African Americans typically have the following expectations of a clergyperson during the illness and death of a loved one:

- Upon notification of the serious illness of a member of the faith community or congregation, the clergyperson will make a personal bedside visit to offer prayers and support to the sick person and the family.
- The clergyperson will encourage others in the faith community and congregation to pray for and be supportive of those who are ill and their families.
- Upon learning of the death of a member of the faith community or congregation, the clergyperson will immediately make a personal visit to the family to offer condolences and assistance with the final arrangements.
- The clergyperson will be present at and support the family during the wake or sit-up that occurs before the funeral service.
- The clergyperson will officiate at the funeral service, delivering a personalized eulogy and offering support and regard for the surviving family members during the service.
- The clergyperson will participate in the committal service.
- The clergyperson will make an appearance at the social gathering and repast that traditionally follows the committal service.

The active and responsive participation of the clergy or spiritual leader during this important and sacred time is a defining moment in the survivors' relationship with and subsequent regard for the clergy and the religious institution.

UNDERSTANDING GRIEF

While African Americans experience grief in similar ways to other ethnic groups, caregivers should understand some particular aspects of African-American grief. Many African Americans have flexible and extended kin networks. Grandparents, noncustodial parents, and fictive kin honored by the titles "aunt" and "uncle" may be an important part of the kinship system. Not only are their losses mourned but their deaths—especially in lower socioeconomic groups—may have considerable effects on the family's structure. In assessing grief, caregivers should carefully explore the nature of these relationships and the effects of the death (Hines & Boyd-Franklin, 2005; Rosenblatt & Wallace, 2005). In addition, African Americans, especially women, may struggle with two contradictory norms: to mourn the death openly and to project strength. Caregivers should be sensitive to the need for clients to "dose" grief—that is, to carefully select the times and places for emotional expression.

Mistrust of the mental health system—especially among lower socio-economic groups—may extend to support groups (Hines & Boyd-Franklin, 2005; Rosenblatt & Wallace, 2005). Given the valued role of clergy, it may be worthwhile to train clergy as both sources of referral and a primary source of bereavement support (Abrams, Albury, Crandall, Doka, & Harris, 2005). This approach allows African Americans to draw on spiritual strengths—strengths that reinforce the notions of a continued bond with deceased relatives (Rosenblatt & Wallace, 2005).

CONCLUSION

A number of sociocultural considerations are important for caregivers working with blacks who experience loss. The following are practical recommendations:

1. Understand the sociocultural influences from both African and Western traditions that combine to influence the attitudes, beliefs, and values of most blacks regarding dying, death, and funeral practices.
2. Acknowledge and appreciate the uniqueness of the subgroups of blacks and African Americans, understanding the fundamental differences between them. When in doubt, ask a client to describe his or her cultural identity.

3. Be sensitive to the fundamental differences in the quality of life and rate of premature death for blacks compared with whites. Recognize that these factors contribute to chronic grief.

4. Understand the impact of collective losses that African Americans often must grieve.

5. Recognize that race alone is not sufficient to understand the experience of loss among blacks and African Americans. Consideration of socio-economic status and spirituality can be helpful to work effectively with African Americans who are experiencing loss and grief.

6. Be sensitive to the consistent role of cultural mistrust with regard to health, wellness, and premature death among African Americans. Be aware of how that mistrust may contribute to an African-American person's being guarded, especially when working with culturally different caregivers and institutions. Well-intentioned caregivers may not be welcomed with open arms, especially by African Americans with a history of betrayal or victimization. A considerable amount of trust building may be needed to establish rapport and build a working relationship.

7. Be sensitive to the culturally ascribed value African Americans place on expressions of condolence. Understand that for most African Americans, a loved one's death is a major moment in the life cycle. Expressions of condolence are extremely important to survivors and have considerable value during a time of loss and grief.

8. Understand the high expectations African Americans may have of clergy and spiritual leaders during dying, death, and funeralization. Because most blacks regard death as a critical spiritual event, their expectations of clergy and other spiritual leaders are higher than their expectations of other caregivers.

I am often asked by those who are culturally different if they can be an effective caregiver for an African American who is experiencing loss and grief. While race, culture, and ethnicity should not be taken lightly, they should not be perceived as insurmountable barriers. Be yourself, be honest, be real, and be open to and teachable about aspects of a person's experience that may be different from your own. Have faith in our common humanity to connect and support one another in our experiences of loss, grief, and pain in spite of our separateness and apparent differences.

NOTE: This revised and updated chapter originally appeared in the 1998 Hospice Foundation of America book Who We Are, How We Grieve.

Ronald Keith Barrett, PhD, is professor of psychology at Loyola Marymount University. His research has focused on the effects of violence on children.

REFERENCES

Abrams, D., Albury, S., Crandall, L., Doka, K., & Harris, R. (2005). The Florida clergy end-of-life education enhancement project. *American Journal of Hospice and Palliative Care, 22,* 181–187.

Barrett, R. K. (1986). Cultural mistrust as a contributor to mental health and psycho-pathology. *ERIC/CADS Resources in Education, 261–296.*

Barrett, R. K. (1993). Psycho-cultural influences on African-American attitudes towards death, dying, and funeral rites. In J. Morgan (Ed.), *Personal care in an impersonal world* (pp. 213–230). Amityville, NY: Baywood.

Barrett, R. K. (1994). Reclaiming and reaffirming African-American funeral rites. *The Director,* 36–40.

Barrett, R. K. (1995). Contemporary African-American funeral rites and traditions. In L. A. DeSpelder & A. L. Strickland (Eds.), *The path ahead: Readings in death and dying* (pp. 80–92). Mountain View, CA: Mayfield.

Barrett, R. K. (1997a). Bereaved black children. In J. Morgan (Ed.), *Readings in thanatology* (pp. 403–419). Amityville, NY: Baywood.

Barrett, R. K. (1997b, May*). Blacks, death, dying and funeral rites: Everything you've wondered about but thought it politically incorrect to ask.* Presentation at the 15th King's College Annual International Conference on Death, Dying, and Bereavement, London, Ontario, Canada.

Dixon, B. (1994). *Good health for African Americans.* New York: Crown.

Hines, P. M., & Boyd-Franklin, N. (2005). African American families. In M. McGoldrick, J. Giordano, & N. Garcia-Preto (Eds.), *Ethnicity and family therapy* (3rd ed.) (pp. 87–100). New York: Guilford Press.

Holloway, K. (2002). *Passed on: African-American mourning stories.* Durham, NC: Duke University Press.

Holsendolph, E. (1997, October). Insurance companies race for the market. *Emerge: Black American News Magazine.*

Irish, D. P., Lundquist, K. F., & Nelson, V. J. (Eds.). (1993). *Ethnic variations in dying, death, and grief: Diversity in universality.* Washington, DC: Taylor & Francis.

Kalish, R., & Reynolds, D. (1981). *Death and ethnicity: A psychocultural study.* Amityville, NY: Baywood.

Nichols, E. (1989). *The last mile of the way: African American homegoing traditions 1890–present.* Columbia, SC: Dependable.

Parry, J. K., & Ryan, A. S. (Eds.). (1995). *A cross-cultural look at death, dying, and religion.* Chicago: Nelson Hall.

Perry, H. (1993). Mourning and funeral customs of African Americans. In D. P. Irish, K. F. Lundquist, & V. J. Nelson (Eds.), *Ethnic variation in dying, death and grief: Diversity in universality* (pp. 51–63). Washington, DC: Taylor & Francis.

Prograis, L., & Pellegrino, E. (Eds.). (2007). *African-American bioethics.* Washington, DC: Georgetown University Press.

Rosenblatt, P., & Wallace, B. (2005). African-American grief. New York: Routledge.

Sue, D. W., & Sue, D. (1990). *Counseling the culturally different: Theory and practice.* New York: J. Wiley & Sons.

Sullivan, M. (1995). May the circle be unbroken: The African-American experience of death, dying and spirituality. In J. K. Parry & A. S. Ryan (Eds.), *A cross-cultural look at death, dying, and religion.* Chicago: Nelson Hall.

Terrell, F., & Barrett, R. K. (1979). Interpersonal trust among college students as a function of race, sex, and socioeconomic class. *Perceptual and Motor Skills, 48,* 1194.

Terrell, F., & Terrell, S. (1983). The relationship between race of examiner, cultural mistrust, and the intelligence test performance of black children. *Psychology in the Schools, 20,* 367–369.

Washington, H. (1997, October). Fear of medical care can become deadly. *Emerge: Black American News Magazine.*

CHAPTER 7

The New Black Migration: Dying and Grief in African and Caribbean Migrants

Penelope J. Moore

Little has been written about the bereavement process among black immigrants coping with death or about the variations among different groups. Only within the past several years have social scientists started to define the diversity among black people in the United States. Distinctions are difficult to discuss because the U.S. Census aggregates black immigrants in the same category as African Americans. Black immigrants are also aggregated with African Americans in health statistics, where—compared with all other racial groups—they have the highest rates of morbidity and mortality for almost all diseases, the highest disability rates, the shortest life expectancies, the least access to health care, and low rates of modern technology use in treatment (Read & Emerson, 2005, p. 181).

The healthcare literature consistently points to factors such as group degradation, brutality, discrimination, poverty, and violence as contributing to mortality. In their article on black funeralization, Moore and Bryant (2003) note that "to be black in America is to be part of a history told in terms of contact with death and coping with death" (p. 598).

Black immigrants and African Americans alike draw on traditional African conceptions in searching for the meaning of death, which is viewed as another phase of life involving a transition from the material world to the spiritual world (Barrett, 1995). Belief in the continuity of life decreases the sting of death for black people, because it brings with it a sense of freedom and peace. Family members take comfort in knowing that their loved one is in a better place. Cultural rituals associated with death provide the family and the larger community with an opportunity to celebrate the life of the deceased and, in so doing, proactively affirm the humanity of black people.

The literature asserts that whether or not they are religious, blacks come from an ancestral tradition that embraces full expression of emotions when grieving the death of a loved one. Rituals and ceremonies are the cultural mechanisms used to express and communicate the experience of loss. In this chapter, I will discuss the cultural and religious context of grief in an attempt to identify what grief counselors need to know to work with diverse populations from the Caribbean and Africa. I will also discuss areas of strength and protective factors that should be considered when planning grief support services.

AFRICAN AND CARIBBEAN MIGRANTS

The population of foreign-born persons in the United States in 2002 was approximately 33.1 million, or 11.5% of the total U.S. population (Campbell et al., 2005). The foreign-born black population doubled from 3% in 1980 to 6% in 2000. More than half (54%) of the black immigrants come from the West Indies or the Caribbean; 16% come from Africa; 6% from South America, 6% from Europe, and 2% from Asia (Read & Emerson, 2005, p. 182). Black immigrants tend to be ethnically and culturally heterogeneous as a result of geography and the varied experiences of European colonialism and African ancestry. The search for economic security is the primary reason for immigration. Other important factors include family reunification, population pressure, limited resources on small islands or in the country of origin, and political or religious persecution (Mahoney, 2004; Parchment-Pennant, 2002).

Caribbean migration has been uninterrupted since the beginning of the 19th century; however, passage of the Immigration Reform Act of 1965 significantly increased the number of English-speaking black immigrants from the Caribbean islands, Guyana, Panama, Costa Rica, and Belize. The 1965 legislation, which favored family reunification and job skills, opened the door for many West Indians and Haitians. Immigrants from the Caribbean appear to gravitate to large cities such as Miami and New York (Waters, 1994, p. 796).

A different set of policies in the 1990s made it possible for a new wave of Africans to immigrate. During that period, the population grew by 174% due to the diversity visa program, the decision to admit more refugees from African war zones, and the intent to provide more opportunities for Africans to pursue graduate study in the United States. Africans from countries such as Nigeria, Ethiopia, Ghana, South Africa, Liberia, Kenya, and Somalia settled primarily in Washington, DC, and New York (Campbell et al., 2005).

Whereas immigrants of northern European descent have the option of assimilating into mainstream society, black immigrants do not have this option because of their skin color, and the impact of racial discrimination is devastating. Residential segregation limits access to socioeconomic goods, which in turn limits access to education and employment opportunities, medical treatment, and other significant areas of life. Racism also increases stress by creating a stigma of inferiority that affects physical and mental well-being. Consequently, mortality outcomes are increased (Bulatao & Anderson, 2001; Read & Emerson, 2005). Equally devastating is racism's impact on the psyche, as it pits immigrants against American-born black people. Coming from societies where black people constitute a racial majority and enjoy high social status, black immigrants expect to attain a higher standard of living than they had in their home country. However, when they experience the limitations imposed on them by labeling and racial prejudice, they may become defensive and try to reject negative stereotypes by disassociating themselves from African Americans; thus, they may contribute to tensions among subgroups of blacks (Takougang, 2002).

Not all black immigrants find themselves blocked in their efforts to attain upward mobility. Well-educated professionals are often sought to fill positions that require specific skills. Less well educated immigrants, for whom survival is of utmost importance, use various strategies to get ahead. Less skilled immigrants are often willing to accept low-paying jobs without medical benefits for an opportunity to establish roots in this country. It is common for immigrants to live near or in households with others from their country and to pool resources to make ends meet. Many women of Caribbean background fill positions as nurses and domestic workers. The usual migration pattern involves a woman coming to live with a friend or relative until she is financially able to send for other family members (Campbell et al., 2005).

CULTURAL STRENGTHS

A spiritual paradigm that gives meaning to life in adversity is a tool of resilience. In the foreword to *Jesus and the Disinherited* (1976) by noted African-American theologian Howard Thurman, Vincent Harding succinctly captures the meaning of spirituality for oppressed groups: "No external force, however great and overwhelming, can destroy a people if it does not first win the victory of the spirit against them." Spirituality is a major factor used by persons of African descent to address concerns about life, death, feelings of hopelessness, victimization, demoralization, and oppression. Blacks who are considered to be acculturated into Western societies still appear to draw on the experiences and expressions—the distinctive qualities, rites, and ceremonies—

of African traditional religions in order to manage grief (e.g., Vodou in Haiti, Santería in Cuba, Shango in Trinidad, and Condomble and Macumba in Brazil [Barrett, 1976, p. 24]).

Black immigrants from Africa and the Caribbean are more closely affiliated than African Americans with indigenous practices of medicine and religion. Often, they have blended indigenous practices with the Catholicism or Protestantism of the colonial rulers in their countries of origin. Central to indigenous religions is a system of ethical norms and conduct; the arts and crafts of healing and folk medicine; the involvement of deities in the moral, social, and emotional affairs of humans; the existence of spirits that can be used for good or evil purposes; the practices of divination, conjuring, and exorcism; a belief in life after death; and the ability to communicate with the ancestors (Hylton, 2002, p. 168).

Barrett (1976) observed similarities between West African religious beliefs and Jamaican folk beliefs in his description of West African conceptions of death. At the core, African conceptions of death hold to the premise that all life returns to a supreme creator. Ideas about the soul of the individual inform the nature of rituals and customs used to release the spirit:

> Among the people of West Africa there is a belief in two or more souls. Among the Yoruba of Nigeria and the Fon of Dahomey, four souls are enumerated including the life-soul which enters one at birth and comes directly from the hand of the Supreme Being. Next, there is the personality-soul which determines the kind of person one is to be. Third is the guardian-soul which may be considered one's protecting spirit or conscience. Lastly, there is the shadow-soul. The last two are almost indistinguishable. At death, the soul that comes from God goes back to God. The personality-soul is reborn in a child of the family; the guardian- and/or shadow-soul remains around until after all funeral rites are completed. The shadow-soul may remain around after the funeral for an indefinite time, depending on the circumstances of one's death. This soul is called a ghost and must be satisfied that the dead has been treated appropriately, especially in funeral rites; otherwise, it can become angry, vindictive, and troublesome. The ghost of someone who has had an untimely death may haunt the community until he or she is dispatched from the land of the living by a religious specialist (pp. 108–109).

In addition to providing guidance about the individual treatment of the deceased, indigenous religions have served both a social and political function by organizing groups into cohesive units and coordinating struggles against colonialism and slavery. They have maintained the identity and legacies of ethnic groups, regions, and customs, and have furthered the establishment of social organizations. These organizations are instrumental in bringing members of the same ethnic group together, encouraging them to communicate with and provide mutual aid to each other, and offering a measure of dignity to all. Community members elect leaders who are invested with authority over designated areas and ethnic groups. In this way, culture in different forms is preserved (Hylton, 2002, p. 175).

Cultural cohesion in the sending country has functioned to maintain a strong sense of ethnic community that contributes to the survival of new immigrant families in the United States. Cohesive ethnic communities act as a buffer against racism and discrimination by providing a sense of purpose and motivation, emotional and practical support, reinforcement of cultural values, maintenance of close interpersonal relationships, and cooperative decision making. Community cohesion is most evident when there is a death, and grievers rely on these bonds to work through feelings of loss. During this time of transition, the extended family, friends, and the community as a whole gather to comfort the family.

The three major rituals are the wake, funeral, and postburial gathering. At the wake, the body can be viewed and family and friends gather to share food, drink, and memories. Participants and observers share stories about the deceased's life, and the surviving family and community members are encouraged to cry, scream, clap their hands, tap their feet, or react as the Spirit moves them (Bolling, 1996).

At the funeral, emphasis is placed on open and full expression of feelings, which is often achieved through the cadences of the preacher's voice, the soulful music, and the symbolic selection of songs and dances. Depending on the age of the deceased, these rituals may be somber or festive. Usually, the death of an infant or young child is experienced as more tragic than the "homegoing" ceremony of elders. The postburial ritual includes going to the home of the deceased for food and drink. Below-ground burial is usually preferred to cremation (Bolling, 1996; Clements et al., 2003).

COMPLICATED GRIEF

Complicated grief refers to the intensification of the pain of loss to the point that the person becomes overwhelmed, resorts to maladaptive behavior, or remains in a state of grief and is unable to progress toward completion of the healing process. A paradigm of complicated grief reactions includes the following: (1) chronic grief reactions that never come to a satisfactory conclusion; (2) delayed grief reactions that are suppressed or postponed; (3) exaggerated grief reactions, in which the person resorts to maladaptive behavior; and (4) masked grief reactions, in which the person experiences symptoms and behaviors that are disturbing but are not recognized as death related (Worden, 1991, pp. 70–74).

Opperman and Novello's (2006) exploratory study examining the influence of context on complicated grief in South Africa led to the hypothesis that "the more prevalent the contextual stresses (i.e., environmental, familial or personal), the greater the possibility that bereavement may develop into complicated grief" (p. 386). Factors that contribute to complicated grief include poverty, unsafe environment, conflict between the community and the bereaved person, loss of income, loss of material security, and macrocontextual factors such as the medical community's response to death. Additionally, contextual factors within the family (including dysfunctional attachment styles, family norms, and absence of extended family) and personal factors that prevent the bereaved from integrating death into his or her worldview undermine a person's capacity to resolve grief.

The experience of immigration itself predisposes black persons to complicated grief reactions, as illustrated in a study of the decisions of Caribbean women to migrate to New York. Best-Cummings and Gildner (2004) interviewed 11 women from nine countries: Antigua, Barbuda, the Dominican Republic, Grenada, Guyana, Jamaica, Panama, St. Lucia, and Trinidad. The study revealed the steps of the decision-making process before migrating, during the migration, and during the initial adjustment in the United States. The authors showed how complicated grief reactions are inherent in the emigration experience by applying Elisabeth Kübler-Ross's theory of death and dying to the decision process of West Indian women. Kübler-Ross's five-stage model of grief includes denial, anger, bargaining, depression, and acceptance. Qualitative research findings show that some immigrant women find it difficult to reach a level of acceptance about losses incurred during the migration process.

During the premigration phase, as one woman became more aware of her intention to leave, she spoke about the pain of losing her children in a divorce, which triggered her desire to explore opportunities and options away from her island. Best-Cummings and Gildner (2004) observe that "it is at this point that she may experience Kübler-Ross's bargaining phase of the grief process. The increased awareness, discomfort, or pain can cause the woman to bargain with herself, with God, or with some higher being to give her a sign or assistance to make things better in her life and to make the separation from her children acceptable" (p. 88). The active planning step is described as having some of the characteristics of Kübler-Ross's anger phase. Active planning involves exerting intense energies to leave in the face of feeling sad about the loss of her children. During migration, actually saying goodbye to crying children is described as traumatic, and women tend to deal with this phase in one of three ways: avoidance, denial, or honest but controlled disclosure. Women in this situation gain the strength they need to say goodbye by keeping their focus on the long-term goal. The adjustment phase—characterized by an internal struggle related to the decision to leave—is when women feel a profound sense of grief. "These women experience grief continually, as they relive the initial feelings of disbelief, the moments of bargaining, the feelings of anger, and the sense of sadness and despair. During the acculturation process, women live and relive their losses and separations frequently" (p. 97).

In another qualitative study, Matthews (2004) explored the interaction of death, immigration status, and social issues observed by social workers who worked with English-speaking Caribbean immigrants following the World Trade Center tragedy. Most of the 41 respondents worked at the Bedford-Stuyvesant Community Mental Health Center and the Visiting Nurses Services in New York City. Study respondents varied in gender, years of employment, and ethnic background. Their primary responsibilities were mental hygiene counseling and case management. The problems or complaints of the study centered on issues of safety and security, psychological stress, and post-9/11 immigration restrictions. This study highlights systemic concerns related to the immigration status of black people that places them at increased risk of complicated grief. Matthews found the following:

> Both permanent resident immigrants and the undocumented felt that safety in the United States has been compromised by the government's implementation of anti-terrorism measures.... The long-term consequences of the new laws and not terrorism

itself appear to be a primary source of anxiety and depression. They were concerned that delays in processing citizenship and permanent residency applications will expose them to deportation procedures. Their concerns about losing their jobs, the incapacity to access services, ethnic profiling and decrease in civil rights led to a reduction in the use of social services. The feeling that the family can handle any problem militates against seeking assistance from agencies beyond the family group. Thus, members of a Guyanese immigrant family, who were mourning the loss of two adult children in the collapsed World Trade Center building, avoided assistance from community and city agencies. Instead, the grieving parents kept to themselves, refusing to accept professional counseling or use of other "outside" resources. One social worker expressed frustration that immigrants, who were obviously distressed over the disaster, did not want to talk about how they really feel (pp. 78–79).

Although two qualitative case studies cannot be generalized to all black immigrant groups, they nevertheless provide insights into the nature of the life crisis brought on by the process of migration, when people are cut off from family, friends, neighbors, support networks, and all that is familiar. Hulewat (1996) observed that three concepts need to be addressed when trying to help families cope with the stresses of resettlement: (1) the five stages of resettlement (pre-immigration, actual migration, arrival in a new home, decompensation with the realization of loss, and the passing on of unresolved conflicts to the next generation); (2) cultural styles and psychological dynamics of the population being resettled; and (3) the degree to which those dynamics create internal dissonance or consonance in one's attempt to adjust to life in the United States. For black immigrants, who tend to receive a harsh welcome in the United States, grief reactions may be exacerbated when a loved one dies.

The literature also documents the psychological stress of children who may be separated from one or both parents for extended periods. A common concern during the reunification process is how well children can deal with yet another primary loss when they are forced to leave a loving caretaker with whom they may have spent several years. During reunification, family relationships must be renegotiated as children become reacquainted with or meet new family members—such as stepparents, stepsiblings, and siblings—for the first time. In reconstituted families, the potential for conflict abounds and may include concerns about parenting roles, school, friends, and household responsibilities (Gaytan, Carhill, & Suarez-Orozco, 2007). Even though resettlement presents opportunities for an improved quality of life, it is stressful and puts immigrants at risk for complicated grief.

USE OF SERVICES BY BLACK IMMIGRANTS

Knowledge about use of health services is derived primarily from research on African Americans, who tend to be mistrustful of the medical establishment. Similarly, Bhopal's (1998) review of the literature on the health status of West Indian immigrants in England revealed that Caribbean people are mistrustful of Western medical practices. He observed that formal healthcare services are mostly staffed by members of the Western European majority and are usually planned and delivered with their needs and preferences in mind, whereas services for racial and ethnic minorities tend to be of poor quality because of poverty and healthcare disparities. Bolling (1996) observed that people may feel anger and resentment against the medical establishment after the death of a loved one if they listened to the advice of nontraditional healers and believe that their family was denied the opportunity to openly and honestly embrace the certainty of death. "There is a feeling of having been robbed of the chance to spend the last moments saying farewell. There is often anger that the deceased was not allowed time to make preparations for death and to settle business affairs that would have made it easier on family members after his or her death" (p. 155).

Additional barriers to accessing health care include language differences and cultural beliefs that differ from the Western medical model. For example, Laguerre (1981) describes the practice of Voodoo by Haitians living in Brooklyn and Miami:

> The Voodooist folk healer is often a Voodoo priest who has had long training in the study of the mythology of spirits and the properties of plants for home remedial purposes. In his treatment he uses both prayers and herbal remedies, which are learned from elders through oral traditions. The transmission of folk medical knowledge from one generation to the next follows specific rules and is often learned during illness episodes.
>
> Spiritual causation may be suspected and Voodoo practitioners are sought. For example, ancestor spirits are believed to cause illness if they have been neglected by a descendant who has not

contributed toward the annual ceremonial meal to commemorate them. Physical deformities, however, are more likely to be attributed to an angry spirit who has been enlisted by an enemy to perform an act of witchcraft. Many psychiatric disorders are also attributed to spiritual causes (p. 195).

For many low-income immigrants, hospitals are considered a last resort after folk medicine remedies have been exhausted. Many immigrants believe that traditional medicine is superior to the treatment they are likely to receive in public hospitals or Medicaid clinics, which tend to be understaffed and to lack bilingual staff who can speak the diverse languages of immigrant people.

CULTURAL COMPETENCE

To conceptualize grief support services for black immigrants, we must begin by recognizing their strengths. Most immigrants arrive in this country with a strong work ethic and a desire to become U.S. citizens. Service providers must consider the larger social and economic factors that may exacerbate their individual reactions and responses to death. To accomplish this task, they should take a multilevel approach, using the microstrategies associated with direct individual and interpersonal intervention as well as the macrostrategies of indirect intervention at the institutional and societal levels. One needs to have the critical skills of advocacy and empowerment. Advocacy implies addressing power imbalances by working to change conditions that may impede the interaction between people and the environment (Daniel, 2004). In the context of bereavement, it would be necessary to advocate for immigrants' rights to secure agency resources and services without fear of deportation, labeling, or insufficient funds to pay for grief support services.

Daniel (2004, p. 142) defines empowerment as "a process whereby persons who belong to a stigmatized social category throughout their lives can be assisted to develop and increase skills in the performance of valued social roles." Working effectively with black immigrants requires an approach that would educate them about their situation, the power dynamics, and the system in which they live, and teach them new skills to access resources and act on their own behalf.

Black immigrants' experience of death and grief must be understood from an Africentric perspective, in which the central focus involves mending the circle of life shaken by death. Grief counseling with this goal in mind is culturally appropriate, as it includes talking about the ancestors, thus keeping them spiritually alive in the family (Sullivan, 1996, p. 171).

Martin and Martin's (2002) *Framework for Incorporating Black Spirituality into Social Work Practice* is instructive for grief counselors working with black immigrant groups, because it incorporates native helping specialists who can assess social problems in terms of spiritual causes and solutions. Professionals improve their helping capacity if they are able to explore black spirituality. Assessment of a client's religious history, background, and worldview can provide valuable insights about both the client and the client's problem. Whether the black client is a Muslim or a Christian, a Rastafarian or a follower of Vodoun, a Yoruba or a Christian fundamentalist, a thorough working knowledge of the client's religious affiliation is necessary. If the helping professional is not knowledgeable about the client's religious and spiritual beliefs, values, and lifestyle, he or she should obtain a religious consultation with a person who is knowledgeable (p. 212).

Assessment of a black client's language, dreams, and perception of God can provide information about his or her problems, personality, and interpersonal relationships. Learning the role of black spirituality in major life events, such as funerals and memorials, can provide insight into spiritual links between the old and the young, the living and the dead, and family history and black history. Spiritual assessment uncovers potential sources of strength and support. Determining whether clients pray, attend church, meditate, or read scriptures can enable helping professionals to assess the potential effectiveness of these techniques in solving grief issues (Martin & Martin, 2002, pp. 211–215).

Finally, carefully planned and well-staffed programs play an important role in the lives of immigrant families. Helping professionals are ideally situated to mobilize resources and enlist the help of cultural guides to link families to bereavement services according to their stage of adjustment, immigration status, available financial resources, preference for traditional healers, and willingness to meet with a grief counselor.

SUMMARY

The crucial aspect of helping black immigrants from diverse regions of the world is investing the time to understand their beliefs and attitudes about health, disease, and death. The second most important aspect is finding bilingual counselors who can understand the nuances of language and meaning, and communicate effectively with persons from various subgroups of the immigrant population. Third, knowledge of a full range of direct and indirect resources and services is required to meet an immigrant's need for practical help and for emotional support in relation to grief and loss. If the immigrant is cut off from a nurturing community, it may be necessary to help him or her create rituals to promote the resolution of grief. Finally, good clinical practices—such as exploring, active listening, presenting oneself in a nonjudgmental manner, and expressing empathy—and a genuine willingness to advocate for immigrants' rights and empower them to help themselves without overtaxing informal networks will go far to provide grief support and other forms of end-of-life care.

Penelope J. Moore, *DSW, ACSW, LCSW-R, is an associate professor of social work at Iona College in New Rochelle, NY. She coordinates the Women's Studies Program and is coordinator of honor societies and convocations. She represents the college on the Village Team, a consortium of human service agencies, and on the Westchester Alliance of Academic Institutions for Aging-Related Content and Workforce Development. She represents her department as a faculty mentor on the Council on Social Work Education, Gero-Education Northeast Curriculum Development Institute (CDI), funded by the John A. Hartford Foundation. As a CDI participant, she coordinates efforts to infuse gerontology content in the undergraduate curriculum of the Social Work Department at Iona and in other programs nationwide. She is an active member of the National Association of Social Workers, Council on Social Work Education, New York State Social Work Education Association, and Association of Death Education and Counseling. Her research interests include intergenerational program development and evaluation, bereavement supports and the black church, and cultural competence with African Americans in health care and educational institutions.*

REFERENCES

Barrett, L. (1976). *The sun and the drum.* Kingston, Jamaica: Sangster's Book Stores Ltd.

Barrett, R. K. (1995). Contemporary African-American funeral rites and traditions. In L. A. DeSpelder & A. L. Strickland (Eds.), *The path ahead: Readings in death and dying* (pp. 80–92). Mountain View, CA: Mayfield.

Best-Cummings, C., & Gildner, M. A. (2004). Caribbean women's migratory journey: An exploration of their decision-making process. In A. Mahoney (Ed.), *The health and social well-being of Caribbean immigrants in the United States* (pp. 83–101). New York: The Haworth Press.

Bhopal, R. (1998). Spectre of racism in health and health care: Lessons from history and the United States. *British Medical Journal, 316*(7149), 1970–1973.

Bolling, J. L. (1996). Guinea across the water: The African-American approach to death and dying. In J. K. Parry & A. S. Ryan (Eds.), *A cross-cultural look at death, dying, and religion* (pp. 145–159). Chicago: Nelson-Hall.

Bulatao, R. A., & Anderson, N. B. (2001). *Understanding racial and ethnic differences in health in late life: A research agenda.* Washington, DC: National Academies Press.

Campbell, J., Cree, L., Engels, J., George, J., Haaga, B., Hayfron-Benjamin, C. A., et al. (2005). African immigrants in Washington, DC. Washington, DC: African Resource Center.

Clements, P. T., Virgil, G. J., Manno, M. S., Henry, G. C., Wilks, J., Das, S., et al. (2003). Cultural perspectives of death, grief, and bereavement. *Journal of Psychosocial Nursing, 41*(7), 18–26.

Daniel, C. A. (2004). Social work with West Indian families: A multilevel approach. In A. Mahoney (Ed.), *The health and social well-being of Caribbean immigrants in the United States* (pp. 135–145). New York: The Haworth Press.

Gaytan, F. X., Carhill, A., & Suarez-Orozco, C. (2007). Understanding and responding to the needs of newcomer immigrant youth and families. *Prevention Researcher, 14*(4), 10–13.

Harding, V. (1976). Foreword. In H. Thurman, *Jesus and the disinherited.* Boston: Beacon Press.

Hulewat, P. (1996). Resettlement: A cultural and psychological crisis. *Social Work, 41*(2), 129–135.

Hylton, P. (2002). *The role of religion in Caribbean history: From Amerindian Shamanism to Rastafarianism.* Washington, DC: Billpops Publications.

Laguerre, M. S. (1981). Haitian Americans. In A. Hardwood (Ed.), *Ethnicity and medical care* (pp. 172–210). Cambridge, MA: Harvard University Press.

Mahoney, A. (Ed.). (2004). *The health and social well-being of Caribbean immigrants in the United States.* New York: The Haworth Press.

Martin, E., & Martin, J. M. (2002). *Spirituality and the black helping tradition in social work* (pp. 193–225). Washington, DC: National Association of Social Work Press.

Matthews, L. (2004). Working with Caribbean immigrants after the World Trade Center tragedy: A challenge for social work practice. In A. Mahoney (Ed.), *The Health and social well-being of Caribbean immigrants in the United States.* New York: The Haworth Press.

Moore, J. L., & Bryant, C. D. (2003). Black funeralization and culturally grounded services. In C. D. Bryant & D. L. Peck (Eds.), *Encyclopedia of death and the human experience* (p. 598). Thousand Oaks, CA: Sage Publications.

Opperman, B., & Novello, A. (2006). The generation of hypotheses with regard to the influence of context on complicated grief. *South African Journal of Psychology, 36*(2), 374–390.

Parchment-Pennant, A. (2002). *Acculturation and quality of life.* Draft of dissertation, Adelphi University Graduate School of Psychology, Garden City, NY.

Read, J. G., & Emerson, M. O. (2005). Racial context, black immigration, and the U.S. black/white health disparity. *Social Forces, 84*(1), 181–199.

Sullivan, M. A. (1996). May the circle be unbroken: The African-American experience of death, dying and spirituality. In J. K. Parry & A. S. Ryan (Eds.), *A cross-cultural look at death, dying, and religion* (pp. 160–171). Chicago: Nelson-Hall Publishers.

Takougang, J. (2002). Contemporary African immigrants to the United States. Retrieved August 15, 2008, from http://www.africanmigration.com/archive_02/j_takougang.htm

Waters, M. C. (1994). Ethnic and racial identities of second-generation black immigrants in New York City. *International Migration Review, 28*(4), 795–820.

Worden, J. W. (1991). *Grief counseling and grief therapy: A handbook for the mental health practitioner* (2nd ed.). New York: Springer Publishing Company.

Death, Dying, and End of Life in American-Indian Communities

Gerry R. Cox

Perhaps you know these people: a very old woman who will never again leave her bed; a not-so-old man bedridden from an accident that has left him dependent on others; parents keeping vigil with their child who is dying from cancer. All are ordinary people in extraordinary situations. The difference is that these people are American Indians who have different values and cultures than most other Americans.

Healthcare professionals visit the sick, the grieving, the aged, and the dying. They offer support and comfort from person to person and help families in their time of need. Unfortunately, many of the patterns and techniques of care that these caregivers have developed over time are not effective with everyone and may actually offend some people. Knowledge of American-Indian culture, values, rituals, and ceremonies can help healthcare and hospice professionals better serve this population.

While hospice has not necessarily neglected this group, American Indians make up less than 1% of those served. Hospice and palliative care programs continue to serve a predominantly white population (Connor, 1998). The values and practices of American Indians are often quite different from those of white America, but American-Indian culture has much to teach hospice and other end-of-life organizations. In return, hospice and palliative care institutions have much to offer American Indians.

MISCONCEPTIONS ABOUT AMERICAN INDIANS

The surviving American-Indian peoples have very diverse tribal cultures. For most Americans, the history of American Indians begins in 1492, with the "discovery" of America by Europeans. However, the tribes were here long before that, and their cultures are not posthistorical; they illustrate ethnogenesis in that their cultures and identities are in flux. They may have largely disappeared from the contemporary awareness of Eurocentric society, but their reality remains a vital one.

The U.S. government recognizes more than 550 tribes, and many more are in various stages of petitioning to be recognized (Utter, 2001). There are also groups that are recognized by states and not by the federal government. The term *American Indian* encompasses many different cultures and groups. Even within groups that share a similar name (given to them by Europeans), there is great diversity.

For example, the Inde or Apache are dynamically evolving today in the United States. Forty-one groups call themselves Apache. For the most part, they still live on a few reservations, including the Jicarilla, Mescalero, Fort Apache, and San Carlos reservations in New Mexico and Arizona. The myth of the vanishing Indian has given rise to the belief that Indians are no longer among us or that they have fully assimilated into the larger society. Those who have left the reservation and nearby areas often have assimilated, but those who still live the traditional lifestyle have very different needs from hospice.

HOSPICE, END-OF-LIFE CARE, AND AMERICAN-INDIAN SPIRITUALITY

Some understanding of American-Indian spirituality is crucial for professionals offering end-of-life care. What is spirituality? To be spiritual means to be involved with the realm of the sacred in thought, action, and social forms. It constitutes a total system of symbols with deep meaning that leads to personal transformation. The ultimate good of human life has to do with relating to the sacred. American Indians' encounters with the sacred often evoke tremendous emotions and responses in the form of music, dance, drama, art, and sculpture.

The sacred can be experienced intellectually, practically, or socially. The intellectual aspect includes theology, scholarship, stories, and myth. The practical aspect involves acting and speaking in spiritual ways. The social dimension involves acts of community and fellowship. Spirituality is not individual; it involves others. At the end of life, the spiritual community—through the clan or other kinship group—needs to be included in the dying process.

American-Indian spiritual groups have sacred stories, historical context, a sense of meaning for humans, ritual, art, and symbols. The stories provide explanations of why things occur in the world, including birth, death, and even existence itself. The spiritual offers a way to manage loss and to transform those who have experienced great loss. For an American Indian, the journey is paramount. Dying and death are part of this process. It may be necessary for hospice and other end-of-life organizations to aid the dying in their journey toward transformation. Change, repentance, seeking help from sacred powers, and following a new path out of a fractured existence are all part of the journey. Hospice and palliative care programs often work with people who focus on the impending death. American Indians live for today, and the dying are still living. The focus is not on dying but on continuing the journey until death. One can be healed spiritually even while dying.

For the American Indian, the life power comes from ritual, sharing with family and community, and living according to the group's model of spirituality. While some are moved to develop an ongoing relationship with the sacred, others seem not to need centers of meaning and purpose in their lives. However, suffering and pain may lead patients and families to call for ceremonies to allow them to return to the sacred way. Healthcare professionals should be sensitive to this need and encourage traditional rituals.

The spirituality of American Indians includes thanking the plants and animals that give up life so they can eat, thanking the soil that nourishes the plants and animals, and thanking Mother Earth. It is also important to thank all in society who contribute to surviving today. American-Indian spirituality is not *something* one does, but rather a part of *everything* one does. For most people, it is difficult to comprehend the depth of American-Indian spirituality. While many people participate in spiritual ceremonies or feel spiritual from time to time, the lives of American Indians are permeated with spirituality.

DEATH AND THE AMERICAN INDIAN

American Indians have a unique view of death. Stories of children dying symbolic deaths, battling mythic monsters, or battling with spirits are commonplace. In funeral rites, the newly dead are often thought to be in an in-between state. The dead person may be welcomed back as an ancestor or feared as a potential source of death for the living. Rituals to manage dead spirits have evolved to cope with grief and loss. Artistic expression may be used to help deal with loss.

American-Indian beliefs and traditions include reverence and respect for every part of life, including death. The dirt, rocks, and trees are sacred. The ashes of the dead rest in sacred ground. Rather than disconnecting, American Indians continue to have relationships with the dead. Some loved ones are perceived as still caring for and protecting those left behind. But if the dead person did not do those things in life, he or she is not expected to do them from the afterlife.

AMERICAN-INDIAN CULTURE

American Indians who live in an urban environment view the world quite differently from those who live on or near the reservation. The unemployment rate on reservations is 49%, resources are limited, poverty is rampant, and inadequate health care is a part of life. Yet people have the support of the clan or tribe and the culture—support that is missing in urban environments, where what one does for a living is far more important than tribal community (Robertson, 2008). Being homeless, unemployed, or underemployed, or lacking health insurance are much bigger handicaps in an urban environment.

American Indians have patterns of sharing along kinship lines. This may include sharing money, childcare, housing, transportation, help with work, or whatever is needed. Generosity and sharing are dominant cultural values, but they are often missing in an urban environment. Accumulation of wealth is not a traditional value on the reservation; rather, goods are to be shared and savings are to be used. Giveaway ceremonies are still practiced among many groups.

Family, clan, tribe, and even the Bureau of Indian Affairs can help on the reservation. Indigenous knowledge and practices are being used to design and deliver services that would otherwise be unavailable (Robertson, 2008). The advantage of the tribal community lies in its simplicity. The child learns a consistent normative pattern, has the security of knowing the people around him or her, and has fewer roles to identify and develop. The extended family has more influence on the person. People know what you do and don't do.

American Indians may communicate differently from people in mainstream American society. They tend to use more nonverbal behaviors and silence. How close does one stand when talking to another person? How long does one pause before responding? Is it necessary to fill the air with words, or is it proper to remain silent? Do people look each other in the eye when speaking? In some groups, a person does not look another in the eye until a bond has been established. American Indians generally value silence more than those in the dominant culture do, and personal space is not as important.

If a person is accustomed to folk medicine, traditional healers, ceremonies, and rituals at home or in the community, he or she may be intimidated by the environment of hospitals and pharmacies. Doctors, nurses, bureaucrats, machines, white clothing, stainless steel, and strange smells may intimidate or alienate patients and family members with whom hospice workers interact. Such fears do not lead to healing or resolution of grief. The homecare model of hospice tends to be more compatible with traditional American-Indian culture.

The dominant culture in Canada and the United States tends to focus on the future. It is not unusual to start making college plans for children who are not even in high school yet. American Indians, on the other hand, tend to live in the present, with a view that the past cannot be changed and the future has not yet happened. Why worry? Healing, illness, and death are present issues, not future or past issues. While the dominant culture tends to focus on the future without the loved one, the traditional American Indian will focus on the person who is still here today. And if drinking, smoking, or another vice has led to the illness and ultimate death, one does not blame the victim or focus on his or her failings. People are accepted for where they are now rather than for past accomplishments or mistakes. American Indians see dying persons as still living, while Eurocentric culture focuses on the fact that they are dying.

WORKING WITH DYING OR GRIEVING AMERICAN INDIANS

It is impossible to say precisely what will work with any individual or group. American Indians do not fit stereotypes and can be found in all walks of life, from professional to shaman. They come in all colors and sizes, and with all value systems. Some are Christian; some are not. Government policies since the 17th century have forced many to adopt the dominant European culture, but immense diversity remains.

Healthcare professionals must respect the dignity of American Indians. They must respect their rituals, ceremonies, and culture without attempting to appropriate the activities. Healthcare professionals must allow American Indians to conduct their death-related activities, and if invited, take part; but always remember that the activities are *theirs* (Pritzker, 1999).

For the American Indian, death is as natural as birth. It is not one's choice to be born or to die; in fact, those who take their own lives may be condemned to wander as spirits in the next life. There is no single American-Indian religion. Communication with mysterious beings is available to all. Dreams and visions provide messages or instructions that all may receive as a gift from the spirits. All life has a purpose, and everyone is here for a reason, but it may take a lifetime to determine that reason. Visions, dreams, rivers, rocks, animals, birds, and spirits can give messages if one listens. Cultures with oral traditions can travel back as far as the chain of memory will allow. In a world filled with spirits, the past provides a guide to the present.

Storytellers' tales of animals that talk, spirits that roam the earth, and rocks that have messages both instruct and entertain those who listen. American-Indian storytellers do not just talk. They may drum, sing, and even dance as they weave their tales. Masks, costumes, regalia, and performance mark the stories. Storytelling can be part of the end-of-life experience. Knowledge of the spirit world is essential to practices relating to dying, death, and grief.

Generally, the stories suggest that all animate and inanimate things are tied together and have souls. The stories teach how people are judged and why they are admired. Each person is responsible for helping and protecting others. This includes following correct ritual, forgiveness, patience, sharing, and living a spiritual life. The dying and their survivors will want to do these things.

Life is to be lived even when dying. The sacred stories and myths teach people how and why to live and die. For example, a Navajo (or Diné) story teaches that the sun must be placated by human death. Each day someone must die or the sun will not move. A part of the story is that those who die and go to the Fifth World must return to live in the Fourth World after death. Death is not the end of life, but rather a change. The coyote, the interpreter of signs, told the Diné that someone had to die every night, though it did not necessarily have to be one of The People. The coyote also said that death would come quickly to those who gazed upon the face of the dead. The Diné therefore cover the faces of the dead and bury them quickly.

It is important to remember that American Indians may not completely trust hospice or other healthcare institutions. Oppression and exploitation of American Indians are ongoing, and many American Indians believe that healthcare organizations are pressuring them to assimilate.

RESPECT FOR ELDERS AND OTHER VALUES

Adhering to cultural norms will enable healthcare professionals to be more effective in working with American Indians. For example, elders are very important and are treated in a special way. Children are taught to respect them and listen to them. Elders may or may not be tribal leaders, but they help make decisions in all things that are important to the group, including education, jobs, health and health care, housing, hunting, fishing, and general living. One of the main tasks of elders is to teach the young. They sing songs, tell stories, and teach children to respect their culture and themselves. They teach the three *R*s: respect, reciprocity, and relationships. A fourth *R* might be responsibility.

When groups gather for events, the elders are always asked to begin the ceremonies, are served first at meals, and are acknowledged before others speak. Hospice and end-of-life workers would do well to ask elders to bless them and their work and to pray for the people involved. Elders try to live in a way that earns the respect of others and to be models so that others can learn to respect themselves. Elders enjoy being active, learning, and teaching.

There are protocols for interacting with elders, such as allowing them to talk first. Adhering to these norms will allow healthcare professionals to be more effective. Other important values include those related to personal sovereignty or autonomy. Elders do not make choices for others, interfere with the decisions of others, or judge them. An elder may offer suggestions, but does not make the decision. A chief or leader may say that a course of action should be taken, but the group or individual makes the final decision. One does not tell others how to live. Hospice and other healthcare workers should not dictate to patients and families but rather should offer suggestions or advice. Elder epistemology suggests that elders are the window to roots of tribal identity, the vision of Mother Earth, and life. They are the teachers who have knowledge to help those who are dying and grieving. Healthcare professionals should take advantage of this resource, not try to supplant it.

Healthcare organizations such as hospice might consider developing a list of elders in their area, along with lists of healers, shamans, singers, medical practitioners, and others who have earned respect in the clans.

Furthermore, the use of alternative medicines and healing ceremonies should be accepted. For example, ceremonies that feature the burning of sage or the use of tobacco or sweet grass may be perceived as vital to healing and are of immense importance to many American-Indian groups. It may be necessary to have an outbuilding or an area without smoke detectors and automatic sprinklers for these ceremonies.

American Indians have a strong sense of humor. All aspects of life, including death, are subjects of humor and laughter. This humor is very natural, even at the end of life.

The naturalistic philosophy of tribes generally means that when it is one's time to die, one should die naturally, without tubes or machines. American Indians are unlikely to use medically futile interventions, and they do not believe in showing love by trying to keep a person alive as long as possible. An important belief is that one does not allow a loved one to die with strangers.

GRIEVING CEREMONIES

Although they view death as natural and inevitable, American Indians still experience a deep sense of loss. Grieving ceremonies are very important to most clans, because they believe that what the living do can affect the dead and what the dead do can affect the living. Golden (1996) suggests that the potlatch ceremonies of the Athabaskan tribes in northwestern North America allow the entire community—not just the grieving family—to move from grief into joy. This is evident as well among the Inupiats, a tribe native to Alaska. They live in the tundra, so burials are by necessity a community affair. All the men dig the grave, usually over several days, pouring water to melt the frozen earth. Women boil the water and cook meals to serve each night at a community gathering to mourn the deceased. Even the carving of the memorial stone is a communal affair. All deaths involve the tribe, for each one takes away from the clan. Thus, each death must be mourned. Some tribes do not even use the word *death;* rather, they say the deceased leave the world and go on a spirit trail, where they will see all their previously deceased relatives and wait for their descendants to join them.

Most American Indians seem to face death without great concern for their actions or failures in life. If one has lived a life of integrity and has respected the dignity of others, one has no reason to fear death. It is the natural end of life, merely a transition into a different world (Steiger, 1974). It is meant to occur. Life cannot occur without death. We live and then we live again. Death is a painful separation for the living, but when one dies, the dead can wait for their descendants to join them.

Conclusion

Those who provide end-of-life care to American Indians should have a genuine interest in their values, culture, and practices. It is also important that health-care professionals be nonjudgmental and try to develop an understanding and empathy for American-Indian ways. It is also useful to acknowledge the role of elders in the dying and grieving process; to respect diversity and differences; to allow ceremonies, rituals, and practices; and to recognize that American-Indian spirituality is all-inclusive and permeates everything people do.

Part of the beauty of ministering to American Indians is the opportunity to learn and grow. In many ways, American Indians can teach the end-of-life community the true nature of holistic care.

Gerry R. Cox, *professor emeritus and director of the Center for Death Education and Bioethics at the University of Wisconsin–La Crosse, serves as host of the International Death, Grief, and Bereavement Conference held annually at the University of Wisconsin–La Crosse. He has published extensively. He is a member of the International Work Group on Death, Grief, and Bereavement, the Midwest Sociological Society, Alpha Kappa Delta, and the American Sociological Association. He serves on the board of the National Prison Hospice Association.*

REFERENCES

Connor, S. R. (1998). *Hospice: Practice, pitfalls, and promise.* Bristol, PA: Taylor & Francis.

Golden, T. R. (1996). *Swallowed by a snake: The gift of the masculine side of healing.* Kensington, MD: Golden Healing Publishing.

Pritzker, B. M. (1999). *Native America today: A guide to community politics and culture.* Santa Barbara, CA: ABC-CLIO.

Robertson, P. (2008). Native Americans, reservation life. In V. N. Parrillo (Ed.), *Encyclopedia of social problems.* Thousand Oaks, CA: Sage.

Steiger, B. (1974). *Medicine power: The American Indian's revival of his spiritual heritage.* Garden City, New York: Doubleday.

Utter, J. (2001). *American Indians: Answers to today's questions.* Norman, OK: University of Oklahoma Press.

Hispanic Cultural Issues in End-of-Life Care

Carlos Sandoval-Cros

INTRODUCTION

What is culture? Culture refers to learned patterns of behavior, beliefs, and values shared by persons in a particular social group. It provides human beings with both their identity and a framework for understanding experience (Marshall, 1990). When we refer to culture in its broadest sense, we usually think about a group of people with similar ethnic background, language, religion, family values, and life views.

Culture and nationality, however, are not synonymous. The United States, for example, is made up of people from many countries and traditions, each with a unique culture. For many years we viewed this country as the great "melting pot" of the world; however, this vision is being rejected (Locke, 1998). The truth is that the United States is a multicultural or pluralistic society, made up of members of different ethnic, racial, religious, and social groups, living side by side, sharing aspects of the dominant U.S. culture but maintaining their own values and traditions.

Since culture provides individuals with a framework for understanding experience, it is of great importance to consider culture in the medical setting. Each cultural group has its own views about health, illness, and healthcare practices (Kleinman, Eisenberg, & Good, 1978). These views affect how people respond to illnesses and their symptoms, including pain; identify and select medical care; and comply with prescribed care (Chrisman, 1977; Wood, Zeltzer, & Cox, 1987; Zborowski, 1969). These views also affect how a person or a group views death and grief. It is culture that guides people regarding the meaning of death and how to respond to it (Moller, 1996).

HISPANIC CULTURAL VALUES

In 1990, the Census Bureau reported that there were about 22 million Hispanic Americans in the United States, comprising about 9% of the total population. In the following decade, the Hispanic population grew an estimated 58% to about 35 million of the country's residents. The 2007 estimate brought the percentage to 15.1% (45.5 million people), surpassing African Americans as the largest minority group in the country (U.S. Census Bureau, 2001).

The term *Hispanic* is a label of convenience for a group with a common cultural heritage stemming from Spain's colonization of the Americas (Talamantes, Gomez, & Braun, 2000). Hispanics can be of any racial group (e.g., indigenous American, black African, Asian, Caucasian) or of multiple racial ancestry. Hispanics include several subgroups, each with important social and cultural differences. The major Hispanic subgroups in the United States traditionally have been Mexican Americans, Puerto Ricans, and Cubans. However, the dramatic increase in Hispanics observed in the 2000 census was fueled primarily by immigration from Central and South America.

Differences among Hispanic subgroups may relate to country of origin, that country's racial/ethnic makeup, different histories of immigration to the United States, or (as in the case of Puerto Rico) the population's experience with colonization (Talamantes et al., 2000). However, for the most part, these subgroups share a common language, religion, traditional family structure, and several common Hispanic values. Brazilians—a product of Portugal's colonization in the Americas—speak Portuguese and are therefore not Hispanic; however, they, too, are immigrating to the United States in significant numbers and share many family values and cultural, racial, and religious characteristics with Hispanics.

In addition to differences among subgroups, Hispanics in the United States also differ in their level of acculturation or assimilation into mainstream culture. Language use is a primary example of these differences. While many Hispanics in the United States are bilingual, the extent to which they speak either Spanish or English varies considerably, from virtually no English in recent immigrants and many of the elderly, to full bilingualism in acculturated Hispanics, to very limited Spanish in second- and third-generation Hispanics. This pattern is observed across various Hispanic cultures.

One value shared by most Hispanics is their religion. Although individual practice and church participation vary, the majority of Hispanics are Christian, predominantly Roman Catholic (McCready, 1994). However, many Hispanics practice other religious beliefs that they have incorporated into their Christianity, such as forms of ancestor worship with rituals dating back to pre-Columbian times among Central-American Indians. Many Caribbean Hispanics practice Santería, a syncretism of Catholicism and the Yoruba religion brought to Cuba by African slaves (Sandoval, 1977). Hispanic religious and spiritual beliefs include views on dying and death. For example, it is common to hold a continued vigil over an older family member with a terminal illness. After death, it is common practice to offer daily masses or light candles in honor of the deceased (Rael & Koete, 1988). These and other practices honor the loved one and form part of the bereavement ritual.

Family plays a very strong role for most Hispanics, with ties among an extended network of uncles, aunts, cousins, grandparents, and family friends. In the concept of *familismo*, family welfare takes precedence over that of the individual.

In addition to language, religion, and family, five other themes influence Hispanic culture:

- *Personalismo:* Trust building over time based on the display of mutual respect
- *Jerarquismo:* Respect for hierarchy and authority
- *Presentismo:* Emphasis on the present, not the past or the future (Cuellar, 1990)
- *Espiritismo:* Belief in good and evil spirits that can affect health and well-being
- *Fatalismo:* The belief that fate determines life outcomes, including health, and that fate is basically predestined (Ferriss, 1993)

Table 1 on page 120 presents a framework of issues to consider with regard to Hispanic patients and palliative care.

Table 1

Hispanic Cultural Themes That Can Influence Care

THEME	MEANING	IMPLICATION
Familismo	Emphasis on the well-being of the family over that of the individual	Include family members in healthcare and end-of-life discussions.
Personalismo	Trust building over time based on the display of mutual respect	Learn about patients and their culture. Use personal and open communication.
Jerarquismo	Respect for authority and hierarchy	Check whether patient is withholding information out of deference to provider. Patient and families may have unrealistic treatment expectations.
Presentismo	Emphasis on the present rather than the past or the future	Patient and families may avoid end-of-life discussions and advance directives.
Espiritismo	Belief in good and evil spirits that can affect health and well-being	Patients may seek spiritual healers such as *curanderos* instead of standard treatment.
Fatalismo	Fate determines life outcomes, including health, and is predestined	Patients may be reluctant to seek care.

Sources: Adapted from Cuellar, 1990; Perkins, Supik, & Hazuda, 1993.

END-OF-LIFE CARE PREFERENCES

How do Hispanic values, beliefs, and practices influence end-of-life preferences? While research is limited, I will review the following: patient autonomy, advance directives, life-prolonging treatments, and the role of hospice.

Patient Autonomy

In a study in Los Angeles comparing Mexican, Korean, African, and European Americans on several issues relating to patient autonomy, researchers found that Mexican and Korean Americans were less likely to believe that a patient should be told about a terminal diagnosis or should make decisions about life support. The researchers found that Mexican and Korean-American elders were more likely than African and European-American elders to want family members to make these decisions (Blackhall, Murphy, Frank, Michel, & Azen, 1995). This study also found differences among Mexican Americans by income, degree of acculturation, and age; that is, younger and more acculturated respondents and those with higher incomes were more likely to favor telling the truth about the diagnosis.

In a series of focus groups exploring general medical treatment decisions with a random sample of 50 Mexican-American elders in San Antonio, Talamantes and Gomez (1996) found that 46% of the elders wanted their doctor to make these decisions, 24% would prefer to make their own decisions, and 18% would discuss the decision with their families. When asked whether it bothered them to talk about these issues with their families, 84% said that it did not.

Advance Directives

The aforementioned Los Angeles study on patient autonomy among Mexican, Korean, African, and European Americans (Blackhall et al., 1995) also compared knowledge about advance directives. The researchers found that while Mexican and European Americans were significantly more knowledgeable than Korean and African Americans about advance directives, only 22% of the Mexican Americans actually had one, compared with 40% of the European Americans.

Miles, Koepp, and Weber (1996) found that the Mexican Americans who had advance directives were more highly acculturated than those who did not. Three years earlier, at the University of Miami in Florida, Caralis, Davis, Wright, and Marcial (1993) conducted a multicultural study examining the influence of ethnicity on attitudes toward advance directives, life-prolonging treatments, and euthanasia. The researchers found that Hispanic Americans (most were of Cuban heritage) were less knowledgeable about living wills than African and non-Hispanic white Americans.

Life-Prolonging Treatments

On the issue of life-prolonging treatments, Caralis and her colleagues found that Hispanic and African Americans were more likely than non-Hispanic whites to want their doctors to keep them alive regardless of how ill they were (42% and 37% versus 14%, respectively). Furthermore, only 59% of Hispanics and 63% of African Americans said they would agree to stop life-prolonging treatment, compared with 89% of non-Hispanic whites (Caralis et al., 1993). This disparity may have been due partly to the biblical commandment: "Thou shalt not kill." A religious Christian might interpret withdrawing or withholding treatment as an infraction of this commandment.

Hospice

A few studies have suggested that Hispanics are low users of hospice services. This may be due to unfamiliarity with hospice, insurance coverage issues, language barriers, or unpleasant experiences with or distrust of the healthcare system (Sotomayor & Randolph, 1988). In addition, Wallace and Lew-Ting (1992) suggest that low utilization of hospice among Hispanics may be due to physician referral patterns; that is, physicians might not refer Hispanic patients to hospice because they see families providing care themselves and believe that hospice might be unnecessary or culturally inappropriate.

INTERVENTIONS

Taking into account Hispanic core values, the aforementioned barriers, and end-of-life preferences, what can the healthcare provider do to improve palliative care for the Hispanic client? Healthcare professionals need to learn about the family, social, and religious values associated with Hispanic culture in general, and become familiar with the history of the subgroups they usually deal with. This, as well as learning to speak Spanish, will help providers display respect and build trust (Talamantes & Gomez, 1996).

The provider should include family members in discussions with the patient about palliative care. In some situations, the patient may not want to include the family in the discussion, and this, of course, should be respected (Cuellar, 1990).

Finally, it is important to have open and clear communication with the patient and the family. The tradition of *jerarquismo* may lead the Hispanic patient to withhold information or hesitate to communicate honestly. The provider must ascertain whether the patient fully understands the treatment being offered and whether he or she fully agrees with the treatment plan (Spinetta, 1984). This is particularly important when it comes to end-of-life decision making and advance directives, as research indicates that several factors may discourage frank discussions on these topics (Blackhall et al., 1995; Caralis et al., 1993; Sotomayor & Randolph, 1988). *Jerarquismo* may lead the patient and family to have unrealistic expectations about what conventional treatment can accomplish. The family may be expecting a miracle cure for the terminally ill patient and thus may refuse to consider palliative care options. Conflicts between the patient's religion and withdrawing or withholding of treatment can be addressed and clarified by including a clergy member in decision making.

The role of community education cannot be overstated, especially in light of the degree of marginalization many Hispanics face because of language, racism, and other socioeconomic barriers, including legal status. Education should be provided directly by the healthcare team because of the value placed on *personalismo*, and the target audience should include the entire community: patients, families, and community leaders, including clergy.

The provider can share with the Hispanic community not only general information about health and specific illnesses, but also information about end-of-life issues, palliative care, and the role of hospice. Healthcare providers should be included in education, because many of them lack knowledge of the broad range of palliative care interventions, especially pain management. One resource for up-to-date training on palliative care is Education for Physicians in End-of-Life Care (EPEC) at www.epec.net. Education can also be enhanced by recruiting members of the community who are living with specific health issues to serve as role models to share their experience with the illness. The provider should not rely on brochures alone for education, since the language used in many brochures may be above the reading level of many Hispanics, or the brochures may only exist in English, or may be poorly translated (Talamantes, 1993).

Community-based organizations should be developed to identify and address the specific healthcare concerns of local minority communities. One such organization is the Harlem Palliative Care Network in New York City, whose specific objectives are as follows:

- To increase access to palliative care services for patients and their families residing in Central and East Harlem who are facing progressive, life-threatening illness
- To overcome cultural and environmental barriers among minority populations in receiving timely intervention
- To enhance the continuity and coordination of care through greater integration of community-based and institutional services
- To improve the quality of life for Harlem patients through better pain and symptom management
- To provide support services to meet the emotional and spiritual needs of the patients and their families (Payne, Payne, & Heller, 2001)

CONCLUSION

While healthcare professionals who work with Hispanics cannot become familiar with every cultural issue related to medicine, they can become more sensitive to the role that culture plays in how people access and experience palliative care services. Recognizing the role of culture and being familiar with the core values of a cultural group will help eliminate barriers to treatment and will optimize patient care, particularly end-of-life care.

NOTE: This chapter draws on work previously published by the author in: O'Neill, J. F., Selwyn, P. A., & Schietinger, H. (Eds.), A clinical guide on supportive and palliative care for people with HIV/AIDS. Washington, DC: U.S. Health Resources and Services Administration.

Carlos Sandoval-Cros, MD, is a psychiatrist in private practice and an Episcopal priest. He earned his medical degree from the Catholic University Madre y Maestra in the Dominican Republic. After attending seminary, he worked as a medical missionary in Quito, Ecuador, and was ordained a priest. Dr. Sandoval-Cros returned to Miami and completed his psychiatry residency at UM/Jackson Memorial Hospital and took a position as assistant professor in the Department of Psychiatry and psychiatrist for The Courtelis Center for Psychosocial Oncology, where he became director in 1998. After 10 years at the University of Miami, he went into private practice and now works mostly with the elderly living in assisted living facilities. Dr. Sandoval-Cros also currently serves as pastor of Saint Simon's Episcopal Church, a bicultural congregation in southwest Miami.

REFERENCES

Blackhall, L. J., Murphy, D. T., Frank, G., Michel, V., & Azen, S. (1995). Ethnicity and attitudes toward patient autonomy. *Journal of the American Medical Association, 10,* 820–825.

Caralis, P. V., Davis, B., Wright, K., & Marcial, E. (1993). The influence of ethnicity and race on attitudes toward advance directives, life-prolonging treatments, and euthanasia. *Journal of Clinical Ethics, 4,* 155–165.

Chrisman, N. J. (1977). The health-seeking process: An approach to the natural history of disease. *Culture, Medicine and Psychiatry, 1,* 351–377.

Cuellar, J. B. (1990). Hispanic American aging: Geriatric education curriculum development for selected health professionals. In M. S. Harper (Ed.), *Minority aging: Essential curricula content for selected health and allied health professions* (pp. 365–413). DHHS Publication No. (HRS) P-DV-90-4. Washington, DC: U.S. Department of Health and Human Services.

Ferriss, S. (1993, January 19). *Fatalismo*: A health threat for Latinos. *San Francisco Examiner.*

Kleinman, A., Eisenberg. L., & Good, B. (1978). Culture, illness and care: Clinical lessons from anthropologic and cross-cultural research. *Annals of Internal Medicine, 88,* 251–258.

Locke, D. C. (1998). *Increasing multicultural understanding: A comprehensive model.* Newbury Park, CA: Sage.

Marshall, P. (1990). Cultural influences on perceived quality of life. *Seminars in Oncology Nursing, 6,* 278–284.

McCready, W. C. (1994). Culture and religion. In P. J. Cafferty & W. C. McCready (Eds.), *Hispanics in the United States: A new social agenda* (pp. 49–61). New Brunswick, NJ: Transaction Publishers.

Miles, S. H., Koepp, R., & Weber, E. P. (1996). Advance end-of-life treatment planning: A research review. *Archives of Internal Medicine, 156,* 1062–1068.

Moller, D. W. (1996). *Confronting death: Values, institutions, and human mortality.* New York: Oxford University Press.

Payne, R., Payne, T. R., & Heller, K. S. (2001). The Harlem Palliative Care Network: An interview with Richard Payne, MD, and Terrie Reid Payne, MA. *Innovations in End-of-Life Care, 3*(5). Available from www.edc.org/lastacts

Perkins, H. S., Supik, J. D., & Hazuda, H. P. (1993). Autopsy decisions: The possibility of conflicting cultural attitudes. *Journal of Clinical Ethics, 4,* 142–154.

Rael, R., & Koete, A. O. (1988). El ciclo de la vida y muerte: An analysis of death and dying in a selected Hispanic enclave. In S. R. Applewhite (Ed.), *Hispanic elderly in transition: Theory, research, policy, and practice.* Westport, CT: Greenwood.

Sandoval, M. (1977). Santería: Afrocuban concepts of disease and its treatment in Miami. *Journal of Operational Psychiatry, 8,* 52–63.

Sotomayor, M., & Randolph, S. (1988). A preliminary review of caregiving issues and the Hispanic family. In M. Sotomayor & H. Curiel (Eds.), *Hispanic elderly: A cultural signature* (pp. 137–160). Edinburg, TX: Pan American University Press.

Spinetta, J. (1984). Measurement of family function, communication and cultural effects. *Cancer, 53,* 2330–2337.

Talamantes, M. A. (1993, March). *Community education on advance healthcare directives.* Paper presented at the annual meeting of the American Society on Aging, Chicago, IL.

Talamantes, M. A., & Gomez, C. (1996, November). *Knowledge and use of advance health directives by Mexican American elderly.* Paper presented at the annual meeting of the Gerontological Society of America, Washington, DC.

Talamantes, M. A., Gomez, C., & Braun, K. (2000). Advance directives and end-of-life care: The Hispanic perspective. In K. L. Braun, J. H. Pietsch, & P. L. Blanchette (Eds.), *Cultural issues in end-of-life decision making* (pp. 83–100). Newbury Park, CA: Sage Publications.

U.S. Census Bureau. (2001, April). Table 4: Difference in population by race and Hispanic or Latino origin: 1990 to 2000. Retrieved October 1, 2008, from http://www.census.gov/population/www/cen2000/briefs/phc-t1/tables/tab04.xls

Wallace, S. P., & Lew-Ting, C. (1992). Getting by at home: Community-based long-term care of Latino elders. The *Western Journal of Medicine, 157,* 337–344.

Wood, P. R., Zeltzer, L. K., & Cox, A. D. (1987). Communicating with adolescents from culturally varied backgrounds: A model based on Mexican-American adolescents in South Texas. *Seminars in Adolescent Medicine, 3,* 99–108.

Zborowski, M. (1969). *People in pain.* San Francisco: Jossey-Bass.

Diverse Spiritualities

Spirituality remains a major source of diversity. Spirituality is the way that one finds meaning in life—the beliefs that are the major organizing principle or worldview that frames how one encounters life's ultimate questions. Spirituality is a major influence in end-of-life care and grief. Every spiritual system defines the "good death" in its own way. Spiritual communities may offer practices and rituals that should be performed when someone is ill or dying, at the time of the death, or throughout a defined period of mourning. Spiritual beliefs may influence decisions at the end of life. Beliefs, practices, and rituals may facilitate, and even at times complicate, bereavement.

In many populations, spirituality can be more of a defining factor than ethnicity or race. For example, in Northern Ireland, the major social division is between Catholics and Protestants. Among many Asian immigrant groups, religious affiliation along with ethnicity is a major source of identity.

Maurice Lamm begins this section with an article on Judaism, affirming that being Jewish transcends even spirituality. One may still self-define as Jewish even if one is secular and religiously nonobservant. Yet, even among the nonobservant, Lamm notes, Jewish identity as well as beliefs and rituals remain important as one faces illness, dying, and death. Lamm offers not only descriptions of beliefs and rituals but also sage advice on the sensitivities that may help caregivers bridge the cultural gap. Barry Kinzbrunner expands understanding of Judaism as he explores the detailed practices and rituals that surround the Orthodox and Hasidic communities. While these communities represent only about 10% of North American Jews, it is a growing population. Moreover, these rituals and practices may be involved by even those less observant.

Hasan Shanawani offers perspectives on the growing Islamic population. This provides another example of the importance of spirituality as a source of diversity. Muslims may have a variety of racial identities. They may come from many countries even if the faith is predominant in the Middle East and many Asian nations. Yet, their shared faith offers common rituals, practices, and beliefs likely to influence end-of-life care and bereavement support. Shanawani identifies the barriers that might affect end-of-life care even as he educates on the critical sensitivities necessary for transcending these barriers.

Eve Mullen's chapter considers Buddhism—another religion growing from both Asian migrants and Western converts. Mullen notes the diversity within Buddhism and the common practices, beliefs, and rituals that reaffirm impermanence and the constant cycle of death and rebirth until transcendence. Mullen makes a number of critical points relevant to diversity. First, she affirms that ethnicity along with spirituality represent important forms of identification among Buddhists. Second, Mullen emphasizes that Buddhism, like many Eastern faiths, is more inclusive than many Western belief systems. Buddhists may also harmoniously adhere to Confucian ideas or Taoist practices, for example. Finally, she notes the many diverse schools of Buddhism.

Kenneth Doka's chapter concludes this section. Culture, it is often remarked, hides from those who know it best. That is, one can often recognize the distinct elements in other cultures even while ignoring one's own. In this light, Doka explores the Christian evangelical movement—a growing movement that claims slightly over a fourth of American Christians. Doka notes the tensions that can exist between evangelicals and hospice and palliative care. While analyzing the history and sources of this conflict, Doka affirms that these conflicts are more perceptual than real and offers suggestions for outreach to the growing evangelical community.

Again, this discussion of spirituality is meant to be illustrative rather than exhaustive. Not all faiths are discussed. Hinduism, for example, is a major world religion but is in the early stages of consolidation in the United States. Other faiths like Jehovah's Witnesses have practices such as refusing blood transfusions or celebrating only certain special occasions that have profound implications for end-of-life care and grief support. Again, though, the number of Witnesses in the United States is limited. The point of this section remains: Any assessment of diversity needs to include an understanding of spiritual identification and a sensitivity for how spiritual beliefs, practices, or rituals influence dying, death, and grief.

CHAPTER 10

Jewish Perspectives on Loss, Grief, and End-of-Life Care

Maurice Lamm

THE JEWISH COMMUNITY TODAY

Judaism is the most ancient of today's cultures, and also the most unfamiliar. There are more than 6 million Jews in the United States. Most are concentrated in the largest cities, and in those places their ways are better known. They are sometimes prominent, occupying university positions, working in the medical and legal professions, owning retail businesses, and overrepresented in the computer and financial industries. But even in these metropolitan settings, the startling lack of knowledge about such a major culture is mystifying.

Exacerbating this lack of knowledge is the assumption that Judaism holds certain truths and practices that it does not and never has. The geographic and stylistic proximity of Judaism to its daughter religion, Christianity, leads some people to assume that they are essentially the same in religious practice, especially regarding death; but they are definitely not. For example, Catholic "Last Rites" are assumed by some to also be fundamental to the Jewish religion. But this is not so. In Judaism, there is a two-line prayer, called *Vidui,* which is similar sounding but theologically vastly different.

This knowledge gap is exacerbated by a curious situation: Authentic Judaism is relatively unknown to many secularized Jews, no matter how educated they are. Secular Jews generally do not identify with the Jewish community's interests except in two circumstances. The first circumstance is when a threat to the Jewish community looms on its horizon, such as personal or institutional anti-Semitism. The second is when a person's own life is threatened, or that of a relative or friend. In these circumstances, Judaism is the old home where the light is always on.

The hospice team may face a two-horned dilemma. The Jewish patient may not know much about even the most basic Jewish practices; but, at the same, he or she may be looking for something transcendent to grasp on to in a time of crisis. The hospice worker must make a complex assessment concerning what part of the Jewish faith and practice this patient might long for and what part he or she would reject out of hand.

CONNECTING TO JEWISH PATIENTS—A CAREGIVER'S PRIMER

The caregiver needs to know that different Jews observe their faith at different levels and that attitudes toward one's Jewish identity hold many facets. The following are some avenues through which caregivers can connect with their Jewish patients.

Although some Jews adhere to all laws and customs, others are totally nonobservant and do not incorporate Jewish ritual into their lives. From the perspectives of both Jewish law and the canons of modern social work, Jews at both ends of the spectrum—from devout to secular—are legitimately Jewish. According to the Babylonian Talmud: "A Jew, even when he sins, is still a Jew." This is unlike certain Christian and Muslim sects that base their acceptance of a person on baptism or belief in one dogma or another.

In working with Jewish patients, the caregiver should be sensitive to the person's self-definition, be it social/organizational, ethnic/cultural, national/Zionist, or straightforwardly religious (Orthodox, Conservative, or Reform).

"Jewishness" is a powerful concept and a strong bond. A volunteer or professional caregiver can uphold the client's identity by:

- Affirming the person's Jewishness—letting him know that you know he is Jewish—unless he expressly wishes to avoid the subject
- Becoming familiar with the Jewish calendar, and mentioning upcoming religious and community holidays
- Discussing a current event involving Israel or a current example of anti-Semitism
- Sharing ethnic Jewish food, if medically permitted, such as a bagel or gefilte fish

If the caregiver is Jewish, he or she might sing a Jewish song with the patient. In a recent case, the family asked a rabbi to help them coax the patient to break his rigid silence. Nothing had worked. The young Reform rabbi sat alongside the bed and simply began to sing "Adon Olam." First the patient and then the whole family joined him in the song. That is true spiritual harmony.

Particular sensitivity is required when clients seek your counsel on death and funeral arrangements. It can be very helpful to recommend that they speak with a rabbi or other Jewish authority and to help them contact such a person.

Hospital libraries should include books on the Jewish way of death, the Jewish funeral, Jewish consolation, prayer books, and such publications as *The Jewish Hospice Manual* (available from the National Institute for Jewish Hospice).

Acknowledging the Lack of Knowledge

The hospice worker should have a basic understanding of the legitimate diversity of customs, basic Jewish practices surrounding death, and words and phrases that are common in Jewish usage and that Jews of all stripes know. Currently, there is a general lack of knowledge throughout the hospice movement about Jewish customs and attitudes toward death.

It goes without saying that one cannot successfully manage a patient's needs in a hospice setting unless one can communicate with the patient. Imagine a Southern Baptist or an Orthodox Jewish caregiver bending over the bed of a faithful Buddhist, searching for spiritual words of comfort for a person whose lifestyle is totally foreign. Cultural incompetence can seriously detract from effective and professional end-of-life care.

Cultural Uniqueness: The Holocaust Patient

Competency extends not only to the *facts* of the faith—the practices and accepted ethics—but also to the *culture.* An 80-year-old woman in a free-standing hospice was a survivor of the Nazi death camp of Dachau. She awakened from an afternoon nap and called for a nurse. The hospice management sent one of its finest nurses—a tall, blond German national with a heavy accent. The nurse innocently stood over the woman, looked down at her, and asked, "Vat can I do to help you?" The woman let out a scream, in Yiddish, that startled all the patients. The hospice had all the provisions for healing and caring, and the nurse had done his best. But, because of a lack of basic cultural sensitivity, the result was abominable.

Barriers to Hospice Admission

One barrier to hospice admission for Jews concerns whether the whole direction of the hospice movement—especially the conventional wisdom about it—is legitimate and aligns with the worldview of the Jewish patient. There may be a communal Jewish uneasiness with regard to hospice's perceived refusal to actively fight death and, in crisis, to surrender to fate.

Holding on stubbornly to life in the face of impending death is not only a function of religious observance but an inbred conviction about the supreme value of life under all circumstances. Most other religious creeds (although not all) also value life highly and hold it to be sacred, given by God, and not to be tampered with. But Jews have faced and resisted death not only in the Holocaust, but in every generation throughout history. For them, Deuteronomy's "And thou shalt live by them" is not simply a scriptural demand. It elicits a visceral reaction, an instinctive, primal response.

Fortunately, the barriers to hospice care for Jews are rapidly evaporating as the idea behind hospice becomes more acceptable among the general population and as patients realize that they can reject the idea of a DNR (do-not-resuscitate order). When the National Institute for Jewish Hospice (NIJH) was created in 1985 in Los Angeles, its first priority was to make hospice acceptable in the national Jewish community. It has been even more successful than expected. Today, hospices exist in virtually all major cities from Jerusalem to Brooklyn, and hospice is used by Jews of all persuasions: left-leaning Reform Jews, middle-of-the-road Conservatives, and even members of the right-leaning Orthodox or Traditional movement. In fact, NIJH was launched in an Orthodox setting. (In the interest of full disclosure, the author of this article is the president of NIJH.)

In the Jewish community, "DNR" is something of a code word for all medical objections to hospice, including the practice of withholding life-sustaining techniques, nutrition, and hydration, and dealing with the "plug-pulling" recommendations of medical staff. An observant Jewish family will want to consult with their rabbis in these situations.

Another sensitive area applies to a specific population within the Jewish community. They are *Chasidim* (from *Chasid*, meaning "pious") and *Yeshivish* (from *Yeshiva*, meaning "religious school"). These persons are distinguished by their clothes—usually black and always modest. Chasidim are customarily dressed in 17th century Polish garb. They are very observant—at the opposite end of the spectrum from Reform Judaism. The primary concern in dealing with them is to observe strict rules for gender-related behavior; a female should not touch a male, and vice versa, even to shake hands. (In health emergencies, of course, these rules do not apply.)

If an admission problem does arise, the caregiver should call the family's rabbi, if they have one. If that is not possible, the hospice chaplain should call a local rabbi, the Board of Rabbis, or the Jewish Federation. If patients need help finding a rabbi, they can call NIJH at 800-446-4448.

Uniquely Jewish Interventions

In the course of 25 annual conferences on the Jewish component in hospice, an immense amount of time and effort has been spent on end-of-life problems, but not nearly enough on the grief process, which affects the family rather than the patient. Some people remain bereaved after 20 years, never achieving closure and sublimating their grief in ways that may lead to extreme behavior. In some cases, this kind of grief can motivate extreme creative and scientific efforts; however, it is more likely to ruin family life and other relationships.

Hospice caregivers who focus on questions of grief have more time to work (months or years rather than weeks) and are usually dealing with otherwise healthy persons. Their work can have a spectacular effect on these clients. Caregivers need to be familiar with certain behavior patterns to design interventions and care that are appropriate for the Jewish community.

Jewish Framework of Bereavement

Judaism has made an extraordinary contribution to the thinking and practice of mourning ritual. It has developed a remarkable store of behaviors, creative rituals, and counterintuitive insights in an effort to alter the environment of the bereaved. It provides embedded but unspoken aid to mourners—aid that is very different in substance and style from what is customary.

Role Reversal

Medical breakthroughs have altered the nature of dying, transforming it from a catastrophic to a degenerative process. Lingering illness burdens relatives for longer periods—caring, worrying, calling, preparing, managing doctors and nurses, and transmitting daily bad news to other relatives. Even mourners who are not directly involved in end-of-life decisions or preparations carry the anticipation of the death as a burden in their hearts for months. After the death, the survivors must notify friends and family members, make major decisions, and deal with myriad details with doctors, hospitals, mortuaries, rabbis, and cemeteries. In Jewish tradition, a reversal takes place at the funeral: The role of victim passes from the deceased to the bereaved at the moment the grave is filled and the mourners turn to leave.

In a way, this role reversal is universal: Everyone who cares for someone and then mourns the person's death experiences it to a certain extent. What Jewish tradition does is highlight the transition as a formal event, one that helps frame the grieving into a beginning and an end, and allows formal closure. As soon as the burial is over, the mourners turn away from the fresh grave.

Now it is *they* who are death's victims and the center of concern, receiving the compassion that until now has been focused on the dying person. The transformation happens in a precise ritual. Those at the gravesite form parallel rows leading out of the cemetery, and the mourners wend their way through the line, receiving consolation. Jewish law creates this formal boundary in the burial ritual. Until the grave is covered and interment is completed, every aspect of the proceedings, including the eulogy, must be directed toward the deceased. After the interment, every expression of compassion must be to ameliorate the grief of the living.

The dying patient was the victim; now the mourners are the victims. The patient withdraws gradually before death; now the mourners withdraw to the place of *shiva*. The patient may have been visited by the mourners; now the mourners are visited by the consolers. The comforters becomes the comforted; the active become passive; those who gave their strength and patience and wisdom are now recipients; and those who fed the sick are now fed their first postburial meal by family and friends. In Talmudic language, in a moment we have gone from "concern for the dead" to "concern for the living." This quick turnaround impels mourners to return to the real world with a sense of purpose, rather than easing into tomorrow.

Time Warp

The tradition of Jewish bereavement also alters the character of time that mourners experience. Between death and burial, mourners experience compressed time—a rush to do everything necessary to bury the person as soon as possible. This compression of time is mandated in the Bible in three separate commandments to avoid leaving the deceased unburied, which, according to the Torah, is shameful disrespect for the dead.

After the burial, the velocity of mourning suddenly slows and time expands. By design, shiva is slow paced, filled with the sitting, talking, and listening that require patience and endurance. If the process of burial seemed too fast, the process of bereavement now seems too slow. Physically, we dispose of the dead in double time; psychologically, we heal only gradually. This time warp, built into Jewish mourning, allows grievers to heal at an emotionally healthy pace.

Space Switch

In Jewish tradition, the dimension of space also changes for mourners. For example, especially in the case of prolonged illness, there is a dramatic switch from the broad landscape of hospital and cemetery to the narrow confines of the home or apartment where shiva is observed. After the burial, the parallel lines formed by family and friends squeeze the grievers funnel-like from the cemetery to the house, and the cavernous space of the cemetery becomes the warm, compact space of the home. From the moment he or she returns home after the internment, a Jewish mourner is channeled by the conduit of tradition.

On the surface, this narrowing space might seem to be a limiting factor that would somehow restrict our expression of mourning. In truth, it is liberating, because being in the comfort of the familiar gives us the freedom to go fearlessly into our selves, to manage the frenzy of our feelings. Mourners find themselves safe in the protective custody of close relatives and friends.

Habitat Shiva: A Safe House for Healing

The phenomena of the role reversal, time warp, and space switch are familiar to most Jews, although they are not really discussed. But the mourning strategies that follow operate in plain sight. Many books have been written about them, and much research has been done on the subject. Jewish law refers only to how they should be implemented.

Levi Eshkol, prime minister of Israel from 1963 to 1969, was once pressured to give an audience to an American industrialist despite being very busy. As the man approached, Eshkol said, "Look, you're busy; I'm busy. Let's start from the end." Let's start at the end to understand the concept of shiva—the mourning ritual of traditional Judaism. Imagine that you are a hospice professional who has had little previous contact with Jews, and you are standing outside the deceased's home, where the relatives are mourning. You look through the window before entering. This is what you see:

The mirrors are covered with cloths. The mourner is sitting on a low stool, while guests sit on normal chairs in a semicircle around him. A 7-day candle is burning, as it will for the 7 days the mourner must spend at home after returning from the cemetery. The mourner is speaking, and the visitors are listening attentively. There is no food (an oddity at Jewish events). Visitors do not say "hello" or "goodbye"; they just mumble indecipherable words in Hebrew or English. When someone enters, he or she is not welcomed, except perhaps by a nod. The mourner is unshaven and is wearing a jacket or sweater that has a prominent tear near the collar. He is fully dressed but wearing slippers.

Without an explanation, the scene appears eccentric, or at least unconventional. It lasts for 7 days (*shiva* means "seven"). It is customarily referred to as "sitting shiva."

Shiva is a sanctuary for grieving. The mourners stay at home—generally with family and for 7 days, if possible—recuperating from the experience of death before they reenter society without the deceased. Shiva does not dismiss suffering by offering assurances of God's goodness and desirable outcomes. It confronts, rather than eases, the pain of loss. It provides a profound regimen that helps lead people out of the entanglements of grief and empowers them to grow.

How can a simple ritual accomplish such enormous tasks? The answer is in the remarkable hidden framework behind the religious practices, which elevates shiva's healing potential. Jewish tradition insinuates sweeping changes in roles, time, and space into the mourning process—all imperceptible and never articulated but implicit in the laws and traditions.

CONTRADICTORY FORCES OF SHIVA

To understand what we glimpsed through the mourner's window, we need to appreciate the Jewish concept of grief. Hospice staffs should be aware that not all Jews—not even most Jews—sense the depth of these rituals. Many simply follow the traditions of their ancestors, as is common in all religions. But *Habitat Shiva* is nothing less than a laboratory of maneuvers for the Jewish mind in its quest for closure. In the Jewish mourning framework, contradictory expressions of grief are a hallmark of shiva. For example, mourners use both silence and storytelling, both solitude and shared grieving—all are important for complete healing. The four basic components of healing in Habitat Shiva are solitude, silence, sharing, and narrative.

Solitude: The Protective Membrane

"I want to be alone." "I can't sort it all out in front of everybody." "I don't need your advice, I need my own." "Give me some space." Coming to terms with loss is difficult and painful, and it is often a solitary journey. Although friends sincerely wish to share the burden, the process is essentially private, full of thoughts and feelings that could not be shared when the loved one was alive. Human beings are the only creatures who can see their own death coming. Instinctively, they prepare for that death by retreating from their outer interests and cultivating their interior gardens, alone and in tranquility.

Solitude is an elegant term—it suggests a person who has a capacity to be alone; in fact, one who is comforted by being alone. Shiva restricts mourners to the home for a week and then allows them the freedom to be alone—apart from society and its hurly-burly of interpersonal relations, frenzied demands, etiquette, and niceties. The Hebrew word for mourner *(avel)* means precisely this condition of solitude—withdrawing to the warm, intimate setting of privacy. Solitude can allow us to regenerate a tired and battered soul.

The urge to separate from society accounts for the temporary abandonment of social niceties during shiva, such as hair cutting, elaborate grooming, tailoring, and so on. Jewish law acknowledges this desire of the mourners; at the same time, it includes practices that will bring them out of the shell of privacy and resuscitate them after their entanglement with death.

Silence: The Numbness Dissolves

The German mystic Meister Eckhart wrote, "There is nothing so much like God in all the universe as silence." Virtually all mourning observances and proscriptions of shiva flow from the complex need for both solitude and silence. This is where the mourner stands at the raw, unprocessed moment after death: wanting to be left alone to commune with his or her own self, undisturbed and quiet. Silence and solitude are also necessary for gradual healing; by themselves, they can help unravel the knots of internal distress.

Silence emulates the profound stillness experienced by the prophet Ezekiel as "numbing." From this biblical observation, Jewish law derives its most familiar mourning bans: There are no greetings at the door, no playing with children, and no participation in any form of rejoicing—no attendance at parties, festivals, or personal celebrations (for a year for the children and 30 days for all other relatives of the one who died). There is even a ban on studying the Torah, because of the joy it brings.

Jewish law formally recognizes the mourner's need for quiet in another way: It tells visitors to wait 3 days before coming to the home to offer consolation, because in the first days a griever's silence must be protected. After the third day, Jewish law relieves the stark solitude by mandating that others go into the mourner's home and share the grief. However, the first thing they must do in the house of shiva is—nothing. The mourner should be the first to break the silence and set the direction of the conversation.

Sharing Grief: Submerging Loneliness

The law has praised solitude and cleared the way for the mourner to exploit it. Now the same authority calls for the opposite—for the mourner to share the grief by having a community of friends visit, commiserate, and listen to the sad tale. What better way to battle the loneliness after a loved one has vanished?

It is fascinating how Judaism, profoundly sensitive and astonishingly streetwise, resolves this paradox. On the one hand, the Torah calls the mourner *avel*, or withdrawn. Then it turns around and instructs friends and neighbors to relieve this solitude in a biblically ordained practice called "consoling the bereaved."

The tradition is clearly saying that mourners need to have other people with whom to share the burden, to draw them out, listen, and not leave them alone. Thus, as much as mourners need to be alone, they also need to be with others. How can both happen at the same time? An anecdote will help. The Oxford theologian C. S. Lewis desperately wanted to be alone after the death of his beloved wife, to contemplate their life together. But he couldn't bear to be alone, so he asked his Oxford colleagues to come to his house after the funeral and speak to each other. He needed solitude in the midst of others.

Narrative: Telling the Story Makes Sense of Sorrow

When mourners talk about the final moments of a life rather than taking refuge in silence, they are airing out a raw wound that otherwise would fester. Talking may leave the mourner disconsolate, but it will slowly strengthen his or her mind and launch the process of objectifying the loss.

Storytelling is a basic source of history and tradition. Society needs stories to define itself. All religions have rituals that involve storytelling, particularly about historical events, the change of seasons, holidays, and the life cycle. From ancient times, the Jews have designed rituals for telling the classic Jewish narratives, like the exodus from Egypt.

We are a narrative species. Telling our story is indispensable for human development. We survive by storytelling, and this is profoundly true for individual survival: Our story defines us, gives us pride and stature, and offers a taste of the immortality we crave.

Shiva provides a framework for telling the story of our loss. We make changes with each retelling, and eventually we get it right, encapsulated in a final edited version. We mourn appropriately only if we believe we are telling our story effectively. Comfort does not come from the diversionary chitchat we often hear in a house of shiva; it comes from a purposive, therapeutic presentation of the facts as we frame them and finally package them.

Not surprisingly, telling a story has the opposite effect of being silent. Silence allows meandering. In silence, intimacies and secrets can be amorphous— floating in memory, passing as shadows. But narrating the details of the death for others crystallizes memory. The mourner-narrator imposes a framework over unrelated details, molding the facts into a sensible, digestible, methodical pattern. And, as with all storytelling, making the narrative acceptable to listeners entails giving it a beginning and an end—rendering a story.

The narrative changes, not only because of the changing audience—the rabbi, a doctor, a close friend, an old aunt—but because remembering is an unfolding process. It reorganizes the teller's universe, giving it coherence and reorienting a life that will now be lived without the loved one. Soon the story will be cast into soothing prose, high-sounding phrases, and homey jokes. The narrative also renders seemingly random events purposeful. Rehearsing and retelling the story convinces the mourner of its integrity and understandability, and the mourner's own life takes on a new shade of meaning. The completed narrative becomes an untouchable part of family memory.

The process of narrative is probably the most effective factor in Habitat Shiva. Without telling the story repeatedly, the mourner may find it more difficult to recover a sense of order. Therefore, caregivers should:

- Encourage retelling the same story as often as possible, because it makes the death more real. Every retelling is a bullet fired at the ghost of denial.
- Rehash the details of the final days; this curtails chatting and brings the talk back to the loved one.
- Encourage talk about feelings, not just facts.

UNDERSTANDING THE RITUALS WE SAW IN THE WINDOW

The Cut in the Collar: Permissible Rage
Biblical law decrees that mourners tear their clothing in response to the death of a relative, teacher, or prominent scholar; a cataclysmic tragedy such as the burning of a synagogue; or a family or community disaster. The rending of the garment is one of the most striking Jewish expressions of grief. It was the custom of its patriarchs, prophets, and kings; Jacob stabbed his clothing when he saw Joseph's bloody coat and thought that his son had been killed.

The fabric of a shirt, suit, or sweater is ripped on the left side directly over the heart at the death of a parent; on the right side, farther from the heart, for the death of other relatives. The law requires that the rending of the garment be performed while standing. The posture of accepting grief in Jewish life is always erect, symbolizing strength in the face of crisis and respect for the deceased. The act of tearing the garment and then wearing it during shiva should be viewed as an act of controlled agony that expresses deep frustration but never sheer vindictiveness.

Covering Mirrors: Fear of Becoming Invisible

The laws of Jewish mourning call for the covering of all mirrors in the house of mourning during shiva. The reasons for this custom are many. Primarily, it serves to diminish the cosmetic component of life during grief and discourages grievers from switching their focus from the spiritual to the physical. But—as in all areas of Jewish religious observance—an ancient tradition elicits new levels of significance and interpretation. The act of covering mirrors addresses a primitive fear, the fear of becoming invisible. Grief teaches a stark but subliminal lesson: Life goes on without the deceased, no matter how worthy he or she may have been. The more intimidating lesson is that life will also go on without us when our time comes. This realization dawns on mourners suddenly, often with a surprising ferocity.

This unspoken fear lodges deep in the mourner's soul: Am I invisible? Am I the deceased, just a few years later? The essence of death is the drama of vanishing—for the mourner as well as the deceased. People may whisper things like "Part of me died with her." We dread the realization that we, too, will vanish. When the mirrors are covered and no images are reflected in the entire house, we feel intimations of our own vanishing.

Sitting Shiva: The Central Metaphor of Jewish Mourning

Sitting on a low stool during shiva—lower than a normal chair—is the characteristic posture of the Jewish mourner. Sitting may be the most widely practiced Jewish ritual of the 7 days.

Despite the fear, anger, isolation, and confusion that accompany the death of a parent, spouse, dear friend, or child, our culture's message is to "move on." In fact, it is almost un-American to stop and think. It is surprising that, in the Jewish faith, the metaphor for mourning is not "move on" but "sit down."

What is the significance of requiring a specific posture—sitting? It is not standing, not walking, not running, not bowing, not prostrating, and not moving on. During shiva, we specifically and purposefully sit. Why? "Walking" implies forward movement, dynamism, goal seeking, and progress. It is a motor function, directional and energetic. Sitting, on the other hand, is a metaphor for thinking, meditating, and contemplation. It is eager only to reach the bottom of the soul. It creates a picture of passivity and pensiveness, of a preoccupied and melancholic mind. Sitting anchors the heart, keeping the griever from losing the sanctity of spiritual experience in a whirlwind of social activity.

Ideally, as they sit in silence, share their grief with those around them, and articulate their feelings of loss, mourners will be able to seize the opportunity radiated from the sad moment. In the midst of the greetings and consolations and farewells, buffeted by uncertainties, a bewildered mind can begin to reset itself and envisage a new world. For this, we need to sit.

Some of the material in this chapter is adapted from the author's book, Consolation *(Jewish Publication Society, 2004).*

Rabbi Maurice Lamm *received his BA, MA, and an honorary doctorate from Yeshiva University in New York, where he is now a professor and the Chair in Professional Rabbinics. In 2004, he was honored by Yeshiva with the Lifetime Professional Achievement Award. He is a senior rabbi at the Beth Jacob congregation in Beverly Hills, California. He is the author of seven books, including* The Jewish Way in Death and Mourning, The Power of Hope, I Shall Glorify Him, The Jewish Way in Love and Marriage, *and* Consolation. *He is the founder and president of the National Institute for Jewish Hospice. As a senior consultant for VITAS Innovative Hospice Care, he helped create the* Jewish Hospice Manual. *He also serves as president of the board of Rabbis–Southern California, dean of AKIBA Academy and Rambam Academy, and vice president of the Rabbinical Council of America.*

Orthodox and Hasidic Perspectives

Barry M. Kinzbrunner

The word *orthodox*, which originates from the Late Greek *orthodoxos*, is defined by the Merriam-Webster online dictionary (2008) as "conforming to established doctrine, especially in religion." When capitalized, it can also mean "of, relating to, or constituting any of various conservative religious or political groups" or "of or relating to Orthodox Judaism."

There are two main groups of Orthodox Jews living in North America: Ashkenazim, who primarily hail from Germany, France, and Eastern Europe; and Sephardim, whose ancestors lived in Spain, North Africa, the Mediterranean nations, and the Middle East (Rich, 2008).

Within Ashkenazic Jewry, a group known as Hasidim arose in Eastern Europe in the 18th century. These Jews, initially led by Rabbi Israel ben Eliezer (known as the *Ba'al Shem Tov* or Master of the Good Name), now consist of at least a dozen or more subgroups, generally named for the European towns where they originated. They can be recognized by their distinctive clothing, which includes dark suits and long coats called *kapote*, which are worn on the Sabbath, and their black hats or, in the case of some, distinctive round fur hats called *shtreimels*. They adhere very strictly to Jewish law. The most well known Hasidic subgroup in North America is the Lubavitcher or Chabad Hasidim, who have established synagogues in many cities and towns throughout North America and the world.

DEMOGRAPHICS

According to statistics compiled in 2001, the Jewish population of North America stands at about 5.65 million. Almost 5.3 million live in the United States, while the remaining 350,000 live in Canada (Singer & Grossman, 2006). Approximately 10% (565,000) of Jews consider themselves to be Orthodox (United Jewish Communities, 2004), of which about 32% (180,000) are of Hasidic affiliation (Hoover, 2006). The Orthodox segment of the Jewish population appears to be growing, especially among younger Jewish adults and in the Hasidic communities (Hoover, 2006; United Jewish Communities, 2004; Weinreb, 2003). This fact highlights the importance of acquainting end-of-life caregivers with Orthodox and Hasidic perspectives on end-of-life care. Even though the majority of patients are not Orthodox or Hasidic Jews, in an increasing number of circumstances the Orthodox child of a patient is the legal healthcare surrogate and is responsible for making end-of-life care decisions for his or her parent. Jewish law will play an instrumental role in decisions made on behalf of the patient by the surrogate.

ORTHODOX JEWISH PRACTICE AND THE DELIVERY OF HEALTH CARE

JEWISH LAW AND THE RABBI

Orthodox Jews believe that Jewish law, embodied in the Torah (the first five books of the Bible), was given by God to Moses on Mount Sinai. They believe that God also gave Moses an oral law, which expounded on the written laws in the Torah and was eventually written down in the Mishnah. The Mishnah and its companion work, the Talmud (which records ancient rabbinical discussions on the Mishnah), are the basis for subsequent works of Jewish law, culminating in the *Shulchan Aruch* (Table of Law) written by Rabbi Joseph Karo in the 16th century. Modern rabbis use this text and its numerous commentaries, in conjunction with the Torah (as well as the rest of the Bible), Mishnah, and Talmud to formulate Jewish legal opinions related to observance in the modern world. This process has been established for many centuries, so it is not surprising that when an Orthodox Jew has questions regarding any facet of Jewish law, including health care, she or he consults with a rabbi (Kinzbrunner, 2004). For the Hasid, rabbinical guidance is even more of an imperative, for one of the characteristics of a group of Hasidic Jews is that it has a rabbinic leader, usually referred to as a *rebbe*, who provides advice and counsel that is generally considered binding on any and all issues raised by his adherents (Weinreb, 2003). For the end-of-life professional caregiver, understanding the importance of the rabbi's or rebbe's counsel to the Orthodox Jew, especially the Hasid, is crucial to understanding how these patients and their families approach the challenges they face when life is coming to its conclusion.

Sabbath and Holidays

On the Jewish Sabbath, Orthodox Jews are prohibited from performing many common activities, including using electricity, cooking, carrying anything in a public domain, and traveling by a motor vehicle. On the many Jewish holidays, most of these activities, with the exception of cooking and carrying, are prohibited as well. All these prohibitions are set aside when someone has a life-threatening illness (Babylonian Talmud Tractate; *Yoma* 85a–b; Karo, *Shulchan Aruch Yoreh Deah* 328:2), so end-of-life care providers should not encounter any major challenges in caring for their patients and families on the Sabbath or a holiday (Kinzbrunner, 2004). However, some Orthodox or Hasidic patients or family members may not know that the prohibitions may be set aside or may believe that the medical situation is not severe enough to warrant violating the Sabbath or holiday. It is important for caregivers to be aware of and sensitive to patient and family concerns about Sabbath and holiday observance.

Jewish Dietary Laws

Orthodox Jews follow the kosher dietary laws outlined in the Torah and elaborated upon by the rabbis in the oral law. These laws include eating meat from only certain kinds of animals and birds that are slaughtered and prepared in a specific fashion, eating only fish that have fins and scales, and not cooking or eating meat and dairy products together. Orthodox homes have separate dishes for meat and dairy foods. Caregivers need to be aware of these restrictions and make sure they do not inadvertently bring nonkosher food into a patient's home (or a kosher nursing home) or use the wrong dishes if they are assisting a patient or family member at mealtime. Even foods certified as kosher may not be considered acceptable to many Orthodox, especially Hasidic, families; the caregiver should always check before bringing any foods into the home (Weinreb, 2003).

MODESTY AND INTERGENDER CONTACT

Orthodox Jews, especially Hasidim, refrain from any physical contact with members of the opposite gender, with the exception of spouses and other immediate family members in the privacy of their homes. Like the laws of the Sabbath, these prohibitions are suspended when someone is ill, but caregivers should be aware that some Orthodox or Hasidic patients may be extremely uncomfortable when care, especially personal care, is provided by a member of the opposite gender. In such circumstances, it is incumbent on the care provider to be respectful and flexible to meet the needs of such patients without subjecting them to undue stress (Weinreb, 2003).

END-OF-LIFE DECISION MAKING

Judaism believes in the absolute sanctity of life to the extent that even the laws of the Sabbath are set aside when a life is at stake. Nevertheless, Judaism also recognizes, as King Solomon said in the Book of Ecclesiastes, that there is "a time to live and a time to die" (3:2).

As noted above, all decisions made by Orthodox Jews are consistent with the will of God as it is expressed in Jewish law. With regard to medical decision making, it can be said that they limit their autonomous decision making to conform to Jewish law (Kinzbrunner, 2004; Lamm & Kinzbrunner, 2003; Steinberg, 1994), with the rabbi or rebbe as the expert who advises the patient and family. Many current medical issues are not specifically covered by Jewish legal opinions from previous eras, so modern rabbis and rebbes have formulated opinions on many of these medical questions. Not surprisingly, opinions, even among the Orthodox, may differ sharply on these issues. For example, while many rabbis have ruled that one may withhold medical interventions from a terminally ill Jewish patient when there is no likely benefit, others have ruled that the mandate to preserve life outweighs all other considerations. Regarding artificial hydration and nutrition, virtually all Orthodox rabbis—even those who allow the withholding of other medical interventions—will mandate that in virtually all circumstances, terminally ill patients should receive food and fluids by whatever means necessary, as they are considered basic human needs (Kinzbrunner, 2004; Lamm & Kinzbrunner, 2003). End-of-life caregivers must learn to respect the relationship between the patients and families and their rabbis or rebbes, and learn how to provide care for these patients within the framework of Jewish law, rather than trying to convince patients and families to make decisions contrary to what their rabbis have ruled.

HOLOCAUST SURVIVORS

The specter of the Holocaust continues to cast its shadow over the last of its survivors, who are now dying of old age. Whether or not Jewish Holocaust survivors are Orthodox, the experience significantly colors how they approach the natural end of their lives and greatly influences their end-of-life care decisions. For example, the mandate to provide artificial nutrition and hydration is not only related to the fact that these are basic human needs but reflects the experience of starvation that was part of life under the Nazi yoke. End-of-life care providers must be aware of this and other potential challenges that Holocaust survivors face as life draws toward its close (Barile, 2000).

CARE OF THE BODY AT THE TIME OF DEATH

Although end-of-life care providers are accustomed to cleaning and preparing the body of the deceased for transport to the funeral home, Orthodox Jews traditionally do this themselves. Orthodox and Hasidic communities have Jewish burial societies called *Chevra Kadisha* that are responsible for the preparation and ritual cleansing of the body before the funeral. As it is customary not to leave the deceased unattended, there is also a *shomer*, or watcher, who stays with the deceased until the burial. When end-of-life caregivers are present at the death of a Jewish patient, it is important that they do not follow their normal routine of preparing the body but merely contact the funeral home, rabbi, or Chevra Kadisha, who will take full care of the deceased (Lamm & Kinzbrunner, 2003).

MOURNING AND BEREAVEMENT

Traditional Judaism has well-defined mourning and bereavement practices covering virtually all facets of the process. They include the requirement to bury the deceased within 24 hours whenever possible, the tearing of the garment *(keriyah),* and the initial week of mourning in the home, known as *shiva,* during which many everyday activities are forbidden as the mourners take time to formulate their lasting memories of the deceased. These and the other rituals of Jewish mourning were designed not only to ensure that proper respect is paid to the deceased but also to allow the bereaved time to memorialize their loved one and gradually reintegrate themselves into their daily lives with the new reality of their loss (Lamm, 1969; Lamm & Kinzbrunner, 2003).

Jewish tradition also provides for a great deal of community participation in the mourning and bereavement process. Some of these activities, which are part of everyday life in the Orthodox and Hasidic communities, include forming and participating in the *Chevra Kadisha*, interrupting virtually any activity to participate in a funeral (Karo, *Shulchan Aruch Yoreh Deah,* 361:1–3), actively participating in the burial, providing the first meal at the house of mourning, and visiting the bereaved and conducting prayer services in the home during *shiva* (as the mourners are not allowed to leave the house). (Lamm, 1969; Lamm & Kinzbrunner, 2003).

Thus, while end-of-life care providers should make themselves available to support and comfort families following a loss, they should be aware that their roles will be relatively minor compared with those of the family and the Jewish community. Care providers can develop support groups and other bereavement activities for families in Orthodox and Hasidic Jewish communities, but only in conjunction with the full participation and support of these communities.

Conclusion

Traditional Judaism as practiced by Orthodox and Hasidic Jews provides a wealth of knowledge and guidance regarding caring for patients whose lives are nearing the end and for their families. It is incumbent upon end-of-life care providers to be aware of these traditions and to tailor the care they offer these patients and families to accommodate them. Caregivers should also be aware that Jews who belong to other denominations or are unaffiliated, and who do not observe Jewish traditions as strictly as the Orthodox do, may, when nearing the end of life, choose to observe some or all of these traditions. Their desires should be accommodated and respected.

Rabbi Barry M. Kinzbrunner, MD, FACP, FAAHPM, is executive vice president and chief medical officer for VITAS Healthcare Corporation of Miami, Florida. He is board certified in internal medicine, medical oncology, and hospice and palliative medicine. He was ordained as an Orthodox rabbi in Jerusalem in 2002. During his 25-year career in hospice and palliative medicine, Kinzbrunner has spoken and published extensively on the care of patients at the end of life; he wrote a textbook titled 20 Common Problems in End-of-Life Care. *He has developed expertise in end-of-life care issues pertaining to patients of the Jewish faith and has published extensively in this area. Since 1998, he has been consulting with JDC-Eshel to help develop hospice and palliative care services in Israel, including the development of spiritual care services in Israel in cooperation with the National Association of Jewish Chaplains.*

References

Babylonian Talmud Tractate. *Yoma* 85a–b.

Barile, A. (2000, March–April). Geriatric study of survivors. *International Society for Yad Vashem, Martyrdom and Resistance,* 14.

Hoover, A. (2006). As Hasidic population grows, Jewish politics may shift to the right. *University of Florida News.* Retrieved October 15, 2008 from http://news.ufl.edu/2006/11/27/hasidic-jews/

Karo, J. *Shulchan Aruch Yoreh Deah,* 328:2.

Karo, J. *Shulchan Aruch Yoreh Deah,* 361:1–3.

Kinzbrunner, B. M. (2004). Jewish medical ethics and end-of-life care. *Journal of Palliative Medicine, 7*(4), 558–573.

Lamm, M. (1969). *The Jewish way in death and mourning.* New York: Jonathan David Publishers.

Lamm, M., & Kinzbrunner, B. M. (2003). *The Jewish hospice manual: A guide to compassionate end-of-life care for Jewish patients and their families.* Miami, New York: VITAS Healthcare Corporation and National Institute for Jewish Hospice.

Merriam-Webster Online Dictionary. (2008). Definition of *orthodox.* Retrieved October 15, 2008 from http://www.merriam-webster.com/dictionary/orthodox

Rich, T. (2008). Judaism 101: Ashkenazic and Sephardic Jews. Retrieved October 15, 2008 from http://www.jewfaq.org/ashkseph.htm

Singer, D., & Grossman, L. (Eds.) (2006*). American Jewish yearbook, 2006.* New York: American Jewish Committee. Retrieved October 15, 2008 from http://www.jewishvirtuallibrary.org/jsource/US-Israel/usjewpop.html

Steinberg, A. (1994). A Jewish perspective on the four principles. In R. Gillon & A. Lloyd (Eds.), *Principles of healthcare ethics* (pp. 65–73). Chichester, England: John Wiley and Sons, Ltd.

United Jewish Communities. (2004). National Jewish population survey 2000–01, Orthodox Jews, presentation of findings. Retrieved October 15, 2008, from http://www.ujc.org/local_includes/downloads/4983.pdf

Weinreb, T. H. (2003). Hasidic and Ultra-Orthodox Judaism. In M. Lamm & B. M. Kinzbrunner (Eds.), *The Jewish hospice manual: A guide to compassionate end-of-life care for Jewish patients and their families*. Miami, New York: VITAS Healthcare Corporation and National Institute for Jewish Hospice.

Dying and Grief in the Islamic Community

Hasan Shanawani and Syed Zafar

As our communities become increasingly multicultural, healthcare professionals face both challenges and opportunities as they work with and treat individuals from diverse backgrounds. The growing number of Muslims in the United States challenges care providers to understand this population's perspectives, experiences, and ways of practicing Islam—especially how Islam relates to health, biomedicine, and dying. An effective caregiver must understand and respect the values of others while maintaining awareness of his or her own values. The promise of a peaceful and dignified death obligates us to fulfill these responsibilities to our patients and their families (Shanawani, Wenrich, Tonelli, & Curtis, 2008).

ISLAM AND MUSLIMS

Islam: The Religion

Islam considers itself to be one of the great monotheistic faiths. *Allah* is the Arabic term for God; Christian Arabs use the same term. Islam believes in a long line of prophets (also recognized in Judaism and Christianity) who are mentioned by name in the Koran; they include Adam, Noah, Abraham, Moses, and Jesus (Nasr, 2005). Muslims believe that the last of this line—the vice-regent of God's final religion and law on Earth—is Muhammad.

For practicing Muslims, religion is a comprehensive way of life. The Koran addresses not only personal faith and theology but also religious and cultural regulations for the individual and the community. The main religious duties of a Muslim are embodied in the five pillars of Islam. These are:

1. The *Shahada* or declaration of faith: "There is no god but God and Muhammad is the Messenger of God."
2. *Salat*, the five daily ritualized prayers.
3. Fasting during the month of Ramadan.

4. *Zakat*, the annual alms tax of one's wealth and assets.
5. *Hajj* (pilgrimage) to the holy city of Mecca in Saudi Arabia once during a Muslim's lifetime.

Each of these pillars depends on the person's ability to perform it. For example, a person is not expected to pay zakat if he has insufficient wealth; prayer may be modified if a person is physically unable to perform it; and Muslims suffering from illness are not expected to perform the ritual fast (Laird, Amer, Barnett, & Barnes, 2007).

Although Islam lays down beliefs and principles, their application is subject to interpretation among Muslims. The majority of Muslims, with some important exceptions, recognize no central authority that uniformly dictates what is and is not Islamic. The practice of Islam is shaped by the cultural influences of the diverse societies that Muslim populations inhabit, although virtually all Muslims agree on the bedrock of belief and practice; for example, salat is universally recognized as central to the practice of Islam. In contrast, the Islamic requirement of modest dress varies according to customs in a particular country or culture. Few people make a strong distinction between culture and faith, weaving the two together in their minds as they live their lives. This blending of culture and religion is not unique to Islam; it is common across religions. The incorporation of cultural elements into religious practice has resulted not just in culturally distinctive expressions of religious traditions, but also in a blurring of the line between religion and culture, as people consider cultural customs to be important parts of their religious practice.

Islam has many denominations, but two dominate worldwide and in the United States. The division between these two groups, *Sunni* and *Shi'a*, stems from the choice made by early Muslims regarding who would be the leader of all Muslims following the death of Muhammad. The Sunnis formed the majority, which accepted Abu Bakr, Muhammad's close companion, as his successor. Followers of the Shi'a tradition (Shi'ites) chose to follow Ali, Muhammad's cousin, son-in-law, and closest relative. With 940 million adherents, Sunni Islam is the largest denomination of Islam. There are approximately 120 million Shi'ite Muslims in the world. Sunnis and Shi'ites are as diverse within their denominations as they are different from one another, as their religious practice varies from region to region and culture to culture.

In the United States, most Muslims are Sunni, but there are large communities of Shi'ites, especially in southeast Michigan and northern California. The best way to determine the religion and denomination of a Muslim is by asking directly.

Muslims

There are an estimated 1.2 billion Muslims in the world, with approximately one-third living as religious minorities in the countries they inhabit. Approximately 52 countries have Muslim majorities, and as a result of immigration, significant minorities exist in many more (Woodrow Wilson International Center for Scholars [WWICS], 2003).

Although Muslims in the United States often are thought of as immigrants, a large proportion of the American Muslim population was born in the United States. Approximately 4.7 million Muslims live in the United States (Nasr, 2005). The largest number of immigrants comes from South Asia, Iran, and the Arabic-speaking countries. The African-American Muslim community makes up 14% to 30% of the total population of Muslims in the United States (Council on American-Islamic Relations, n.d.), and it deserves special mention. Africans were the first true wave of Muslims to enter the United States, coming by way of the slave trade. Estimates are that 10% to 20% of African slaves were originally Muslim. Most slaves were forbidden to practice their religion, however, and were forcibly converted to Christianity (WWICS, 2003).

In the United States, one distinct group, known as the Nation of Islam, arose in the 1930s. Founded by Wallace Fard Muhammad and made famous by Elijah Muhammad, the Nation's ideas attracted many African Americans. The Nation of Islam considers itself to be very different from the larger and older Sunni and Shi'a denominations of Islam.

MUSLIM CULTURE AND BELIEFS: IMPORTANT POINTS FOR THE HEALTH PRACTITIONER

It would be inappropriate to discuss Muslims in America without addressing the cultural diversity that exists among them. It is tempting to focus on the considerable number of cultural similarities in a group and discount their differences. Also, geographic origin and culture cannot be inferred solely on the basis of religion, nor can a person be assumed to be Muslim on the basis of geographic origin. Many Muslim-majority regions have considerable non-Muslim minorities that share many cultural traditions with their Muslim neighbors. Religion, geographic origin, and culture are separate entities, and we cannot assume one on the basis of the others.

One element binds all Muslims, however: their common faith and its reliable features of belief and practice. The following summary of elements of Islam that are shared across cultures (despite variation among individuals) can suggest to providers what issues they might need to consider in dealing with a Muslim patient or client. Providers need to formulate a "cultural brokering" approach to Muslim clients—a way to evaluate their needs and wishes regardless of their backgrounds.

Autonomy and Independence in Muslim Culture

Islam gives people great autonomy in determining their course of action. Thus, Muslims generally believe it is not permitted to force a person to experience a treatment he or she does not want. Islamic tradition says that the Prophet Muhammad was angry at his family when they forced him to drink some medicine as he lay weak on his bed in the last days of his fatal illness.

Islamic encouragement of individual autonomy should not be confused with a strict sense of independence. Although Islam places great emphasis on each person's individual responsibility to choose right over wrong, it does not recognize individualism in the sociological sense as a good thing. A sense of responsibility for family, neighbors, and community is highly valued in Islamic ethics and law. For example, in Islamic law, adults are legally responsible for the economic support of their parents if they are in need. In most cases, the same responsibility entails for grown siblings. Muslims are socialized with a strong belief that human society is only possible through mutual support and dependency. Shame is avoided by making assistance to the ill and needy a legal and moral responsibility, not an act of charity (Mattson, 2002).

Many immigrant Muslims rely on their families for support and avoid institutionalized care. This may be less a reflection of a faith tradition than immigrant suspicion of institutional care or unfamiliarity with available resources. However, the aversion to institutional care may be expressed in religious terms. The distrust of institutionalized care can make providing support to Muslim families a challenge for end-of-life care providers. The families most likely to refuse outside help are also those most likely to be overwhelmed and least likely to ask for the help they need. The concerns of such patients and families should be addressed to encourage greater involvement with the hospice and palliative care services in the community.

The Importance of Continued Worship Among Religious Muslims

Muslims believe that Islam supports the dignity of those who are ill by recognizing their continuing obligation to remember God and worship him as much as they can (Mattson, 2002). As long as they are conscious, even the bedridden are expected to perform the five daily ritual prayers. If a Muslim is too weak to perform the physical aspects of the prayers, such as standing and kneeling, he or she may pray in a seated or even supine position. Even a paralyzed Muslim is required to pray by imagining the movements of prayer and moving his or her eyes in the proper direction at the proper times. By requiring the continued performance of acts of worship to the extent that a person is able, Islam seeks to prevent ill adults from being reduced to the level of children, who lack such obligations. As long as they are lucid, adults are recognized as essentially competent.

Family Structure and the Role of the Family in Health Care

Among most Muslims—as in other religious and ethnic groups—the family is considered the fundamental social unit. Even as adults, Muslims rely on their parents and other family members for many necessities of life, such as food, clothing, and housing. A major emphasis on maintaining family harmony and stability can lead to efforts to avoid conflict and defer decision making to a hierarchical figure in the family. In such traditional families, members relate to one another on the basis of hierarchies (the older the member, the more authority and respect he is afforded). Within this structure, obligations are more important than rights, and family interests outweigh personal interests (Stone, 2005).

Islam emphasizes taking care of the weak and disabled. The Koran stresses respect for parents and the duty of children to care for them in the frailty of old age. Given the cohesiveness of family life among Muslims and across the life span, the care of children and the care of one's parents is a lifelong obligation. Such traditional families have stereotyped roles for and expectations of their members, especially by gender. The mother is typically the primary caretaker of the children, especially those with severe illness. Men tend to be less involved with childcare responsibilities.

Gender Issues

Muslims may have views concerning proper interactions between the genders that differ from those held by mainstream American society, but these views are usually neither difficult to understand nor hard to accommodate. Many Muslims would accept an opposite-sex provider but would be more comfortable and open with a same-sex provider. This preference should be accommodated, if possible, to improve the quality of the interaction, the patient's satisfaction and comfort with it, and the patient's compliance with recommended treatment. Another option is to have a same-sex third party present, especially during a physical exam (Hathout, n.d.).

Modesty is highly valued in Islam, and many Muslims consider dress to be an important expression of modesty. Both men and women are instructed to dress modestly and to avert their gaze when they encounter a person of the opposite sex. Clothing is generally, but not always, expected to be loose for both men and women. For men, the most commonly stated rule is that in public they must be covered from the navel to the knees; women must cover their whole body except for their face and hands. The issue of modesty can provoke significant debate, and individual Muslims may adhere to varying levels of what they consider modest dress (e.g., South Asian women wear saris). Regardless of what that level is for an individual, many Muslims (and many non-Muslims) feel exceedingly uncomfortable when they are forced to wear garments that provide less cover, such as hospital gowns. The Maine Medical Center made news by redesigning its hospital gowns to provide better coverage after learning that Somali Muslim patients were canceling their appointments because they feared having to wear revealing gowns during outpatient procedures and in public areas (Hathout, n.d.).

Muslims hold a diversity of views on the precise details of how to put their religious principles into practice. Opinions and patterns of interaction vary widely; providers should follow their patients' lead and ask about their preferences. Patients should be encouraged to openly discuss what level of interaction they find comfortable. It should be obvious that, at the very least, interactions between males and females must maintain a professional distance and allow sufficient personal space. This does not preclude friendliness, but excessively familiar interactions are generally discouraged. The directive for modesty includes modesty of character; overly informal interactions may be felt to violate a religious sense of personal space. For example, shaking hands with a person of the opposite sex has varying levels of acceptance among Muslims; some patients will accept medical care from a member of the opposite sex but would prefer not to shake hands.

Important Holidays
The Islamic year follows a lunar calendar with no leap year; thus, Islamic dates rotate throughout the Gregorian year. Islam's three main holidays are the month of Ramadan and the two holidays of Eid al-Fitr and Eid al-Adha. Friday

is considered a mini-holiday of sorts and is the day on which congregational prayers are held.

Ramadan is the ninth month of the Islamic calendar and one of the most highly anticipated times of the year for Muslims. Tradition says that Muhammad had his first revelation during Ramadan; Muslims commemorate this event with fasting throughout the month. While this practice often seems very rigorous to non-Muslims, Muslims generally greet it as a time of spiritual renewal. They perceive fasting as beneficial in several ways. It helps them strengthen the control of their intellects over their physical desires. Their hunger also helps them remain conscious of God and their submission to his will throughout the day. Finally, it helps them feel sympathy for the poor, who experience hunger without the comfort of knowing when they will have their next meal.

In addition to fasting, Ramadan gives Muslims more opportunities for acts of worship. Many perform extra prayers, and many increase their donations to charity during the month. Ramadan is also a month of community and socializing: Muslims often gather in the evenings to share in fast-breaking meals.

Several concerns related to health, severe chronic and terminal illness, and religious practice arise in connection with Ramadan. As people abstain from food and drink, their energy levels can drop significantly, particularly toward the end of the day. Depending on the degree of illness, they may not have the necessary physiologic reserve to tolerate a day without food or drink. Blood pressure may also drop during the day; people who take blood pressure medication may need to reduce their doses during this month (Athar, n.d.). After a day of fasting, it can be easy to binge, leading to poor dietary choices and weight gain or weight loss. According to Laird (2006), a review of health-related literature pertaining to Ramadan showed both positive and negative effects of fasting on existing medical conditions, and as a precipitating factor for adverse conditions, such as pregnancy complications.

Medications can pose another issue during Ramadan. Consuming anything by mouth, including medication, breaks the fast, so patients may be reluctant to take scheduled medications during the day. Some people may stop taking medication entirely, while others may try to fit in all their doses in the evening or early morning when they are permitted to eat. This may not matter for some medications, but it may change the effect of others. It is very important for healthcare providers to discuss medication scheduling during Ramadan, so patients/clients can work out a system that is satisfactory from both a religious and a medical perspective.

Non-oral medications—those that are inhaled, applied, or injected—also pose a challenge. In general, the rule is that such medications do not break the fast unless they are providing a source of nutrition. Some patients may be concerned about intravenous medications, but unless they are providing nutrition, these are allowed and will not break the fast (Hathout, n.d.).

Most patients in hospice are likely to have conditions that make it medically unsafe to fast. Fasting can induce unsafe levels of dehydration, and insulin-dependent diabetics must strictly control their food intake. Such persons are not required to fast, and because Islam prohibits doing harm to oneself, most Muslims will discourage them from fasting. Still, Muslims have a deep attachment to Ramadan and are often extremely resistant to forgoing the fast. Involving the local imam may help encourage such persons to follow medical advice.

Eid al-Fitr (the holiday of fast-breaking) marks the end of Ramadan. Eid al-Adha (the holiday of sacrifice) occurs at the end of the pilgrimage and commemorates Abraham's submission before God and his willingness to sacrifice his son. These holidays are marked with a congregational prayer in the morning, and people generally spend the rest of the day at gatherings with family and friends. Inpatients may be disappointed to miss these festivities, the traditions they have built around them, and the company of friends and family. They would likely be grateful to service providers who acknowledge the holidays and would welcome the chance to share their traditions. If family members cannot be with them on these holidays, the local Muslim community may be able to locate people who can visit and help them celebrate.

The Shi'ite community has an additional important holiday: Ashura. It commemorates the death of Hussain, the grandson of the prophet. Shi'as mourn Hussain's death. This holiday centers on the defining event that led to the schism between Sunnis and Shi'as. Sunnis also celebrate Ashura, but for very different reasons, and this difference can lead to conflict between the two communities. Service practitioners should be aware of this sensitive time, which can ignite passionate feelings in their patients.

Congregational services for Muslims are held on Fridays during the time of the midday prayer. They consist of a sermon followed by the ritual prayer. Men are required to attend Friday prayer, and many women attend as well. Providers should make every effort to allow patients to attend. Many U.S. hospitals set up services for Muslim patients and staff or arrange transport to services. If such arrangements are not available, the local Muslim community may be able to help.

Suffering, Death, and Bereavement in Islam

Bereavement and adjustment after death in the Muslim community is an underresearched area, and the role of bereavement service provision to Muslims is still uncertain. A look at the Muslim tradition in the area of loss and bereavement can provide a practical foundation. An important belief in Islamic doctrine is that during life in this world, as part of their preparation for the next life, people face a series of tests and challenges. Muslims are encouraged to keep God in mind during all actions in this world. Islamic teachings emphasize that all challenges are surmountable and that God never gives a person more burdens than he or she can bear. Thus, bereaved family members may not see their suffering after the loss of a loved one as a negative experience to be avoided. Although this is one of the most distressing human experiences, it can be an opportunity for family and friends to reflect on social and spiritual relationships, and to strengthen their spiritual and religious beliefs. The key is the concept of *sabr* (patience) among family and friends. *Sabr* is an Arabic word that means a state of constant and unconditional contentment with divine decree (Sheikh & Gatrad, 2008).

Mourning is usually for 3 to 7 days, during which time relatives and community members visit the home of the deceased and offer prayers for the survivors' prosperity. A woman who has lost her husband may mourn for a longer period: 3 months or, if she is pregnant, until the baby is born. Islamic death and bereavement customs are strongly shaped by local culture as well as religious teachings, so the role of healthcare providers can be challenging. Knowledge of religious tradition and rituals can be helpful to provide appropriate care for the dying Muslim patient and bereavement services to the family.

Food Restrictions and Preferences

Diet is a key area in which religious practices can affect treatment plans. Muslim dietary preferences can often be accommodated, and they should be. Muslims are forbidden to consume pork, blood, carrion, or alcohol. Slaughter of an animal for food requires a certain ritual. Meat from a properly slaughtered animal is called *zabiha* or *halal*, which simply means "allowed." Some Muslims will eat only meat that has been prepared in this manner, although some will also accept kosher food. Seafood is almost universally allowed, regardless of how it has been prepared.

Many Muslims object to food or medications that are indirectly derived from pigs or non-zabiha animals. For example, some Muslims will not eat cheese unless they are certain it was prepared with enzymes that were not derived from pigs. Certain medicines, such as cough syrups, contain alcohol and thus are forbidden. Muslims may avoid gelatin, which is often derived from non-zabiha animals; this can be problematic, as it is present as an inactive ingredient in many pills. Muslims may object to medications such as Lovenox that are derived from pigs. In such cases, a frank discussion with the patient about the health effects of refusing a medication may help; after all, forbidden foods are permissible when the alternative is starvation. The local imam may be able to resolve such difficulties.

ISLAM, MUSLIMS, ILLNESS, AND DEATH: RITUAL ASPECTS

Like all religions, Islam offers perspective on suffering and dying. The Koran says, "Every soul shall taste death" (2:185). A central notion in Islam is that human beings have no choice but to eventually return to God. For a Muslim, death marks a transition from one form of existence to another (Sheikh & Gatrad, 2008), and only God decides when it will happen (Puchalski & Hendi, 2004). The dying experience occurs in this world, but it is only a small part of a person's whole reality. Death is part of the continuum of existence that includes life before conception, the intermediate realm, the day of judgment, and the afterlife. Death is not a taboo subject in Muslim society; in fact, Muslims are encouraged to reflect on it (Al-ghazali, 1995).

The following paragraphs describe some important ritual aspects of death and dying in Islam; however, different Muslims may follow different rituals, depending on denomination and geography.

The Sick Muslim

Visiting the sick is considered a religious responsibility, and being visited when you are sick is an essential right of a Muslim. During these visits, friends and family may encourage the patient to pray for him- or herself and others, as illness is considered an opportunity to be forgiven for one's sins. Visitors may recite Koranic scripture with or for the sick, and remind them of the importance of the oneness of God.

As much as functional status allows, patients are encouraged to perform prayers and other required acts of faith. *Wudu* or ablution (the ritual washing of certain parts of the body before prayer) is a prerequisite for prayer; caregivers can help weak or frail patients with this ritual.

When a Muslim Is Dying

As Muslims approach their final days, they are expected to seek forgiveness from others and settle debts—either material or of conscience—as well as seek forgiveness from God. Recitation of the Koran is a source of comfort and solace for the terminally ill, and is often performed by close family members at the bedside. Any caregiver who might have a Muslim patient should have a copy of the Koran. Access to a Muslim chaplain may also be helpful, but this is not always possible (Sheikh & Gatrad, 2008).

When a Muslim is near death, the position of the body is of great importance. Muslims believe that it is important at this time to face the *qiblah*, the direction of the holy shrine in Mecca, Saudi Arabia. In North America, this is usually northeast—the qiblah can be easily determined with a quick Internet search or by asking a local Muslim. The caregiver might want to turn the bed so the patient can lie on his or her right side, facing northeast.

If the patient is still able to speak, the *Shahadah* is of great importance. Muslims believe that if their last words are the declaration that "there is no lord worthy of worship except God, Allah," they will be forgiven on the day of judgment. Patients may recite the Shahadah repeatedly.

Many Muslims believe that the time of death is not a time for comfort. As he lay dying, the Prophet Muhammad supposedly said, "Truly, in death there is oppression," referring to the suffering that is part of the body's failure during death. To alleviate this suffering, Muslims may recite specific chapters of the Koran. With proper preparation and discussion among healthcare providers, the patient, and the family, the distress and suffering at the time of death can be ameliorated in acceptable ways.

Immediately after the moment of death, the patient's mouth and eyes should be closed, and the body covered. Every effort should be made to make arrangements for a quick burial; Muslims try to bury their dead before the next sunrise or sunset, if possible.

The Muslim Burial

In Islamic tradition, burial of the dead is carried out without unnecessary delay, and funeral rites are somewhat ascetic. Muslims do not cremate, nor do they embalm their dead, and few rituals surround the burial.

The body undergoes a *ghusl* or ritual washing by members of the family, designated members of the Muslim community, or as part of a service provided by a Muslim funeral home. After the ghusl, the body is wrapped in a shroud, and the funeral process begins.

The Muslim funeral ceremony, or *janazah*, is very short. There is no memorial service, eulogy, or elaborate ceremony. The body is brought to the front of the prayer area of a mosque. A brief ritual prayer is performed, lasting only a few minutes, and then the body is taken to a graveyard for burial. Here the deceased is laid to rest with a final prayer. These funeral services are considered spiritually beneficial and fulfilling for the dead and for those who participate.

Islamic ritual dictates that the body should be placed directly into the ground, with no casket. If a casket is required by local regulation, it should be plain, without ornamentation or decoration.

Autopsy, Organ Transplantation, Withdrawal of Life Support, and Physiologic Definitions of Death

There is tremendous controversy in the Muslim community on some issues surrounding death. National organizations such as the Islamic Medical Association of North America (IMANA) endorse neurological criteria for death (brain death), withdrawal of life support in terminal cases, and organ transplantation (IMANA, n.d.). IMANA also permits autopsies if medically indicated or required by law. However, some Muslim denominations strictly forbid the use of do-not-resuscitate orders, limits on resuscitative measures at the end of life, and neurological criteria to determine death. For example, Shi'ite Muslims who follow Imam Sistani believe that any withdrawal of life support before cardiac death is tantamount to murder (Sistani, 1994).

Although numerous organizations besides IMANA have made formal statements on these and other topics, there is no central authority among the majority (Sunni) Muslims, which results in a wide range of opinions. There is no replacement for a direct conversation with the patient and his or her family about every aspect of the plan for end-of-life care.

CONCLUSION

The most important point is that, like people in other faith communities, Muslims hold a wide variety of opinions and follow many different practices. The Bosnian immigrant, the child of South Asian immigrants, and the American-born African-American Muslim may have widely different understandings of Islam. This chapter can serve as a springboard to help caregivers explore their Muslim patients' religious and spiritual needs, and build a partnership leading to the mutual development of an optimal, patient-centered care plan.

Several parts of this chapter were previously published in the primer Disability and the Muslim Perspective: An Introduction for Rehabilitation and Health Care Providers, *part of the CIRRIE (Center for International Rehabilitation Research Information and Exchange) Monograph Series.*

Hasan Shanawani, *MPH, MD, is an assistant professor of pulmonary and critical care medicine at the Wayne State University School of Medicine in Detroit, Michigan. He is a faculty member of the Wayne State University Center to Advance Palliative Care Excellence. He is also a research fellow for the Institute for Social Policy and Understanding. He advises the Association of Muslim Health Professionals and the Islamic Medical Association of North America on professionalism, bioethics, and patient needs in North America. Shanawani's research and teaching interests relate to barriers to communication between physicians providing end-of-life care and critically ill patients from minority ethnic and religious backgrounds.*

Syed Zafar, *MD, is a third-year resident in internal medicine at Wayne State University. He earned his medical degree from Dow Medical College in Karachi followed by postgraduate clinical training in Pakistan. His career interests include gastrointestinal oncology with special emphasis on end-of-life care in the cancer patient population. He has won numerous teaching and clinical awards during his residency. He has participated in various research studies ranging from basic/preclinical to clinical in various oncologic areas. He is also involved with community outreach projects with the Arnold P. Gold Foundation and he serves as a member of the Gold Honor and Humanism Society.*

REFERENCES

Al-ghazali, A. (1995). *The remembrance of death and the afterlife*. Cambridge, UK: Islamic Texts Society.

Athar, S. (n.d.). Ramadan fasting and Muslim patients. Retrieved August 1, 2008, from http://www.imana.org/mc/pagedo?sitePageId=7720

Council on American-Islamic Relations. (n.d.). American Muslims: Population statistics. Retrieved December 10, 2005, from www.cairnet.org/asp/populationstats.asp

Ethics Committee of the Islamic Medical Association of North America. (2005). Islamic medical ethics: The IMANA perspective. *Journal of the Islamic Medical Association, 37,* 32–42.

Hathout, H. (n.d.). Frequently asked medical ethics questions. Retrieved December 10, 2005, from http://data.memberclicks.com/site/imana/IMANAEthicsPaperPart2_FAQ.pdf

Islamic Medical Association of North America. (n.d.). Retrieved October 15, 2008, from http://www.imana.org

Laird, D. L. (2006). *Muslims and the cultures of healing.* Unpublished manuscript. Boston University School of Medicine.

Laird, D. L., Amer, M. M., Barnett, E. D., & Barnes, L. L. (2007). Muslim patients and health disparities in the UK and the US. *Archives of Disease in Childhood, 92,* 922–926.

Mattson, I. (2002). Dignity and patient care: An Islamic perspective. *Yale Journal for Humanities in Medicine.* Retrieved June 1, 2008, from http://yjhm.yale.edu/archives/spirit2003/dignity/imattson.htm

Mujahid, A. M. (2001). *Muslims in America: Profile.* Retrieved May 1, 2007, from http://www.allied-mediacom/AM/AM-profile.htm

Nasr, S. H. (2005). Islam. In K. Park (Ed.), *The world almanac and book of facts 2006* (pp. 14–16). New York: World Almanac Books.

Puchalski, C. M., & Hendi, I. Y. (2004). Spirituality, religion and healing in palliative care. *Clinical Geriatric Medicine, 20*(4), 689–714.

Shanawani, H., Wenrich, M. D., Tonelli, M. R., & Curtis, J. R. (2008). Meeting physicians' responsibilities in providing end-of-life care. *Chest, 133*(3), 775–786.

Sheikh, A., & Gatrad, A. R. (2008). Death and bereavement: An exploration and a meditation. In A. Sheikh & A. R. Gatrad (Eds.), *Caring for Muslim patients* (pp. 103–113). Oxford: Radcliffe Publishing.

Sistani, A. (1994). *Islamic laws.* World Federation of KSI Muslim Communities.

Stone, J. H. (Ed.). (2005). *Culture and disability.* Thousand Oaks, CA: Sage.

Woodrow Wilson International Center for Scholars. (2003). *Muslims in the United States: Demography, beliefs, institutions.* Proceedings of a conference sponsored by Vision of United States Studies. Retrieved May 19, 2008, from http://www.wilsoncenter.org/topics/pubs/DUSS_muslims.pdf

CHAPTER 12

Buddhist Perspectives on Death, Grief, and Loss

Eve Mullen

A FICTIONAL CASE

A 50-year-old Buddhist lymphoma patient is dying in a hospital. Her breathing must be aided by a machine, and she is incoherent when she is awake. Her husband and adult children, also Buddhists, call a meeting with her doctors and ask that life support be removed, citing not the patient's wishes (which are unknown and unexpressed) nor their desire to keep her with them or to end their own pain, but instead citing the Buddhist concept of right intention and their wish to end her suffering. What issues should be considered? What course of action should be followed? In Buddhist ethical terms, what is the good to be pursued?

Buddhism is a well-established and fast-growing religion in the United States. Immigrant and transnational families from Asia, as well as American popular interest in Buddhism, contribute to a diversity of Buddhist practices and worldviews in the American religious landscape. Some people estimate that there are more than 1.5 million Buddhist practitioners in the United States—more than a 175% increase since 1990 (Kosmin, Mayer, & Keysar, 2001). With numbers like these, hospice care providers should be prepared to respond to the needs of Buddhist patients.

To serve Buddhist clients effectively, end-of-life care workers should first explore the religious worldview and the diverse ethical interpretations possible within Buddhism. What must we know when working with dying and grieving persons in the Buddhist population? I will describe the basic Buddhist doctrines, worldview, beliefs about death, and contemporary movements in Buddhist care for the dying, then conclude with a return to the fictional case above and a review of some points to remember when working with Buddhist patients and families.

THE BUDDHIST WORLDVIEW

The origins of Buddhism predate Christianity and Islam, and approximately coincide with the births of Confucian and Taoist philosophies. In the sixth century BCE, a prince in what is now northern India or Nepal was born. A great seer predicted that he would become not the next king, but an important teacher. The prince, Siddhartha Gautama, became the man we know as the *Buddha* or "awakened one." Siddhartha, a protected youth, went against his father's wishes and ventured out, away from the pleasures and luxuries of royal life, to see the world as it was. This journey into the world of suffering marks the beginning of the Buddhist path to enlightenment: Siddhartha saw illness, death, and old age for the first time in his life, and he was moved to find an escape from such suffering. He operated within a Hindu-Brahmanical religious context in which rebirth is the assumption about life and death. He found the path he sought in intense meditation and discovered the Four Noble Truths. These truths form the basis of Buddhist enlightenment, an awakening to a new way of seeing reality that allows one to escape rebirth and redeath.

The Buddha's first insight was that all life is suffering. Suffering includes not only the pains of life (such as hunger, disease, and grief) but also the pleasures (such as food, health, and happiness), which, by the joy they give us, make us crave them all the more. Thus, the second noble truth is desire. We crave that which makes us happy, but as all happiness is fleeting, the cravings are endless, driving us to seek out pleasure again and again, and turning us into slaves to our desires. It is a Buddhist goal to become free from that slavery—the lusts that make us self-absorbed—because desire is the cause of suffering.

Third, there is a way out of suffering, out of the cycle of desire. This is known as *nirvana*. Its literal translation from Sanskrit is "blow out," perhaps pointing to the path to peace as blowing out the world of rebirth, the world of suffering, as one would blow out a candle. Nirvana is not a heaven or a paradise; it is the state of nonbeing. Consider the notions of karma and rebirth in the Indian-origin religious traditions. Karma, or "action," is the force that builds up good and bad as we perform good and bad actions in our lives. Karma must work itself out in a person's life. If it does not, the person is reborn into *samsara*—the world of "returning" or "going through." Samsara is our world, the world we see around us. It is the world of birth, suffering, death, and rebirth. The goal of Buddhism is to get out of samsara, to escape the clutches of karma. In short, the goal is to "blow out" of life. This is the true meaning of nirvana.

It is vital to understand one key element of Buddhism: the concept of no-self (Sanskrit: *anatman*). Just as all pleasures are fleeting, so is the self. Part of the basic Buddhist worldview is that nothing lasts. Things we might take for granted—like a home, a mountain range, or a beautiful lake—simply do not last. In Buddhism, the impermanence of all things is applied to one's ego as well. And here is the joy of Buddhism: If there is no self, why worry about oneself? The freedom gained from a realization of no-self is bliss.

If one knows there is no self, one has no reason to be attached to one's actions, desires, or negative emotions, such as hate or greed. Karma operates only on attachments and intentions, so the person who is free from attachments is also free from karma. Karma can no longer affect the life cycle, and nirvana is one step closer. Meditation is the tool for deep realization of no-ego. Looking inward to search for the self ideally results in the knowledge that the self does not exist. The realization of this truth is the highest goal of the Buddhist practitioner.

The fourth noble truth is the Eightfold Path to nirvana. This set of guidelines is the ethical system for Buddhism and a way of living that minimizes the accumulation of karma and can lead to an end to rebirth. The eight prescriptions are right understanding and right thought, which lead to wisdom; right speech, right action, and right livelihood, which lead to correct ethical conduct; and right effort, right mindfulness, and right concentration, which cultivate the mental abilities necessary for meditation. Again, it is through meditation that the Buddhist practitioner can cut through the illusions of craving and desire and find enlightenment. The Eightfold Path has compassion as a basic prerequisite: Because we are all equal in suffering, we must realize that we are equal in all matters. No person is greater than another. For the Buddhist practitioner, this realization should lead to an outpouring of compassion toward others. After all, if there is no self, why would one assert that he or she is better than another? The doctrine of no-self logically leads to humility.

BUDDHIST DIVERSITY AND IDENTITY

The Four Noble Truths and the other Buddhist basics mentioned above are common to all forms of Buddhism, and there are many forms. We cannot speak of Buddhism as a monolithic religion but must instead recognize the global diversity of Buddhist traditions.

From their Himalayan origins, the foundational *dharma*, or teachings, of the Buddha spread throughout Asia. Mahāyāna (Great Vehicle) Buddhism spread to Tibet, China, and Japan, among other locations. In each culture, the religion flourished and diversified, often adapting to existing beliefs in order to compete or harmonize with other philosophies. For example, China gave rise to distinct forms of the religion, such as Pure Land Buddhism and Chan Buddhism. Chan Buddhism is an anti-intellectual tradition emphasizing the arts over books. In Japan, it is known as Zen. Pure Land Buddhism, or Jodo Shinshu, maintains that all one must do to reach nirvana is to call upon a Buddha named Amitabha (Omituo in China; Amida in Japan). The reward for devotion to Amitabha is birth into a paradise known as the "Pure Land" before a final life and freedom from samsara. The Tibetan Buddhist tradition is the Vajrayāna (Diamond Way or Lightning Bolt Way). The Tibetan tradition is very popular in the West and has enjoyed the leadership of the charismatic Dalai Lama, an enlightened being believed to be the same person he has been since the 16th century, purposefully reincarnated to aid the Tibetan people. The current Dalai Lama is a symbol for peace and a highly recognizable figure in Buddhism globally; he has written on grief and bereavement related to the Tibetan experience of homeland invasion and loss. Finally, Theravāda (Way of the Elders) Buddhism grew from its Indian roots to Sri Lanka, Burma, Thailand, and Southeast Asia in general. This is a far more conservative, authority-oriented tradition. For instance, Theravāda has no nuns, as the patriarchal orthodoxy upholds the male-only rule for monastic life. Again, while the formal institutions of these countries and cultures may vary, the basic Buddhist worldview—including no-self and the Four Noble Truths—does not.

Many varieties of Buddhism exist in America as well, and nonimmigrant Buddhist traditions contribute to further diversity. What some scholars of religion call "elite Buddhism" or "white Buddhism" refers to American Buddhist groups (often with an ethnic monk or nun as teacher) that may or may not fall under a clear category of tradition but are successful and prolific nonetheless. Identification across religions is often the norm in Buddhism around the world. In modern China, for example, the boundaries between Buddhism, Taoism, and Confucianism are not well defined and often overlap in folk religion or *mixin*. In Japan, the question of one's religion is sometimes nonsensical, as most people identify with more than one type of Buddhism, as well as with Shinto, the indigenous tradition of the Japanese islands. "What is your religion?" seems to be a distinctly Western question, too limiting in its assumption that identity can be categorized. Western assumptions about religions, strictly defined and categorized, often do not apply to Asian cultural identities. It is important to be sensitive to such basic differences in religious identification, especially when working with persons from Chinese and Japanese cultures. As a side note, it is also vital to recognize that Tibetans are not Chinese in religious, lingual, or ethnic definitions. Tibetan Buddhism is distinct from Chinese forms of Buddhism, and the identification of a Tibetan as Chinese is considered hurtful and offensive in Tibetan communities.

BUDDHIST VIEWS OF DEATH AND DEATH RITUALS

What can generally be said about Buddhist attitudes toward death? Common to all Buddhist traditions is the story of the grieving woman and the mustard seed. Krisha Gotami was overcome by grief at the death of a child. She begged the Buddha to return the child to her. The Buddha instructed her to go to the village and bring back a mustard seed from a household that had not experienced a family member's death. The woman sought the magical ingredient that would restore the child but when no such household could be found, the Buddha's intended lesson became clear: no one is untouched by suffering or death. Death is a reality for all. Sogyal Rinpoche regards this story as a foundational Buddhist lesson: "A close encounter with death can bring a real awakening, a transformation in our whole approach to life" (Rinpoche, 1992, p. 29).

With such gentle teachings in mind, we can view death as an opportunity for awakening to the Buddha's teachings and the reality of no-ego, as well as an opportunity for enlightenment itself, the ultimate awakening. Confronting death can cultivate a peaceful joy for life. It is as a human being that one can best learn of spiritual and other matters, because human beings have the greatest capacity for focus and concentration. Of all the existences that can be one's fate in the world of rebirth, human existence is best.

There is no one Buddhist view of death, but the basic ideas of rebirth and no-self shed light on underlying Buddhist assumptions. A dying person is not a permanent soul that will be lost. After one short lifetime of constant change, death and rebirth only mark more change and another transformation in a universe of almost unending movement. This is an obvious point of difference between the Buddhist perspective and typical Western perspectives on the individual. Western religions generally posit a human soul that survives after death. Buddhism does not. In addition, Buddhism is not a theistic religion; this can be a potential stumbling block to a Jewish, Christian, or Muslim monotheist attempting to understand Buddhism. The thoughtful clinician would do well to cultivate an awareness of these fundamental differences and adjust language appropriately. Words like "soul," "afterlife," "God," "judgment," and "creator" are not meaningful in the Buddhist worldview. "Karma," "rebirth," "nirvana," "enlightenment," "impermanence," and "no-self" are far more useful.

Ritual in all religions facilitates transformation. In a bar mitzvah, a boy becomes a man. In a wedding, two people become one. A funeral is also a rite of passage: The funeral ritual eases the transformation from one state of being to another, usually—in a religious context—from this life to the next. Funerals are also valuable for the living, most commonly to facilitate grief. Buddhist funeral rituals are specifically meant to ease the transition from one life to good rebirth, or ideally, to nirvana. Buddhist funerals provide a space for grief, even as they discourage attachment to the dead.

The diversity inherent in Buddhism applies to rituals as well. In Japan, a Buddhist funeral may involve burial or cremation, a Buddhist priest or a Shinto priest, belief that the deceased is subject to rebirth, or belief that the deceased has become a godlike *kami*. In China, a Buddhist funeral might not be a transition to rebirth or godlike status for the deceased but perhaps an elevation to ancestor status or to a sad existence as a ghost. As a general rule, Southeast Asian Buddhists cremate the body, but even in the orthodox Theravāda, rituals can vary.

Nonattachment to the body is a key element in all Buddhist funerals. Cremation, a method of body disposal Buddhists inherited from the Hindu-Brahmanical traditions of India, is the norm in many Buddhist cultures. Cremation leaves no corpse to tempt the spirit into staying behind or on which a grieving loved one might become wrongly focused. The body is a physical form that—like all else—is impermanent. Any attempt to preserve a corpse (for instance, through embalming) is seen as a fundamental error. The decay of the body is not only inevitable but is sometimes regarded as a useful lesson in Buddhist truth. One form of meditation practiced in Theravāda, Mahāyāna, and Vajrayāna alike is the concentrated consideration of a rotting corpse: The meditator may sit next to a corpse for extended periods of time and in this visceral manner contemplate the transitory nature of the flesh. This may be impractical, but any meditation that considers the impermanence of the body can be a useful exercise.

Particularly in Buddhist communities that lack a strong monastic community, funeral rituals are conducted increasingly by lay people. Still, many communities prefer to rely on an authority appropriate to their tradition, normally a monk who can perform the rituals and recite or read pertinent sacred scripture. The Tibetan Buddhist *Bardo Thödol (Book of the Dead)*—

used by many Western Buddhists since its translation into English in 1927—is an excellent example of a ritual text in the Vajrayāna that can be read by either a lama (monk) or a lay person.

CONTEMPORARY BUDDHIST CARE MOVEMENTS: TWO MODELS

Immigrant and transnational Buddhism in the United States is affected by host culture, and care for the dying is similarly affected. Many Buddhist organizations and communities in the United States engage in good work for terminally ill patients, prisoners on death row, and grieving families. In urban centers where immigrant and transnational groups are large and well organized, religious and secular leaders address the need for care from a Buddhist perspective for their Buddhist-oriented communities. Nonimmigrant traditions of care are also employing Buddhism's vast scriptural resources, views, and approaches to care for the dying. Two of these contemporary Buddhist care institutions in the United States stand out for their originality and popularity: the San Francisco Living and Dying Project and the New York Zen Center for Contemplative Care. Their approaches are described here as examples of the wide range of Buddhist end-of-life care that clinicians can draw on for use with patients.

The main focus of the San Francisco Living and Dying Project, founded in 1977, is defined in the mission statement: The project encourages the use of life-threatening illness as an opportunity for spiritual growth and cultivation of Buddhist virtues such as compassion, patience, and wisdom. The programs draw on sources from many religions, including the Tibetan *Book of the Dead*. The sacred text is read aloud, in keeping with Tibetan tradition, to the dying person. The person is led through three main stages or planes of existence between this life and the next, with the goal of either reaching enlightenment and ending rebirth or at least successfully traversing the planes so that he or she can be born into a good human existence—one that will allow for spiritual progress toward nirvana in the next life.

Reading the *Book of the Dead* to Tibetan Buddhist patients can be a soothing ritual. Although reading has traditionally been the job of a monk, lay people are increasingly stepping into the role, so the clinician need not worry about issues of religious authority if he or she wishes to read aloud. The book offers comfort, careful guidance, and a unique Buddhist perspective on the individual's progress through a suffering-filled world. The Living and Dying Project provides a model for how one can creatively incorporate the text into a religious and spiritual blend of care.

The New York Zen Center for Contemplative Care offers an innovative Buddhist Chaplaincy Training Program. Founded in 2007, the center offers approximately 30 clinical praxis internships each year to students in the contemplative care chaplaincy education program. The program is not limited to Zen Buddhist studies or religious services. It emphasizes general Buddhism and includes a nonreligious outreach to people of other faiths. The program philosophy was described by founder Koshin Paley Ellison as "having the community take care of people in the community"—an idea that crosses religious boundaries. The program focuses on a certain kind of comfort for patients, emphasizing basic human actions such as listening and providing a space for emotion. The contemplative care approach involves no rituals, no texts, and no explicitly religious advice. The absence of such things is quite anti-intellectual and Zen in character.

The ideal result for patients and their loved ones is an atmosphere of intimacy in which they can be human without worrying about theology. Ellison is quick to point out that the Buddha had no theology; he awoke to the facts of sickness and death and found a way out of suffering for all beings. In the same way, Ellison says, we should regard ourselves as equal to the suffering person for whom we are caring, and approach that person with moment-by-moment patience and openness to the changes through which he or she is going. In the view of contemplative care, each of us has the ability to care for our neighbors.

The Zen Center approach to Buddhist end-of-life care is entirely different from, and even conflicts with, that of the San Francisco Living and Dying Project. The former is decidedly antitextual and assumes no certainties about what happens after death, while the latter is text-based and assumes the existence of a plane between this life and the next. However, both of these creative institutions offer comfort with the explicit goal of caring for the dying in today's world. Their programs are informed not only by Buddhism's diversity of traditions but also by contemporary work in psychology and the healthcare field, and they answer the needs of people living in a pluralistic society, often on the margins of the mainstream. They provide support through a modern application of Buddhist teachings. Both approaches are valid under the large umbrella of practices known as Buddhism. Numerous resources are available that we can draw on to better serve our Buddhist patients. No special religious authority is necessary; a clinician generally can engage in "Buddhist" care without being a Buddhist. We need only ask those we serve what is best for them.

END-OF-LIFE ETHICAL CONSIDERATIONS AND BUDDHISM

The most common arguments regarding the practical application of Buddhist ethics hinge on the Buddhist concept of intention, particularly as it relates to earning karma. If one's intentions are selflessly compassionate, one's actions can be seen as accumulating no karma and are thus acceptable. On the other hand, a selfish attachment to one's actions and their desired outcomes is unacceptable. An example illustrates this idea. If a person trips and falls down while walking past us, we might rush to help, but think, "This person will reward me" or "Maybe this person will like me more." These are attached actions, motivated by selfish desires. In Buddhism, these are incorrect actions. The correct action would be a natural, compassionate effort with no thought of what we might gain from it.

Ethical issues pertaining to end-of-life care can be similarly interpreted according to intent. Thus, several viewpoints are possible on one action meant to alleviate a person's suffering. Buddhist author Peter Harvey says that suicide and killing under any circumstances are against Buddhist teachings. But he also says, "The increase of painkillers, with the foreknowledge that this may cause death, may be acceptable if the intention is genuinely to ease the pain, and not to kill it by killing the patient" (Harvey, 1999, p. 412). Even within one religious family, individuals may come to different conclusions on end-of-life care issues.

A RETURN TO OUR FICTIONAL CASE

Returning to the case with which we started this chapter, we can see some important Buddhist elements at play in the ethical question of best action. The wife and mother who is dying of lymphoma did not express her wishes regarding life-extending technologies. Her family has communicated their wish to remove the breathing aid. The Buddhist issues we have explored are central in this case. We need to differentiate between selfless and selfish motivations in a karmic world. The possible results are attached or nonattached actions that may earn karma for those involved. The family expressed their compassion in their wish to end their loved one's suffering. For them, the decision is clear: Ending a life is not a negative act in this situation but a karmically neutral one based on the selfless wish to end suffering. The good to be pursued in Buddhist ethics is not good karma, but no karma at all. The determination that one is motivated in the purest way possible, with only compassion in mind, allows for a course of action that earns no karma. The life-support apparatus can be removed with no fear of committing a negative act.

By the same Buddhist logic, *not* removing the life support could be the most detrimental act possible. If the family's desire to preserve the woman's life were rooted in selfish fears of missing her in their own lives, bad karma would result, and their loved one's suffering would be prolonged. Once again, intention is key.

The woman's own karma is not in question here. Her good and bad karma will play out in this life or the next life or lives, unaffected by the family's decision. In the general Buddhist worldview, ending suffering in this way does not mean robbing a person of her chance to eliminate bad karma via "cleansing" suffering.

There are many interpretations of such situations in Buddhism, just as in any modern, internally diverse world religion. But one conclusion is always the same: Just as we must not ignore the person who has fallen on the sidewalk, we cannot simply turn away from suffering.

CARING FOR PATIENTS AND FAMILIES

There are several helpful tips to remember when dealing with Buddhist patients and loved ones, on both the personal and professional levels.

1. Generally, Buddhist attitudes toward death are defined by the concept of no-self. A living person does not possess a soul or a permanent ego. The self is an illusion to be overcome. It is a common Western misconception that the Buddhist belief in no-self must be negative, even nihilistic. On the contrary, in Buddhism the notion of no-self is freeing. Comprehending the lack of a permanent self is considered a joy that leads to the further joy of selfless actions on behalf of others.

2. A related misconception is that Buddhists devalue human life because the ultimate goal of the spiritual path is to escape rebirth. In truth, Buddhists highly value birth as a human being, for it is as a human that one can best understand spiritual matters. While Buddhists respect all life, including animal life (most Buddhists are vegetarians), they cherish human life.

3. In the Buddhist worldview, there is no concept of an eternal afterlife. While there are many levels of existence to which a person may be reborn, none last. The thought of repeated rebirths is generally not comforting. Just as one would not want to live through the same day repeatedly, neither does one want to be caught in an endless rut of repeated lives.

4. Theodicy—the attempt to explain suffering or evil in the world—is as controversial in Buddhism as it is in theistic religions. Buddhism is a nontheistic belief system, so innocent people's suffering cannot be blamed on a higher power. However, the impersonal, universal force of karma is sometimes invoked. Actions return to the person who selfishly performed them, so that person him- or herself is the culprit. More commonly, however, people are not harshly blamed for their bad karma; rather, there is a less judgmental resignation to simple bad luck.

5. Buddhist practices, sacred texts, rituals, and histories of traditions vary greatly. From the devotional Pure Land and ritualistic Tibetan traditions to the conservative Theravāda and artful Zen, there is no one way to be Buddhist. We must respect the heterogeneity of Buddhism, making no assumptions about the patient's personal practice of the religion. By the same token, there is no one Buddhist authority on morality. Interpretations of and judgments on controversial issues such as assisted suicide, definitions of life, and euthanasia are highly varied, and arguments surrounding controversial topics tend to center on intention and selfless motivation as they relate to karma and right action.

6. Particularly in Chinese and Japanese cultures, Buddhism is often only one part of a person's religious identity. The question "What is your religion?" is thus problematic. A better question is "How can we approach this spiritually in the best way for you?" In addition, Tibetan religious identity is distinct from Chinese or other Buddhist identities. Chinese Buddhists generally do not recognize the Dalai Lama of Tibet as a valid authority, and Tibetan Buddhists resist identification with Chinese forms of Buddhism.

7. Many of the immigrant and transnational Buddhists we meet in our hospice work are already all too familiar with loss and grief on a large scale: People of Tibetan, Vietnamese, Cambodian, and other heritages carry with them the legacies of war, disaster, or genocide. Many families have stories of lost loved ones, friends, villages, and perhaps entire homelands. Sensitivity to these personal and shared tragic histories is essential.

8. Meditation is a Buddhist tool for overcoming illusions of self and ego. Meditation can also be a calming, revitalizing exercise. For patients who are coping with pain or on medication, a few minutes of concentration may be all that is possible. But Buddhist authors such as Sogyal Rinpoche

and Chokyi Nyima Rinpoche remind us that even novice meditations, such as concentrating on one's breath for a few minutes at a time, can be beneficial to a patient.

9. Buddhist funerals take many forms. They may incorporate elements from other religions, particularly in Japanese and Chinese traditions, as well as in American Buddhist circles. They may include burials, but most commonly cremation is the preferred method of body disposal. As a general rule, Buddhist funerals emphasize nonattachment to the body.

10. In Buddhism, it is a compassion-inspiring truth that we are all equal in suffering. We are also all equal in grief. Despite what may seem like a very different worldview than what we are accustomed to in other religions, Buddhists are subject to the same anxiety, anger, denial, and coping mechanisms as everyone else. Buddhist patients and their loved ones must be allowed room to express emotions.

We are all human, after all. As Sogyal Rinpoche (1992, p. 175) writes,

> Look at the dying person in front of you and think of that person as just like you, with the same needs, the same fundamental desire to be happy and avoid suffering, the same loneliness, the same fear of the unknown, the same secret areas of sadness, the same half-acknowledged feelings of helplessness…. I think you would find that what the dying person wants is what you would most want: to be really loved and accepted.

CONCLUSION: THE GOOD DEATH

Perhaps the ideal Buddhist life is one led in awareness of death: Everyone is subject to death, and thus everyone is equal in death. Ideally, Buddhist compassion for others flows naturally from this awareness. What is the ideal Buddhist death? Is suffering meaningful in Buddhism? Suffering becomes meaningful through its opportunities for cultivating compassion and for practicing kindness toward others. We can conclude that a good death is one of calm awareness of potential. In a religious tradition of no-self, death is not an end to an individual person but an opportunity for selfless compassion, as well as for liberation from samsara in the light of the Buddha's Four Noble Truths. The clinician who understands the basic Buddhist views on life and death can better serve Buddhist patients simply by being sensitive to these ultimate beliefs and goals.

Eve Mullen is an assistant professor in the Pierce Program in Religion at Oxford College of Emory University. She earned a BA in religion at Washington and Lee University in 1990, an MTS from Harvard in 1992, and a PhD in religion from Temple University in 1999. Her areas of expertise include Buddhism in America, Asian religious traditions, religion's role in identity construction, and death and dying in Buddhism. Mullen is a Fulbright U.S. scholar and a Fulbright senior specialist in American studies and religious studies, and recently lectured in the Center for Religious and Cross-Cultural Studies graduate program at Universitas Gadjah Mada, Yogyakarta, Indonesia. She has also been a guest lecturer at Universitaet Hamburg, under a grant from the Gustav Prietsch Foundation for Religious and Ideological Tolerance in Germany. She is the author of The American Occupation of Tibetan Buddhism: Tibetans and Their American Hosts in New York City, *as well as numerous articles and book chapters on topics related to Buddhism.*

REFERENCES

Harvey, P. (1999). A response to Damien Keown's "Suicide, assisted suicide and euthanasia: A Buddhist perspective." *Journal of Law and Religion, 13*(2), 407–412.

Kosmin, B. A., Mayer, E., & Keysar, A. (2001). *American religious identification survey.* New York: Graduate Center of the City University of New York.

Rinpoche, S. (1992). *Tibetan book of living and dying.* San Francisco: Harper San Francisco.

CHAPTER 13

Christian Evangelicals: The Challenge for Hospice and Palliative Care

Kenneth J. Doka

W*hen a hospice is committed to the original mission of hospice, its services can be a great relief for both a patient and family members.... Unfortunately some hospices and hospice organizations are actively promoting actions that hasten death, including terminal sedation, withdrawal of nutrition and hydration, and "by delivering pain relief sufficient to cause death by incidentally suppressing breathing"*[1] (Illinois Right to Life Committee, 2008).

This statement by the Illinois Right to Life Committee exemplifies the ambivalence that some Christian evangelicals have toward hospice care. On one hand, there is recognition that hospice care offers a needed service— providing compassionate care to those who are dying. In some cases, evangelical congregations have founded hospices or have been part of coalitions instrumental in beginning local hospices. Yet, there is also an anxiety that some practices of hospice may hasten death.

The suspicion and fears about hospice within the evangelical community are both unnecessary and unwarranted. Evangelical Christians are emerging

---

1 This unsourced quotation is taken from the chapter "Rational Suicide in Terminal Illness" by Thomas Attig in Hospice Foundation of America's 2005 book, *Living with Grief: Ethical Dilemmas at the End of Life*. The entire passage reads, "And, although the ethics of euthanasia is not the subject of this chapter, it is well known that hastening death is practiced and approved in many ways in contemporary terminal care when suffering is extreme and irremediable—for example, by terminal sedation, by delivering pain relief sufficient to cause death by incidentally suppressing breathing, or by withdrawing nutrition and hydration. Given the obligation to relieve suffering, such practices are not incompatible with the physicians' oaths" (Attig, 2005).

as a major spiritual culture in the United States. Hospices and palliative care units need to be sensitive and reach out to them as they would any distinct cultural entity.

This chapter seeks to facilitate that process. It begins by attempting to define the largely amorphous evangelical movement, noting the basic beliefs that define evangelicals. Second, the chapter explores the cultural issues that might arise as hospices interact with evangelicals in their own communities. Finally, the chapter offers suggestions for hospices to improve communication, alleviate needless fears, and better serve the evangelical community.

The Culture of Christian Evangelicals

It may seem odd to describe Christian evangelicals as a cultural group. However, culture is best defined as a way of life characterized by shared values, beliefs, and behaviors. Such an inclusive definition transcends ethnicity or race as the sole determinant of culture. Under this definition, many faith communities—including Orthodox Jews, Jehovah's Witnesses, conservative Muslims, and evangelical Christians—can be considered cultures.

The evangelical movement is amorphous and somewhat difficult to define. Generally, it consists of a variety of Christian church bodies such as Southern Baptists or Pentecostals that are regarded as traditional or conservative in their approach to scripture. The term *evangelical* is usually attributed to Harold John Ockenga, who in a 1947 essay used the term *neo-evangelicals* to describe a split in the fundamentalist wing of Christianity (Henry, 1947). The evangelicals wished to distinguish their beliefs from those of liberal Protestants (whom they perceived as departing from historical Christian views in an attempt to accommodate to the larger, secular culture) and fundamentalists (whom they perceived as too separatist and unconcerned with the social implications of faith).

The evangelicals were not opposed to ecumenical involvement and discussion, provided such dialogue did not involve the surrender of core beliefs. The Reverend Billy Graham, for example, was often criticized by fundamentalists for his willingness to work with groups such as Roman Catholics. In fact, the evangelicals often looked at themselves as a movement that sought to revitalize Protestant churches by helping them develop both a clear Christian identity and a committed mission to change their general culture.

The evangelical movement can also be distinguished from the religious or Christian right, although many evangelicals are involved in it. The religious right is essentially a coalition of Christian political and social organizations that espouse a conservative political agenda. The coalition includes active right-to-life groups (often including conservative Lutherans and Roman Catholics not generally identified as evangelicals) and fundamentalists. In addition, some evangelicals are active in other movements, such as environmentalism, efforts to combat poverty, and attempts to care compassionately for persons with AIDS—positions not usually associated with the religious right. However, in many ways, the Christian right includes the most active and visible manifestation of the evangelical approach to political life, even though other political strains exist within the evangelical movement.

The evangelical movement is large. Slightly more than 25% of Americans define their religious affiliation as evangelical (U.S. Census Bureau, 2007). The culture is marked by church involvement, private piety, and modest dress, as well as shared values and beliefs. Most evangelicals believe that Jesus is the promised messiah and that eternal salvation is only possible for those who personally accept Jesus as their savior. Most evangelicals consider themselves "born again"; that is, they believe that their acceptance of Jesus as their savior represents a new birth as a child of God. Evangelicals also believe that witnessing to their faith is an essential responsibility. Their view of Christian scripture is both literal and authoritative.

Many evangelicals believe that the Bible is divinely inspired and historically and scientifically accurate. Thus, as the word of God, scripture is to be consulted in every aspect of life. Because of this perspective on the Bible, many evangelicals espouse beliefs that support traditional gender roles. In fact, Brown (2002) notes that the fight against feminism and the Equal Rights Amendment was one of the first forays of the religious right in the political arena—it offered both a common cause and a common enemy. Most evangelicals believe that homosexuality is morally wrong and oppose same-sex marriage. Many also oppose policies and initiatives that would interfere with parents' rights to raise their children according to biblical principles. Many support, for example, the right of parents to home-school their children.

Evangelicals as a whole tend to see the separation of church and state as contrary to the wishes of the founding fathers. In many ways, evangelical views of history emphasize religious reasons for colonial migration and tend to focus on American exceptionalism; that is, the notion that America was to be a Christian New Zion—a model to other nations. This spiritual interpretation stresses the religious affiliations of the founding fathers, ignoring the influence of the Enlightenment and the largely Deist views of these early leaders. In this view, the separation of church and state simply meant that churches were not to be publicly supported, nor was any particular denomination officially favored.

To many evangelicals, secular influences have eroded this exceptionalism. Hence, most evangelicals favor school prayer and would allow religious symbols, such as Christmas crèches, to be displayed in public places. Most oppose efforts to remove religious mottos such as "In God We Trust" from coins or "under God" from the Pledge of Allegiance. Many see the use of terminology such as *winter break* or *spring break* in schools instead of *Christmas* or *Easter* as unnecessary surrenders to pluralism or humanism.

Central to evangelical belief is a strong sense of the sanctity of life, which comes from scriptural interpretations rooted in Judeo-Christian history. Judaism historically has strongly emphasized the sanctity of life: Life was a gift of God that could only be surrendered when God willed it. Many biblical scholars hold that God's rejection of the Jewish patriarch Abraham's sacrifice of his son Isaac represented a clear rejection of human sacrifice prevalent in the fertility cults of the time. When the first Christian disciples (Jewish adherents of the new faith) reached Rome, they found many practices—suicide, infanticide, and abortion—that offended their sensibilities. Hence, early Christian literature strongly reaffirmed these historic beliefs.

Even the evangelical rejection of evolution follows not just from a literal interpretation of scripture but also from a belief in the sacredness of life. To accept evolution would make humans little more than highly evolved animals subject to the same laws of nature, rather than a special creation of God, answerable to God's laws.

This belief that life is created by God and hence sacred is behind much evangelical opposition to abortion. It also underlies evangelical objection to embryonic stem cell research, as they consider embryos living beings, and the use of embryos for research suggests a philosophy of utilitarianism that denies the sanctity of life.

At life's end, most evangelicals would oppose suicide, including physician-assisted suicide when a patient nears death. Many evangelicals also oppose practices such as palliative sedation, decisions not to artificially hydrate or feed a patient, and even among some, do-not-resuscitate orders. A smaller segment of the evangelical community is wary of pain management if it has the effect of hastening death, and some might even hold that suffering at the end of life is both natural and perhaps even salutary. These positions have led, in some cases, to suspicion of hospice.

For example, Ron Panzer, president of Hospice Patients Alliance, whose blog posts are often cited both by evangelicals and the right-to-life movement, claims, "While many in the hospice movement assert they will neither hasten death nor prolong death, hospice staff around the country may misuse common end-of-life interventions to hasten death.... They die of dehydration while sleeping, thereby allowing for a 'pretty' or 'peaceful' but unnatural death, i.e., murder.... The National Right-to-Life Committee has known about these hospice killings for years, yet has refused to expose these killings" (Abbott, 2005). Abbott finds conspiracy in the interrelationships of varied groups in the end-of-life movement, such as the National Hospice and Palliative Care Organization (NHPCO) and Choice in Dying (formerly known as the Euthanasia Society).

While Panzer's views may be extreme, the Terri Schiavo case crystallized evangelical suspicion of the hospice movement. Ambivalence and underlying suspicion were evident when many right-to-life groups and Christian evangelicals joined to maintain vigils around the central Florida hospice that was caring for Schiavo. Technically, hospice care was not the issue; rather, the legal case revolved around who could decide to end such care. However, hospice care was forced to center stage in the struggle between Schiavo's parents and her husband over whether or not to withdraw artificial nutrition. As the case was vigorously contested in the political and legal realms, prominent evangelicals such as James Dobson and Jesse Jackson joined pickets outside the hospice where Schiavo resided.

While Panzer and the Schiavo case have raised evangelical concerns about hospice in general, these concerns have not necessarily translated to local hospices. Many evangelical churches have been active in creating or supporting hospices in their communities, even serving as chaplains.

HOSPICES AND EVANGELICALS: AN UNNECESSARY DIVIDE

Evangelical suspicion regarding hospice is unnecessary and unwarranted. Ironically, the roots of hospice have a strong connection to Christianity in general and evangelical Christianity in particular. Cicely Saunders, the founder of the first modern hospice, was a deeply religious woman who, though originally agnostic, converted to Christianity after having a religious experience while vacationing with a friend in 1947 (Richmond, 2005). She was a member of the Church of England, but she often spoke admirably of evangelical leaders such as Billy Graham, noting that she served as a volunteer during one of his crusades (Klass, 2008).

Saunders's spiritual motives and religious symbolism are evident in her choice of the word *hospice*. Hospices originally were maintained by religious orders as places of rest for people on pilgrimages. In the 19th century, a religious order used the term for facilities designed to care for the indigent dying in both England and Ireland. Saunders selected the name St. Christopher's for the facility she designed, as St. Christopher was the patron saint of travelers. Thus, in designing the first modern hospice, she deliberately selected a term steeped in Christian history and symbolism. In fact, she initially hoped that the hospice would be a mission outreach of the Church of England, but diverse sources of funding required that it be open to all faiths. Saunders described it as a religious foundation of an open character (Richmond, 2005).

Beyond these strong religious roots, hospice embraced a philosophy that encompassed spiritual care. To Saunders and those who followed her, the central purpose of hospice was to relieve suffering at the end of life. She understood suffering in a holistic way: Pain was not only physical but also psychological, spiritual, social, and familial. Saunders and her staff at St. Christopher's pioneered palliative medicine and pain management, but her hospice philosophy emphasized that care should always address spiritual, psychological, social, and familial needs. Chaplains and spiritual care were (and are) a critical component of hospice. Saunders emphasized that life should be lived fully until it ended, and she stressed that the end of life could be a time of great spiritual growth.

Saunders was a vigorous opponent of euthanasia. Some of her opposition arose from her beliefs as a committed Christian (Richmond, 2005); however, she also strongly believed that effective pain management and holistic care obviated any need for assisted suicide or other forms of euthanasia. Indeed, in her later years she sometimes claimed that her motivation for starting hospice was her opposition to assisted or unassisted suicide of those suffering terminal illness (Klass, 2008). Hospice itself was an answer.

The spiritual emphasis of hospice continued as hospice crossed the Atlantic and developed in the United States. Most of the early pioneers were both inspired and trained at St. Christopher's hospice. They shared the philosophy of holistic care—a philosophy that clearly acknowledged the importance of the spiritual.

However, two factors in the importation of hospice into the United States may have affected the evangelical perception of hospice. The three people who developed the first hospice in the United States in Branford, Connecticut—

Sylvia Lack, Florence Wald, and the Reverend Sally Bailey—were committed Christians, but they came from a more mainline Protestant tradition, one rooted in New England Protestant culture and heavily influenced by the Yale School of Divinity. Hence, their spiritual approach was more liberal and their language somewhat different from the evangelical tones of Saunders.

In addition, they embraced more pluralistic notions of patient diversity, autonomy, and choice. For example, Wald believed that patients should have a range of options available to them at the end of life—hospice care being one (Friedrich, 1999).

This respect for patient autonomy was evident in the position of the Oregon Hospice Association. In 1994, the Oregon Hospice Association opposed the Death with Dignity Act—an act that, with certain restrictions, essentially legalized physician-assisted suicide in Oregon. However, in the 1997 vote on whether to repeal the act, the association declined to endorse repeal, seeing it as an issue of patient choice. In 1999, Ann Jackson, executive director and CEO of the Oregon Hospice Association, testified in opposition to the proposed Pain Relief Promotion Act of 1999, sponsored by Representative Henry Hyde (R-IL) and Senator Don Nickles (R-OK), which would have essentially nullified Oregon's law. Jackson's position was not in support of assisted suicide; rather, she emphasized that the implementation of such a law might create even more legislative oversight that would inhibit effective pain management. Even on this topic, the lack of consensus should be noted: Samira Beckwith, CEO of Hope Hospice in Florida, representing the National Hospice Organization (now NHPCO), testified in favor of the bill.

The core of disagreement is not whether assisted suicide should be legalized; rather, it reflects more nuanced positions regarding pain management, patient autonomy, and freedom to choose options at the end of life. Unfortunately, these nuanced positions do not translate well to some segments of the evangelical community that tend to see issues in a polarized frame.

EVANGELICALS AND GRIEF

One of the core aspects of hospice philosophy is that the family is the unit of care, and that care continues after the death of the patient in the form of grief support. Evangelical perspectives and approaches toward grief may vary. Evangelicals firmly believe in resurrection—that anyone who accepts the saving grace offered through Christ will enter heaven. For some evangelicals, then, a death is to be welcomed and a funeral service is a homecoming—a celebration that the person has returned to his or her creator. With such a belief, grief can be perceived as self-centered or even a sign of lack of faith.

Most evangelicals, though, have a more nuanced view. While affirming the resurrection of the dead, they acknowledge the feelings of grief and loss experienced by survivors. Such feelings would simply be perceived as an expression of love and attachment that exist along with the belief in eventual reunion. The Christian writer Helmut Thielicke expressed this paradoxical view well: "I walk into the night of death, truly the darkest night; yet I know Who awaits me in the morning" (1970, p. 198). Such a view affirms both the promise of faith and the reality of grief. Some evangelical churches have participated in special services held at the winter solstice. These services allow bereaved persons to come together on "the darkest night" to hear a message of hope, validation, and comfort for those experiencing loss and grief in the midst of the Christmas season.

Bridging the Cultural Gap

While substantive conflicts may not exist between hospice and the values of the evangelical community, hospices may need to approach evangelicals as another distinct cultural group that merits outreach.

Outreach can begin as a local hospice examines its own cultural milieu. Hospices are not monolithic; some hospices are a very good fit with evangelical culture. Their roots may lie in evangelical churches or other culturally compatible groups. Their language, materials, policies, and approaches may be consonant with evangelicals. Their staff and chaplaincy may be rooted in the evangelical community.

Other hospices may have different histories, approaches, or philosophies. They may have roots in other religious traditions—liberal Protestantism, even Buddhist or New Age spiritualities. Such hospices might well serve evangelicals at the end of life, but the fit with evangelical culture might not be as comfortable. In situations in which the hospice culture is not congruent with the evangelical culture, the hospice should openly communicate its philosophy, approach, and policies, even as it offers care.

Outreach can be done in a number of ways, depending on community demographics. In communities with megachurches, the hospice might give special presentations to the pastoral and church staff. Where there are many smaller evangelical churches, personal contacts and events such as clergy breakfasts can be useful forms of outreach. Evangelicals should know about hospice's attractive points: for example, its history of strong religious roots and its contemporary emphasis on holistic (including spiritual) care. Naturally, evangelical clergy should be represented among hospice chaplains and spiritual care communities, and even on hospice boards. Effective communication between hospice staff and evangelical churches when members enter hospice also engenders trust.

As with other groups, hospice staff may initially encounter mistrust among evangelicals who harbor suspicions about hospice. Clearly defining policies in nondefensive ways should clarify hospice's mission.

Counseling services, whether in the dying process or through grief counseling after the death, might be another point of mistrust. Many evangelicals favor Christian counseling, in the belief that people will only find contentment when their actions are aligned with God's will. Christian counseling often is highly directive, seeking to apply biblically based principles to the person's struggle. This approach is very different from the way most counselors function. Some highly religious persons may be very sensitive to any perception that their spiritual beliefs are being discounted or disrespected, and may even believe that seeking or accepting counseling in the first place is a sign of a lack of faith.

Counselors should reassure clients by showing interest in and respecting their religious beliefs; in fact, they might be able to use the beliefs, rituals, faith practices, and even communities in their interventions. For example, it can help to cultivate sensitive clergy and chaplains in the evangelical community who may be appropriate contacts when clients struggle with spiritual issues at life's end. Grief bibliographic resources should include material that evangelicals might find useful. C. S. Lewis's *A Grief Observed* (1961) is one such resource. Lewis is generally accepted in the evangelical community; this book is a graphic and powerful account of his own spiritual struggles with loss and grief as his beloved wife died. Finally, counselors should be aware of their own issues as they counsel evangelical clients. Many issues and beliefs—for example, those having to do with the role of women—can raise significant countertransference issues for counselors.

CONCLUSION

In a way, evangelicals can be a hidden culture, and membership may not be visible, but it is a large culture. As hospice continues to serve communities, outreach to diverse groups should certainly encompass the evangelical community. For some in this community, who believe that life is a divine gift and a person should fight death until the last moment, hospice may not be an appropriate alternative. For most evangelicals, though, the gift of hospice—a peaceful death, neither hastened nor forestalled—is what Cicely Saunders intended it to be: a place of respite on a continuing journey.

Kenneth J. Doka, PhD, *is a professor of gerontology at the Graduate School of the College of New Rochelle and senior consultant to the Hospice Foundation of America. A prolific editor and author, Doka's books include* Living with Grief: Children and Adolescents; Living with Grief: Before and After Death; Death, Dying and Bereavement: Major Themes in Health and Social Welfare; Pain Management at the End-of-Life: Bridging the Gap between Knowledge and Practice; Living with Grief: Ethical Dilemmas at the End of Life; Living with Grief: Alzheimer's Disease; Living with Grief: Coping with Public Tragedy; Men Don't Cry, Women Do: Transcending Gender Stereotypes of Grief; Living with Grief: Loss in Later Life; Disenfranchised Grief: Recognizing Hidden Sorrow; Living with Life Threatening Illness; Children Mourning, Mourning Children; Death and Spirituality; Living with Grief: After Sudden Loss; Living with Grief: When Illness Is Prolonged; Living with Grief: Who We Are, How We Grieve; Living with Grief: At Work, School and Worship; Living with Grief: Children, Adolescents and Loss; Caregiving and Loss: Family Needs, Professional Responses; AIDS, Fear and Society; Aging and Developmental Disabilities; *and* Disenfranchised Grief: New Directions, Challenges, and Strategies for Practice. *In addition, Doka has published more than 60 articles and book chapters. He is editor of* Omega *and* Journeys: A Newsletter to Help in Bereavement.

REFERENCES

Abbott, M. (2005). Is hospice care safe? Retrieved October 1, 2008, from http://www.renewamerica.us/columns/abbott/050330

Attig, T. (2005). Rational suicide in terminal illness. In K. J. Doka, B. Jennings, & C. A. Corr (Eds.), *Living with grief: Ethical dilemmas at the end of life* (pp. 175–197). Washington, DC: Hospice Foundation of America.

Brown, R. M. (2002). *For a "Christian America": A history of the religious right*. Amherst, NY: Prometheus Books.

Friedrich, M. (1999). Hospice care in the United States: A conversation with Florence Wald. *Journal of the American Medical Association, 281*, 1683–1685.

Henry, C. (1947). *The uneasy conscience of modern fundamentalism.* Grand Rapids, MI: Eerdmans.

Illinois Right to Life Committee. (2008). *Hospice checklist.* Retrieved October 1, 2008, from http://www.illinoisrighttolife.org/HospiceChecklist.htm

Klass, D. (2008). Personal communication, August 13, 2008.

Lewis, C. S. (1961). *A grief observed.* New York: Bantam Books.

Richmond, C. (2005). Dame Cicely Saunders [obituary]. *British Medical Journal, 331,* 1509.

Thielicke, H. (1970). *Death and life.* Philadelphia: Fortress Press.

U.S. Census Bureau. (2007). *The statistical abstract of the United States.* Washington, DC: U.S. Government Printing Office.

Other Sources of Diversity

This final section of this book reviews some additional sources of diversity—reaffirming that diversity transcends race, ethnicity, spirituality, and class. Disabilities remain a major source of diversity. Claire Lavin begins this section by reviewing the sensitivities required to work with persons with intellectual disabilities suffering from loss and end-of-life issues. Lavin notes that many of the characteristics of this population, such as memory and language deficits, diminished abstract reasoning, and social/emotional limitations, may create challenges for the end of life. For example, Lavin describes the ways that these characteristics may complicate pain management, ethical end-of-life decisions, and grief support.

Frank Zieziula explores another disability—deafness. Again, Zieziula notes the diversity within diversity, dividing those with hearing loss into three categories: *hard-of-hearing people, late-deafened people,* and *Deaf people.* Each varies in their own attitudes toward their own hearing losses, interactions with the hearing world, and communication modalities and support systems. The hard-of-hearing individuals suffer hearing loss that they regard as an impairment that should be corrected. Their cultural identification is with the hearing world. Late-deafened people are those that experience total or near-total hearing loss later in life, perhaps in adolescence or adulthood. Their deficits are not correctable. They are often marginal, neither fitting in the Deaf culture nor fully participating in the hearing world. Deaf people are those who identify with Deaf culture. The *D* is capitalized by these groups to affirm their strong sense of identification. It is truly a culture with a distinct way of life that centers on the shared language of American Sign Language. Zieziula reminds hospice and palliative care workers to be aware of *audism,* which defines and evaluates persons on their abilities to hear and verbally communicate.

There can be cultures based on occupation. This is particularly likely in military and paramilitary organizations such as the police. Vyjeyanthi Periyakoil writes from the perspective of military culture, noting the sensitivity that palliative care professionals ought to have toward the symptoms of Posttraumatic Stress Disorder (PTSD). PTSD may be triggered by the stresses or inherent life review that occurs with the diagnosis of a life-threatening illness. Periyakoil's chapter also has relevance for other cultural groups, especially those immigrant groups that might be refugees of conflicts and war.

Brian de Vries's chapter on the lesbian, gay, bisexual, and transgender (LGBT) population adds another dimension of diversity—sexual orientation. De Vries describes some of the characteristics of the LGBT population, including those that may complicate care: the relative absence of caregivers for those who live alone or are childless, conflicts over care between the biological family and chosen or logical kin, and the historic roots of insensitivity that breed discrimination. De Vries's conclusion is an apt conclusion for the book: All people deserve sensitive care, and by studying the unique characteristics of each diverse group and committing to sensitively serving the unique needs of each population, we can offer more inclusive and holistic care that will benefit all.

Persons With Intellectual Disabilities: Facing Dying and Loss

Claire Lavin

The population of older adults with intellectual disabilities poses both a challenge and an opportunity for service providers. The challenge is to meet the emerging needs of a group that has battled many obstacles over their lifetimes. The opportunity is to learn more collaborative ways of dealing with all people at the end of life. Fifty years ago, people with intellectual disabilities seldom survived into old age. Now their life spans have increased, and they, too, face the issues of grief and loss in old age. This article will address the classification, historical treatment, and characteristics of people with intellectual disabilities, and the implications for service providers in hospice and community settings.

CLASSIFICATION

The term "intellectual disabilities" has been used in recent years as a replacement for the older term "mental retardation." The American Association on Intellectual and Developmental Disabilities (AAIDD) states, "Intellectual disability is a disability characterized by significant limitations both in intellectual functioning and in adaptive behavior as expressed in conceptual, social, and practical adaptive skills. This disability originates before the age of 18" (AAIDD, 2008). People with an intellectual disability have significantly below average intellectual ability—at least two standard deviations below the mean as measured on an individual intelligence test. They must also evidence impairment in adaptive behavior—the social and pragmatic skills needed for everyday activities.

This legal definition has several implications. The first is that the disability affects the person's ability to function in society in an age-appropriate manner and requires supports that fit the person's profile of strengths and needs. The second implication is that the disability will affect the person throughout life. The third, and most important, is that the disability is simply one aspect of a person who also has strengths. Estimates of the number of persons with intellectual disabilities vary, but approximately 3% of the population is affected.

The number of older adults with intellectual disabilities is estimated at approximately 600,000. This number will increase to several million by the year 2030, as the baby boom generation ages (AAIDD, 2008).

HISTORICAL CONTEXT

Fifty years ago, there would have been little need for this chapter. Most people with intellectual disabilities were either confined to institutions or lived at home with their parents and other family members. They rarely lived long enough to face old age and its vicissitudes. People with intellectual disabilities often had medical complications such as heart and respiratory problems that shortened their lives. With the closing of large institutions, such as Willowbrook in Staten Island, people with intellectual disabilities moved into community settings. Between 1977 and 2005, the number of people with developmental disabilities who lived in institutions decreased by 74%. Most moved to small settings of six or fewer people. As people moved out of institutions and into the community, they accessed services there (Lakin, Prouty, & Coucouvanis, 2006).

Medical advances have improved life expectancy for people with intellectual disabilities. A 1999 study of mortality and morbidity found that the mean age of death for those with intellectual disabilities excluding Down syndrome was 66.1 years; it was 55.8 years for those with Down syndrome; while it stood at 70.4 years for the general population. The authors predicted that in successive generations of people with intellectual disabilities, the mortality rates would be the same as those of their peers (Janicki, Dalton, Henderson, & Davidson, 1999).

The growing population of older adults with intellectual disabilities has posed challenges for both families and service providers. For those who live with family members, the ability of caregivers to meet their needs falters as life expectancies increase. Parents can no longer be certain that they will outlive their children with disabilities, and as parents age, they may not be physically able to cope with the needs of their adult children with disabilities. People with Down syndrome in particular display early onset of Alzheimer's, increasing the challenge of caring for them at home (Zigmond, Schupf, Haverman, & Silverman, 1995).

People with intellectual disabilities have seen major, positive changes in their lives. They can live in communities, not institutions. They live longer and have healthier lives. They are able to participate in more activities with their nondisabled peers. At the same time, necessary community supports are not always in place. Group homes fall prey to the not-in-my-backyard reaction. Community service providers, such as dentists and doctors, are not always trained to deal with this population (Read, Jackson, & Cartlidge, 2007).

CHARACTERISTICS AND IMPLICATIONS FOR SERVICE PROVIDERS

It is important to remember that persons with intellectual disabilities are people first. The disability does not define the person. In most respects, they have the same needs, feelings, and reactions common to all people. Thus, in making decisions, service providers can ask themselves what they would wish for themselves and use the answer as a guideline.

Those with a mild or moderate intellectual disability differ from those with severe disabilities. The former group is more verbal, comprehends more complex information, and is more likely to have lived in the community and developed a repertoire of coping skills. The cohort now entering older adulthood probably lives at home with family members, although they might have spent some early years in institutions before the deinstitutionalization movement of the 1970s and might have subsequently moved into other community settings. As they age, people with disabilities bear more resemblance to their nondisabled peers; in both groups, cognitive acuity lessens, social networks shrink, mobility falters, and communication skills weaken (Forbat & Service, 2005). Those with more severe disabilities will become even less verbal and are likely to have more medical complications that affect their ability to communicate and function independently.

Cognition and Learning

People with intellectual disabilities tend to have difficulty with abstract concepts. They deal more comfortably with the concrete and with a hands-on learning style. Thus, they would be likely to learn more about death from personal experiences with the death of a plant or pet than from a philosophical discussion. It is better to demonstrate and have them do something step-by-step than to simply tell them to do something.

They also need more direct instruction than their nondisabled peers. Most people learn social conventions from observing family and friends. People with intellectual disabilities do not learn as much from such situations. The amount of incidental learning they get from simply living in an environment is limited. One cannot assume they have learned certain skills from experience; often they must be specifically taught.

Memory is also problematic. Many repetitions are required for material to be encoded in their memories. Concepts and behaviors must be reinforced in multiple ways. For example, one exposure to a story about a hospital will not be sufficient for true understanding. A person with an intellectual disability might need to read the story, watch a film and talk about it, role-play with medical instruments, and explain the concepts to a family member. At each step, misconceptions can be clarified and correct knowledge reinforced. In teaching new behaviors and skills, a step-by-step method is most effective. Tasks should be broken down into components and each modeled for the person; otherwise, a complex task may seem overwhelming.

People with intellectual disabilities also have difficulty transferring learning from one situation to another. When taught to respond in one setting, they may not realize that they should respond the same way in other settings.

Language and Communication

Language skills are also affected by disability. With limited vocabularies and restricted life experience, people with intellectual disabilities may not understand complex medical terms and concepts. Many do not read very much and thus do not have a store of knowledge regarding medical treatments and hospitals. They may be reluctant to reveal that they do not understand and may say they do. Service providers need to ask them what their understanding is to be sure they comprehend.

Language weaknesses place more responsibility on the listener. People with intellectual disabilities may not express their thoughts well because of poor vocabulary, so the listener may have to intuit meaning from short utterances.

Those who are nonverbal will have developed signals to communicate, such as pointing to their mouths to indicate hunger or pointing to areas of pain. Understanding their communications regarding pain and distress requires careful observation. An increase in activity can signal either well-being or a response to pain. Those who know or have worked with the person are best able to interpret these signals. Service providers need to work closely with family members and caregivers to learn the person's individual language. In communicating information, providers can use pictures and gestures to explain procedures. Demonstrating actions, such as holding on to the bed rails or coughing, may be clearer than telling the person what to do.

Some tools are available for interpreting nonverbal communication. Regnard and colleagues (2007) developed a Disability Distress Assessment Tool (DisDat) to measure pain expressed nonverbally. It includes careful observation of facial expressions, posture, vocal utterances, and appearance in both contented and distressed states.

Physical Factors

The health of people with intellectual disabilities has improved markedly over the past 50 years. Improved medical care and better nutrition have lengthened the life spans of this cohort. The chief causes of death are cardiovascular diseases, respiratory infections, and cancer. High levels of dementia are found in the group with Down syndrome. On the other hand, people with intellectual disabilities have a much lower death rate due to risky behaviors such as accidents, homicide, smoking, or alcohol use (Janicki et al., 1999). Many have age-related problems of poor mobility, hearing, and vision. People with severe disabilities tend to have multiple medical conditions. Some are immobile or fed through feeding tubes. Some are in semivegetative states, responding only to sounds or tactile stimulation. Many rely on extraordinary measures to survive.

Social-Emotional Factors

Social-emotional skills are generally below age expectations. People with intellectual disabilities require assistance with the activities of daily living and are accustomed to being directed by others rather than acting independently. Their social networks are restricted and consist mainly of family members or live-in companions. They tend to depend on a small circle for support. They may behave in an immature manner, seeking reassurance and affirmation from others. They have a stronger need for approval than people who may have experienced success in various areas of life. They are used to following directions and are likely to acquiesce to the wishes of others. Service providers must actively engage them in discussions of their wishes regarding medical interventions and end-of-life events. Social skills and interactions need to be directly taught and modeled.

ISSUES RELATED TO HOSPICE CARE

There are many points of congruence between the hospice and intellectual disability systems. Both focus on individual and person-centered planning; both consider the whole person—seeing people not as medical conditions but in all aspects of their being. Both focus on providing supports that will enhance the person's functioning and quality of life. Hospice personnel need to be sensitive to several issues related to serving persons with intellectual disabilities.

Informed Consent

People with intellectual disabilities may not be able to make informed decisions regarding their care. Those who hold legal guardianship may make these decisions for them. However, both parents and guardians in group homes need to know the options, services available, and the impact of the decisions they make. Advance directives, powers of attorney, and healthcare proxies should all be in place and should be prepared with as much input as possible from the persons themselves. Having an intellectual disability does not mean that a person is incapable of expressing preferences. Those who are verbal and less severely impaired should be encouraged to express their wishes. A study of a group with mild and moderate impairments found that all the people interviewed could express wishes and comprehend end-of-life services (Tuffrey-Wijne, Bernal, Butler, Hollins, & Curfs, 2007). The interviewees identified as important having someone to listen to their wishes, being comfortable, having family and friends around, and participating in enjoyable activities. They also expressed pleasure at being asked their opinions in the study. While this was a small study, it demonstrated that adults with intellectual disabilities can understand death and end-of-life issues and can express preferences. The authors concluded that those affected by these kinds of decisions must be heard regardless of their impairments and that ways can be found to elicit their opinions.

Best Interest

What is best for clients in terms of promoting well-being, and how do we decide that? Nelson (2003) discusses how to make decisions about treatment for persons with intellectual disabilities on the basis of best interest. He presents case studies that illustrate decisions that diminish pain and suffering, treat people as individuals, and provide a meaningful quality of life. Nelson says that providers must evaluate pain and suffering, probability of restoration of functionality, and the extent to which life can be prolonged. One man on a ventilator with a gastrostomy tube experienced repeated seizures and infections. He was unable to enjoy music and the tactile stimulation that had previously given him pleasure. Nevertheless, he continued to receive treatment.

Nelson concluded that the tendency to do everything possible to prolong life was partially the result of liability issues. No one wants to be accused of withholding treatment just because someone has a disability. However, persons with disabilities should not be denied the right others have to refuse treatment. Baumrucker and colleagues (2008) reviewed a decision to perform surgery on a cancer patient with trisomy 21 from a legal, ethical, social, and medical perspective. They advocated looking at the whole person and comparing the decision with a decision made for a person without a disability.

Years of mistreatment have led to fears that the rights of people with disabilities will not be respected and that treatment may be withheld because their lives are devalued. Safeguards have been put in place mandating death reviews by state authorities. However, some of these processes can hinder delivery of hospice care. Death reviews can affect the willingness of staff to allow the person to remain in the group home and receive hospice care. The staff may avoid the review by moving the person to a nursing home, where he or she may die in an unfamiliar setting (Botsford, 2000). Some states have begun to distinguish between untoward and anticipated deaths and to draft regulations and memoranda related to end-of-life and hospice settings (Craig, 2005).

Quality of Life

What is the meaning of "quality of life"? Some people may believe that a person with an intellectual disability has a poor quality of life, while the person him- or herself may feel content. AAIDD (2008) lists four basic principles to use in making end-of-life decisions for people with intellectual disabilities: (1) dignity, which involves treating all people regardless of mental condition or age, and recognizing that all lives are of equal value; (2) autonomy, which requires that the wishes of the individual be determined and followed; (3) life, which means that the best-interest standard is followed to protect and promote the life of the individual; and (4) equality, which means that adequate and equitable resources are made available to the person.

These principles have several implications for care. The wishes of the person should be ascertained and followed wherever possible, and the bias should be toward preserving life. Treatment should be withheld only if the person has clearly expressed this preference without doubt. Where competence is an issue, the legally designated next of kin should make the decision; if there is any doubt, judicial determination should be sought.

However, decisions are filtered through the prisms of both the decision maker and the patient. Goldsmith, Hendrix, and Gentry (2006) describe cases in which the decision to withhold treatment was affected by the contextual factors of the situation, which included the age of the parents.

Organizational Coordination

Providing hospice services to persons with intellectual disabilities involves federal, state, and local agencies in the fields of developmental disabilities, medicine, and aging. Coordination is necessary to deal with questions about who controls access and who pays for services. Funding issues related to Medicaid, Medicare, and community facility reimbursement must be addressed. When a person is removed from an intermediate care facility (ICF), there is a financial impact on the facility. In some cases, the person cannot stay at the group home because staff cannot revise the service plan to fund the necessary level of end-of-life care. Medicaid funding must be flexible so people with intellectual disabilities can remain at home as those without disabilities can.

Those who care for the person with a disability, at home or in an ICF, may feel protective of him or her and may not be willing to relinquish control to hospice. Additionally, staff at hospices may not think they can provide adequate services to this population. Forbat and Service (2005) present a case study in which care decisions are viewed from a medical, social service, and family context. Each set of principles affects the care of a person who is unable to voice his or her opinions and wishes.

Family members who have cared for a person with disabilities for a lifetime may be suspicious of institutions and may believe that no one will care as much as they do. They have lived with the person, sometimes for decades. It is crucial that hospice staff involve these parents and caregivers in the care of the client. They can interpret nonverbal communication and know how to soothe the person. They can help with the task of life review by recalling, verbally or though pictures, the highlights of the client's life. In many cases, the parents are quite old, with health needs and concerns of their own. They may need extra support in the areas of transportation, counseling, and information.

Training

While hospice workers have extensive training, their training may not have touched on the topic of intellectual disabilities (Read et al., 2007). They may have little contact with this population and may not feel prepared to treat them.

Tuffrey-Wijne, Hollins, and Curfs (2005) conducted a survey to determine the training needs for palliative care staff who work with persons with intellectual disabilities. The key area of need was communication: understanding the patient's communications and making sure the patient understands staff explanations. Pain assessment and ethical issues were also concerns. Blackman (2002) described systematic training that improved staff skills and sensitivities in dealing with grief reactions.

Persons with intellectual disabilities need training to help them deal with end-of-life issues. They can be helped to understand the natural cycle of life and what the end of the cycle means. Death and loss, receiving or withholding treatment, where to die, memorials, and funerals should be discussed with them. Without training, this population (like most people) will not address the issues until a crisis occurs, and then it may be too late for their wishes to be expressed and honored.

Family members also need training. When they are faced with decisions about hospice placement for their loved one with intellectual disabilities, they may not understand the nuances of living wills, advance directives, do-not-resuscitate orders, and healthcare proxies. They may wish to make a decision for their loved one but be prevented from doing so because they have not obtained the needed authority. Botsford and Force (2004) have produced a guide for caregivers to address these issues and help them make informed decisions.

Dealing with Grief and Loss

The death of someone close has the potential to disproportionately affect those with intellectual disabilities. They tend to be less prepared and to receive fewer supports than their peers for dealing with grief and loss (Clements, Focht-New, & Faulkner, 2004).

Proactive Measures

People cope better with grief when they have had preparatory experiences. When a crisis strikes, it is too late to thoughtfully address the many issues related to end-of-life care and to help persons with disabilities deal with death. Because of their restricted life experiences, these persons may have not participated in wakes, funerals, burials, or memorial services. They may not have had models for coping with death, and caregivers may have been reluctant to broach the topic of death and dying with them. They would benefit from preparation integrated into their day-to-day experiences (Botsford & King,

2005). Activities can include observing the cycle of life in nature, caring for pets, and using books and videos to make death more concrete and accessible. Read and Elliott (2007) propose a systems approach to helping people with intellectual disabilities cope with loss. It begins with support in the family, proceeds to support from a network of counselors and social service agencies, and includes national initiatives.

An important part of preparation is to experience the rituals connected to the death of someone not so important to the client. While we can never be fully prepared for the death of a person we love, those who are completely unprepared can be more adversely affected. Dodd and colleagues (2008) found that people with intellectual disabilities who received no preparation for participating in rituals evidenced more complicated grief. Expected behaviors and words of sympathy can be taught and practiced. A trusted caregiver can accompany the client to the service or viewing, model the expected behaviors, and provide support as needed. Afterwards, the caregiver should go over the event with the client, emphasizing how well he or she dealt with the situation. Reinforcing the idea that people can cope with such difficult experiences strengthens them for future trials. This is also an opportunity to discuss questions the client may have about whether he or she—or you—may die, what it is like, and so on. It is a chance to reinforce the ideas that much is unknown about death, that everyone experiences it, that people who care will help when the time comes, and that religious beliefs may help. It is important to give the client a chance to express his or her beliefs about death and clarify any misconceptions, such as that the person died because he was bad, that it was somehow the client's fault, and so on.

Many losses are not as severe but are precursors of the loss we experience in death. For example, people who live in group home facilities may have to say goodbye to many caregivers over the years. Learning to express feelings of sadness and loss, and, more important, learning that life goes on are key lessons. People can also have experiences with pets or through books and movies that can be helpful when a real loss occurs (Lavin, 1989).

Reactive Measures
When a death occurs, everyone needs both practical and emotional support. Persons with intellectual disabilities are more likely to receive practical support than emotional support (Gilrane-McGarry & Taggart, 2007). Most of the people interviewed in this study were included in funeral rituals, although

none were present at the actual death. Most interviewees did not ask questions at the time of the death, but some wished they had been able to discuss it later. The biggest lack was in counseling support. Most of those interviewed said they believed staff needed to listen to them more and try to understand their needs and feelings. Many people in the general population have had a similar experience—they are expected to have gotten over the death after a certain period of time, but feelings of grief and loss persist or recur. Unfortunately for those with disabilities, irritable or noncompliant behaviors may be attributed to the disability rather than to grief reactions.

Rituals are very important to help the person with a disability cope with death. Participation in funeral services can help assuage feelings of loss. Unfortunately, people with disabilities may be excluded from these rituals because others think they will not understand or will be traumatized. It is a mistake for family members or staff to try to hide or deny the strong emotions that accompany the death of a family or group home member. Persons with intellectual disabilities who sense that something is wrong but are not told about the death suffer more than those who are brought into the process and receive an explanation of what happened.

Persons with intellectual disabilities, both verbal and nonverbal, can participate in memorializing the deceased. They can place a flower on a memorial table or on the coffin, collect photographs, draw a picture, or find a special memento of the person. Manuals with suggested activities, phrases to use, and resources to consult can help caregivers address the topic with their clients.

Counseling

Counseling is an important, yet often overlooked, part of dealing with grief. Because persons with intellectual disabilities may not verbally express their need for assistance, caregivers may attribute grief reactions such as withdrawal or aggression to the disability. While we know that most people do not quickly recover from a death, some may believe that persons with intellectual disabilities do not need counseling because they are not as deeply affected by the death and will soon forget. This is not necessarily the case. Dowling, Hubert, White, and Hollins (2006) found significant improvement among persons with intellectual disabilities who participated in a series of 15 weekly counseling sessions. The sessions included active listening, normalizing grief reactions, drawing, looking at photographs, reading stories about death, and making life story books and memory boxes.

Grief work with this group can be verbal for those with mild impairments and more hands-on for those with poorer verbal skills. Those who are verbal need opportunities to ask questions. Many are reluctant to do so or may only broach the subject long after the event. They need people to listen to them, which takes time in a hectic environment. A number of resources are available for grief counselors to use with this population. Blackman (2002) described the Resource for Opportunity and Change program, which combined caregiver training with therapeutic interventions. Family and staff caregivers were taught how to break the news, involve the client in planning activities, validate grief reactions, use direct and simple language, and replace lost supports related to companionship and social interventions. The program consisted of an assessment to identify appropriate techniques followed by sessions. Yanok and Beifus (1993) also developed a program to help people with intellectual disabilities cope with death.

Art therapy is a good medium for expressing sadness—art therapists are skilled in interpreting meaning from pictures, which can well serve the nonverbal population. Music and dance therapy can also help nonverbal persons express and release feelings of sadness and anger related to loss.

FACING THE FUTURE
Much progress has been made in serving the growing population of older adults with intellectual disabilities. Coalitions have been formed among agencies for the aging and developmental disabilities, and legal agreements have been prepared that spell out the process, funding, and ethical review for placing people in hospice care. Training programs have been developed for persons with intellectual disabilities, their caregivers, and hospice service providers.

Manuals and programs are available to help prepare this population to deal with issues of grief and loss. The Last Passages Project, initiated by the Volunteers of America and continued by the National Hospice and Palliative Care Organization, has developed educational materials and encourages cross-disciplinary collaboration to serve this population (Craig, 2005). We are becoming much better prepared to help people with intellectual disabilities deal with issues of dying and loss.

Claire Lavin is a professor of psychology at the College of New Rochelle in Westchester County, New York. A licensed clinical and school psychologist, she works with children and adults with disabilities in facilities and school districts in the greater New York City region. She has written articles and presented papers on older adults with disabilities.

REFERENCES

American Association on Intellectual and Developmental Disabilities. (2008). Frequently asked questions on intellectual disability and the AAIDD definition. Retrieved September 1, 2008, from http://www.aaidd.org/content_185.cfm?navID=62

Baumrucker, S., Sheldon, J. E., Stolick, M., Morris, G. M., VandeKieft, G., & Harrington, D. (2008). The ethical concept of "best interest." *American Journal of Palliative care, 25*, 56–62.

Blackman, N. J. (2002). Grief and intellectual disability: A systemic approach. *Journal of Gerontological Social Work, 38*, 253–262.

Botsford, A. (2000). Integrating end-of-life care into services for people with an intellectual disability. *Social Work in Health Care, 31*(1), 35–47.

Botsford, A., & Force, L. (2004). End-of-life care: A guide for staff supporting older people with developmental disabilities. *Advocacy Monograph No. 3* (2nd ed.). Delmar, NY: New York State Association for Retarded Citizens, Inc.

Botsford, A. L., & King, A. (2005). End-of-life care policies for people with an intellectual disability. *Journal of Disability Policy Studies, 16*(1), 22–30.

Clements, P. T., Focht-New, G., & Faulkner, M. J. (2004). Grief in the shadows: Exploring loss and bereavement in people with developmental disabilities. *Issues in Mental Health Nursing, 25*, 799–808.

Craig, L. (2005). *End-of-life care initiatives: Available resources and training.* Paper presented at the Rehabilitation Research and Training Center on Aging with Developmental Disabilities Conference, Washington, DC.

Dodd, P., Guerin, S., McEvoy, J., Buckley, S., Tyrrell, J., & Hillery, J. (2008). A study of complicated grief symptoms in people with intellectual disabilities. *Journal of Intellectual Disability Research, 52*(5), 415–425.

Dowling, S., Hubert, J., White, S., & Hollins, S. (2006). Bereaved adults with intellectual disabilities: A combined randomized controlled trial and qualitative study of two community-based interventions. *Journal of Intellectual Disability Research, 50,* 277–287.

Forbat, L., & Service, K. P. (2005). Who cares? Contextual layers in end-of-life care for people with intellectual disability and dementia. *Dementia, 4,* 413–431.

Gilrane-McGarry, U., & Taggart, L. (2007). An exploration of the support received by people with intellectual disabilities who have been bereaved. *Journal of Research in Nursing, 12,* 129–144.

Goldsmith, B., Hendrix, C. C., & Gentry, J. (2006). Providing end-of-life palliative care for the developmentally disabled and their families. *Journal of Hospice and Palliative Nursing, 8*(5), 270–275.

Janicki, M. P., Dalton, A. J., Henderson, M., & Davidson, P. W. (1999). Mortality and morbidity among older adults with intellectual disability: Health services considerations. *Disability and Rehabilitation, 21*(5), 284–294.

Lakin, K. C., Prouty, R., & Coucouvanis, K. (2006). Changing patterns in size of residential settings for persons with intellectual and developmental disabilities. *Mental Retardation, 44*(4), 306–309.

Lavin, C. (1989). Disenfranchised grief and the developmentally disabled. In K. Doka (Ed.), *Disenfranchised grief: Recognizing hidden sorrow* (pp. 229–237). Lexington, MA: Lexington Press.

Nelson, L. J. (2003). Respect for the developmentally disabled and forgoing life-sustaining treatment. *Mental Retardation and Developmental Disabilities Research Reviews, 9,* 3–9.

Read, S., & Elliott, D. (2007). Exploring a continuum of support for bereaved people with intellectual disabilities. *Journal of Intellectual Disabilities, 11*(2), 167–181.

Read, S., Jackson, S., & Cartlidge, D. (2007). Palliative care and intellectual disabilities: Individual roles, collective responsibilities. *International Journal of Palliative Nursing, 13*(9), 430–435.

Regnard, C., Reynolds, J., Watson, B., Matthews, D., Gibson, L., & Clarke, C. (2007). Understanding distress in people with severe communication difficulties: Developing and assessing the Disability Distress Assessment Tool (DisDat). *Journal of Intellectual Disability Research, 51*(4), 277–292.

Tuffrey-Wijne, I., Bernal, J., Butler, G., Hollins, S., & Curfs, L. (2007). Using nominal group techniques to investigate the views of people with intellectual disabilities on end-of-life provision. *Journal of Advanced Nursing, 58*(1), 80–89.

Tuffrey-Wijne, I., Hollins, S., & Curfs, L. (2005). Supporting patients who have intellectual disabilities: A survey investigating staff training needs. *International Journal of Palliative Nursing, 11*(4), 182–188.

Yanok, J., & Beifus, J. A. (1993). Communicating about loss and mourning: Death education for individuals with mental retardation. *Mental Retardation, 31*(3), 144–147.

Zigmond, W., Schupf, N., Haverman, M., & Silverman, W. (1995). *Epidemiology of Alzheimer's disease in mental retardation: Results and recommendations from an international conference.* Washington, DC: American Association on Mental Retardation.

CHAPTER 15

Death and Loss in Deaf Culture

Frank R. Zieziula

WHAT IT MEANS TO BE DEAF

You know that you are deaf "when you're at an airport and you miss your plane because you failed to hear the last call on the P.A." (Holcomb, Holcomb, & Holcomb, 1994, p. 108). "When waiting in a busy doctor's office, you sit in a strategic location where you can easily lip-read the caller and be as visible as possible so that you will not miss your turn" (p. 13). "You feel that the local stations do a good job serving their deaf viewers by captioning their news programs. However, when a natural disaster hits your area, you are routinely left in the dark with no captioned emergency broadcasts" (p. 46). "At a meeting with an interpreter, a question is directed to you. Everyone in the room has to wait until the question is relayed to you. Just hope you get the question right the first time" (p. 91). These snippets of experience from *Deaf Culture: Our Way* reveal a life that is very unfamiliar to many of us. Multiply these examples a thousandfold and you begin to sense what it is to be a person with a hearing loss trying to traverse a hearing world.

One of the main goals of this chapter is to provide end-of-life care workers with guidance on how we can best serve this population—a population we will encounter now and in the future. We must begin our discussion by asking, "What does it mean to be deaf?" The answer, in today's culturally diverse world, is interestingly complex. To be deaf means different things to different people, including deaf people themselves. This chapter will attempt to unravel the question and offer guidance to hospice workers on how to provide services to a variety of deaf people.

I will begin by using the generic term "hearing loss" to refer to a person whose interaction with others is affected by an inability to hear speech. The National Center for Health Statistics (NCHS) (1994) of the U.S. Department of

Health and Human Services estimates that approximately 9% (20,295,000) of the U.S. population has hearing losses serious enough to negatively affect daily functioning (work, school, or play). The elderly constitute 28% of this group. The causes of hearing loss for the other 72% are attributable to loud noises, ear infections, birth defects, and ear injuries. According to the NCHS, of the 20 million hearing-impaired people, less than 0.5% (approximately 1.5 million) cannot hear or understand words by speech alone. Of that population, only 2.48% are over the age of 65.

The prevalence of hearing loss appears to be similar in Canada. The Canadian Association of the Deaf estimates that there are 310,000 culturally Deaf Canadians and 2.8 million hard-of-hearing Canadians (Canadian Census, 2008). There is no credible census of deaf people in Mexico, but the numbers are probably proportional to those of the United States and Canada. Thus, the number of people with hearing loss in North America is large (the largest category of disability in the United States), so hospice workers are bound to come in contact with persons with hearing loss in their service to their communities.

To add to the diversity issue and the confusion of identification, various labels have been used throughout the history of our country to categorize and differentiate people with hearing loss, including *hearing impaired, hearing handicapped, deaf, Deaf, hard of hearing, deaf mute, adventitiously deaf, pre-lingually deaf, pre-vocationally deaf, late-deafened,* and others.

One of the reasons for confusion is that, unlike blindness, there is no legal definition of deafness. Deafness is often used as a blanket term that encompasses everyone with a slight, moderate, or severe hearing loss—from the elderly who are losing their hearing as a result of old age, to adults who lose the ability to understand speech because of an accident or illness, to babies who are born profoundly deaf from genetic causes.

People with hearing losses come in all shapes, sizes, degrees of deafness, ages of onset, communication modalities, and self-identities. Some people with a hearing loss do not consider themselves deaf. Not all people with a hearing loss use a hearing aid. Not all people with a hearing loss need sign language or use the same sign language system. Not all people with a hearing loss identify their circumstances as a disability. This population is not only large but also diverse.

How can a hospice professional make sense of the variability of auditory deafness and, more important, prepare to be of service to this diverse population? In this chapter, I will use the term *deaf* (lowercase *d*) to refer to any and all people with a mild to severe hearing loss. In addition, I will use three terms to define different subgroups of people with hearing loss, knowing that I am granting myself a great deal of latitude by placing all people with hearing loss in three boxes. The three terms are *hard of hearing, late-deafened,* and *Deaf* (with a capital *D*). Each of these subgroups has a different attitude toward their hearing loss and different attitudes and behaviors in their interactions with the hearing world. They vary in communication modalities and support systems. Each group requires a different approach to providing comprehensive human, medical, religious, and practical hospice services.

The largest population of people with hearing loss, and the population most likely to be served by hospice workers, is *hard-of-hearing* persons. Many elderly people (the most likely clients of hospices) are hard of hearing. The identification of a person as hard of hearing is based on the fact that the person has a noticeable loss of hearing, specifically in the range of hearing used to differentiate speech, yet these people maintain communication primarily through speech (Moores, 2001). Visual cues are secondary. This group identifies itself culturally as part of the hearing world. They consider their hearing loss as an impairment that needs correction. Most often, the hearing loss is lessened, even corrected, with the use of a hearing aid. Although hard-of-hearing people rely primarily on speech and hearing for interaction, they are very attentive to visual cues, often require added time in service because of the need to repeat things, and are easily distracted by peripheral noise, large group conversation, and lack of or dim lighting.

The term *late-deafened* is used to identify people who, in their late teens or even later, suffered a severe hearing loss that prevents them from understanding spoken language, even with the use of a hearing aid (Moore & Levitan, 2006). This loss usually occurs because of trauma (e.g., soldiers in combat), side effects of medication, accidents, or unknown causes. These people must rely on visual cues as the primary mechanism to communicate with the world, using whatever hearing remains to supplement their vision. Speech is usually intact, but it may change over time, depending on their age when they lost hearing. People in this group often deal with identity issues. They are not hard of hearing by strict definition, because they must rely almost solely on visual cues for communication. They identify with the hearing world, but do not feel safe in that arena, because they have severe difficulty in auditory communication. They do not consider themselves members of Deaf culture (see below). Most are not at ease using a sign language communication system; in fact, some never learn sign language. Like hard-of-hearing persons, late-deafened people often require added time in service because of the need to repeat things. They are easily distracted by peripheral noise and large group conversations. They rely heavily on watching mouth movements, and most use hearing aids.

Finally, there is a statistically small but politically important group of people with a severe hearing loss who identify themselves as *Deaf* with a capital *D*. According to Padden and Humphries (2005), the word *Deaf* describes a group of people within the larger community of those with hearing loss who have common cultural practices and use American Sign Language (ASL) as the primary means of communication with the outside world. Many of these Deaf people were born with a severe hearing loss or suffered a hearing loss before the acquisition of spoken language.

In further explaining this use of the word *Deaf*, Padden (1989) says, "The type or degree of hearing loss is not a criterion for being deaf. Rather, the criterion is whether a person identifies with other deaf people and behaves as a deaf person" (p. 8). This group is probably most misunderstood by the general public, and these are the people who deserve more complete understanding by social service professionals.

CHARACTERISTICS OF DEAF CULTURE

According to Moores (2001), today's Deaf culture can be traced back to residential schooling of deaf children in Connecticut in 1817. The schools brought deaf people together who otherwise would have been isolated in their hearing communities. Through this association in education, a unique Deaf culture developed. Interestingly, cultural identity became so strong that in 1830, graduates of the first school formed an association and attempted to establish a Deaf state. A similar idea surfaced in 1850. People who consider themselves members of the Deaf culture share a number of characteristics that hospice workers should be aware of as they provide services to deaf clients and family members.

First and probably most important is Deaf people's respect for American Sign Language. It is the language of choice in their homes, schools, and social lives. It is estimated that as many as 2 million Americans use ASL for everyday communication (Lane, Hoffmeister, & Bahan, 1996). According to Stokoe, Casterline, and Groneberg (1976), ASL is distinct from English, with its own rules of grammar and its own syntax. It does not use the same word order as

English. Facial expressions, hand and body movements, and space around the signer and between signers are all used to create linguistic meaning between communicators. According to Liddell (2003), no parallel for this exists in spoken language. ASL is not only a means of communication for many deaf people; it is a symbol of the cohesiveness of the Deaf community—the fabric that bonds the community.

Some deaf people use a communication system known as total communication or simultaneous communication. This system (it is not language) incorporates English language syntax (signs and finger spelling) along with speech. In the past, this combination has had strong advocates in the special education community (mostly hearing professionals), who believed that total communication encouraged a better understanding of the English language by deaf children and assimilation of deaf people into the hearing culture (Moores, 2001). The data do not support these beliefs, but many older deaf people continue to use a total communication approach in their interaction with the hearing world.

Another important characteristic of the Deaf community is disassociation from speech—that is, communication without using the voice—called *voice off*. This communication strategy is very difficult for hearing people to understand and accept. The primary reason for voice off is that ASL does not follow English word order. Speech does not lend itself to ASL and, in fact, confuses communication for deaf people. Words mouthed do not follow visual cues. Second, and equally important, speech for a deaf person is an art. It is a very difficult skill to learn for a person with a severe hearing loss who has not heard words and sentences as a child. It is not similar to learning a second verbal language like French or Spanish. Also, it is potentially embarrassing for a deaf person to mouth words he or she cannot hear and to receive looks of disgust from hearing people who do not have a clue how difficult it is to pronounce words without auditory feedback.

Group social loyalty is another profound characteristic of the Deaf community. It is based not only on similarity of language but on relationships formed in schools for the deaf, clubs, sports activities, and marriage. There is a rich social and sports culture among deaf people, created in part by communication barriers which exist in many hearing activities. These unique social and sports cultures are illustrated in deaf performing arts and signed songs, the activities of the Deaf Olympics and the American Athletic Association of the Deaf, the performances of the National Theatre of the Deaf, the alliances and allegiances to state residential schools for the deaf and their social and athletic activities, and participation in deaf social clubs, which exist in most states. The Internet and text messaging have opened another link among deaf people through national and international blogs and websites that focus on Deaf culture.

The Deaf community is currently involved in a controversy with the medical world over a procedure for some deaf children and adults known as *cochlear implantation*. Each year, more than 1,000 deaf people (and the numbers are increasing annually) are surgically implanted with a device that directs electrical impulses to the cochlea to stimulate hearing. Not all people with hearing loss are candidates for a cochlear implant. Once implanted, the person begins a long course of rehabilitation and education that tailors the electronic device to the capabilities of the individual (Padden & Humphries, 2005). The results of this surgery, in terms of ability to hear speech, vary.

Many within the Deaf culture perceive cochlear implantation as the ultimate invasion of the ear; that is, the ultimate denial of deafness (Moore & Levitan, 2006). This concept is very difficult for hearing people to comprehend. According to Lane, Hoffmeister, and Bahan (1996), 14 national associations of the deaf around the world have published position papers disapproving of implant surgery on deaf people. Further, Lane, Hoffmeister, and Bahan (1996) state: "It is a tenet of Deaf culture that deaf people do not have an impairment merely by virtue of limited hearing. Deaf children in general are healthy, and it is unethical to operate on healthy children" (p. 401). Numerous deaf adults, even seniors, are being implanted. Hospice workers will be in contact with people who are implanted as well as some deaf people who have very strong negative or positive opinions about cochlear implantation.

THE GRIEVING PROCESS AND DEAFNESS

Is the impact of a hearing loss—whether for a Deaf person, hard-of-hearing person, or a late-deafened person—so profound that it negatively affects the person's psychosocial development, thinking, and feelings? The answer is debatable. Studies of the psychological development of deaf people have never shown a difference in basic psychological and social needs, drives, and ambitions between them and hearing people. Specific to the process of grieving related to end-of-life events or death, no studies indicate that people with hearing loss are any different from hearing people in their desire to survive illness; their need for support and companionship in dealing with a crisis; their fear of dying; their need to understand the meaning of life, death, and an afterlife; or their wish to provide a personal legacy for the future. In his inaugural address as the first deaf president of Gallaudet University (the world's only liberal arts university for deaf students), I. King Jordan said, "Deaf people can do anything a hearing person can but hear" (Gannon, 1989, p. 174). Fernando (2004), writing about the psychodynamic considerations in working with people who are deaf, notes that there is a tendency among hearing clinicians to overemphasize the differences between hearing and deaf people, and to minimize the similarities. In truth, there are more similarities among us, specifically in relation to the psychological dynamics of tragedy and death, than differences.

Nonetheless, for people born with a severe hearing loss and those who suffer a severe hearing loss later, the loss of auditory stimulation creates a very different life experience compared with that of their hearing peers, specifically in meeting their psychological and social needs and adapting to life crises. The loss of auditory stimulation specifically affects the style of interaction with the outside world, which can have a negative impact on the person's ability to accept a serious illness or impending death, to heal and recover, and to find a new way of life.

For people with hearing loss, when life-threatening illness or death of a family member occurs, complications can arise in receiving necessary information that can alter perceptions and behaviors, responding to situations or events through group activities or communication with others, and adapting to family and community life. It is not the medical condition of having a hearing loss per se that affects these processes of grieving. It is the deaf person's interaction with the hearing world (e.g., with hospitals, nursing homes, hospices, churches, and the community) that profoundly affects how he or she accomplishes grief-related activities. To provide the best hospice care for this population, healthcare workers must be sensitive to the nuances and possible difficulties of interaction as the deaf person proceeds through the processes of grief.

The following example will illustrate the difficulties of healing as a deaf person interacts with the hearing world. I worked with an elderly deaf male whose wife, also deaf, was dying and in the care of a hospice. Both of them used ASL as the major means of communicating with the world. The man described to me the impact his wife's death would have on his world. He told me that he would not only be losing his soul mate of 40 years and the mother of his children, but he would be losing his primary communication companion. He was about to experience a social and communication void that hearing people cannot comprehend. He gave me a vivid example.

This couple loved to cruise and had been doing so for the past 20 years. And yet, when they cruised with 200 other passengers, they might as well have been the only two people on the ship, because they were almost always the only people using ASL. During a 10-day voyage, they interacted only tangentially with their shipmates. Their enjoyment of a wonderful cruise was almost completely confined to themselves. This man asked me, "How can I go on without her? She was my communication link to our social lives, to happiness, and to my sense of being."

Deaf people are very much like hearing people in many ways. And yet, the world is a hearing world, and traversing through it is difficult at best for someone who is Deaf, hard of hearing, or late-deafened. It is our responsibility to be cognizant of the barriers deaf people face and adjust our services so they can achieve the same psychological comfort and healing as hearing clients in times of personal and family crisis.

How Hospice Workers Can Provide Support for Deaf People

The following specific, realistic recommendations and reminders are based on the variety of medical conditions that may exist among people who have a hearing loss, an understanding of the Deaf culture, and the technological and environmental needs of late-deafened and hard-of-hearing people. Hospice institutions and personnel should consider these recommendations in dealing with this population of clients.

Overcome audism. Eliminate audism in your practices, policies, and personal life. Humphrey and Alcorn (1995) define audism as "an attitude based on pathological thinking which results in a negative stigma toward anyone who does not hear—like racism or sexism. Audism judges, labels, and limits individuals on the basis of whether a person hears and speaks" (p. 85). Lane (1999) identifies "audists" as hearing people who discriminate against people who cannot hear, and makes the point that this attitude often exists among hearing people who have never even met a deaf person. In a recent book of essays and news columns on Deaf culture, Jon Heuer (2007), a self-identified member of the culture, frames the attitudinal concern in this way: He differentiates between hearing people with a small *h* and hearing people with a capital *H*. Heuer defines the *hearing* person as one who can hear, knows nothing about deafness, and admits it. He has no preconceived notions about what deaf people can or cannot do. On the other hand, Heuer defines *Hearing* people as those who have definitive opinions about what deafness is all about; opinions that are, most likely, in opposition to reason and logic.

Hospice workers individually, as well as hospice organizations systemically, must join the rest of society in working to eliminate audism, just as we work to eliminate sexism and racism. And just as combating sexism and racism is difficult, eliminating audism is equally difficult. The fact that some deaf people do not consider their deafness or their children's deafness as a medical disability is hard for hearing people to understand and accept. Embracing a visual communication system such as ASL as a language equal to the English language is also difficult for many hearing people to accept. But we must understand and accept that a change in attitude is the first and most important step hearing people can take to provide appropriate services to the Deaf, hard-of-hearing, and late-deafened clients we will meet in our social service positions.

Deal directly with the deaf person, not through hearing family members or friends. Interacting and communicating with people with a hearing loss takes more time and requires more preparation. Whether the issue is understanding the sign language system or speaking with someone who uses an auditory aid, the hospice worker will need to devote more time to preparing for the encounter and communicating directly with the person. Often, it is much easier to obtain the necessary information from a hearing family member or friend. But this is an insensitive approach, one that many deaf people are all too familiar with. The deaf person is left out of the communication loop, and decisions are made *for* him or her, not *with* him or her. Deaf people are quite capable of providing information and making life decisions when they are given the opportunity. Allow the deaf person the dignity of being directly involved in the process of hospice care.

If you use an interpreter, do so appropriately. A sign language interpreter will probably be necessary if the hospice client or a family member uses sign language. It is imperative that a qualified interpreter be hired. Most qualified interpreters are certified by the Registry of Interpreters for the Deaf, a national professional organization. The deaf person can probably tell you how to locate a qualified interpreter. It is important to solicit the deaf person's input; for example, does the deaf person prefer an ASL or simultaneous communication interpreter? Is there a specific person he or she has used previously, or an agency or interpreter to use—or to avoid? Be aware that some interpreters have expertise in medical or mental health situations and may be more appropriate choices to interpret in a hospice setting.

In an article about using interpreters in mental health settings, Turner, Klein, and Kitson (2000) describe three issues relevant to hiring interpreters for hospice services. First, the interpreter must maintain strict confidentiality. Second, the interpreter must communicate exactly what is being said and must not summarize or alter what is being said. Third, the interpreter must not inject his or her own feelings or opinions about what is being said. Hospice workers must address these issues when using sign language interpreters in their work with deaf clients.

Finally, except in emergencies or very brief encounters, avoid using family members or friends to interpret. Family members and friends certainly have the best interest of the deaf person in mind, and they often want to be helpful. But they are prone to answer for the client rather than interpret. In addition, confidentiality may be an important issue with loved ones or friends. Ask the client's permission before you allow a family member or friend to interpret.

All deaf people are not alike. Like any group, Deaf people, late-deafened people, and hard-of-hearing people are as diverse as the general population. The deafness facet is very important, but it does not overshadow other aspects of a person's life and background, such as gender, race, religion, economic status, education, age, and geography. All these elements play a vital role in the wants and needs of a deaf person. Expect diverse needs, customs, and behaviors in relation to end-of-life care and grief intervention strategies.

Communication is key. When all is said and done, a deaf person will tell you, "It's all about communication." Every effort should be made, by any means possible, to ensure that the client is fully aware of what is happening and is a participant in his or her plan of service. Use direct communication with the client, and pay attention to tangential communication as well. For example, professionals (hearing and deaf) who work around deaf people who sign are taught that any time a deaf person is present, they should use sign language, even if the conversation has nothing to do with the deaf person. Communication should be made as accessible as possible for the deaf person. In a perfect world, a hospice worker would be fluent in ASL or simultaneous communication. This is a goal that someday may be a reality.

Make your office accessible. The lives of deaf people have improved immensely as a result of technology. For more than 30 years, deaf people had no access to television and no access to telephone conversations with hearing people. For a long time, the only technology was the Telecommunication Device for the Deaf (TDD), an inexpensive piece of electronic hardware that attaches to the receiver of a land phone and transmits communication via the written word.

Young deaf people today tell me that the TDD is a relic of the past, but many older deaf people continue to use it. It is an excellent idea to have one in your office. Most elderly deaf clients will have a TDD in their homes and use them on a daily basis. Be aware also that telephone relay service is available nationwide. It is possible to make a voice phone call by dialing 711 to access a relay operator, who will communicate with the deaf person using a TDD.

The two forms of communication most used by educated deaf people and many young deaf people are text messaging and the videophone (VP), also called the picturephone. A BlackBerry or pager is a familiar piece of technology for deaf people. Most deaf professionals have access to this technology, although some older people may not. The VP is the communication technology of choice among educated professionals and young people. This technology allows live sign communication between two or more people, unlike the TDD and pager, which are limited to the written word. Access to these technologies can be very helpful to keep lines of communication open between deaf people and hospice personnel. As with the other recommendations, it is the responsibility of the hospice personnel to ask the deaf client what his or her preference is regarding means of communication.

Adjust the environment and eliminate bad personal habits. Eliminating auditory and lighting distractions can significantly help a deaf person communicate. Background music and office chatter can interfere with auditory aid transmission, and some personal habits can interfere with communication. A person who is trying to lip-read can become confused if the professional is chewing gum or talking with her hand over her mouth. In group situations, two people talking at once is confusing. Talking with your back to the deaf person will prevent him or her from participating in the dialogue. Small behavioral adaptations related to bad communication habits can be a great help to someone who must rely on visual cues to understand what you are saying.

Ensure that people understand written materials. Our ease in using the English language is based on auditory input and feedback. Many people who are born deaf have difficulty with the written word; the average person in this group reads at the sixth to eighth grade level. Thus, written hospice materials can be confusing. It is incumbent on the hospice staff to be sensitive to this concern and make sure that deaf people understand written materials. This issue is usually not a concern with late-deafened or hard-of-hearing persons.

Consider including a member of a disability group on your advisory board. Having a member of a disability group—perhaps a deaf person—on your advisory board is a powerful symbol of your organization's commitment to diversity and empowerment. It sends a clear message to the community of your organization's concern and willingness to serve all people. While it can be time-consuming and possibly costly (you may have to hire interpreters on a regular basis), it shows your commitment to provide appropriate services to this large and important segment of your community.

CONCLUSION

Hospice workers are bound to come in contact with deaf clients through their work. I believe most hospice workers and agencies want to ensure that all clients—including deaf people—receive the most competent, thorough, and qualified services possible. A better understanding of this population, along with some small changes in attitude and behavior, can make a big difference in ensuring the best hospice care for the next deaf person you serve.

Frank R. Zieziula, PhD, LPC, is a professor of counseling in the graduate school at Gallaudet University in Washington, D.C. For more than 30 years, he has trained mental health and school counselors to work with deaf children, adolescents, and adults. He is a graduate of New York University and a licensed professional counselor in the District of Columbia. He holds national certifications in clinical mental health and professional counseling. In addition to his teaching responsibilities, he has been a consultant to the National Fallen Firefighters Association in Emmitsburg, Maryland, and the Wendt Center for Loss and Healing in the District of Columbia. He has been a member of the Association of Death Education and Counseling (ADEC) for more than 15 years and has taught a number of ADEC certification courses in grief counseling. He has edited a book on psychological assessment of deaf people and has published a number of articles in professional journals, including American Annals of the Deaf.

REFERENCES

Canadian Census. Retrieved on July 8, 2008, from http:///www.CAD.CA/en/ issues/Canada_census.asp

Fernando, J. (2004). Psychodynamic considerations in working with people who are deaf. In S. Austen & S. Crocker (Eds.), *Deafness in mind: Working psychologically with Deaf people across the lifespan* (pp. 75–88). London: Whurr Publishers Ltd.

Gannon, J. R. (1989). *The week the world heard Gallaudet.* Washington, DC: Gallaudet University Press.

Heuer, C. J. (2007). *Bug: Deaf identity and internal revolution.* Washington, DC: Gallaudet University Press.

Holcomb, R. K., Holcomb, S. K., & Holcomb, T. K. (1994). *Deaf culture: Our way.* San Diego: DawnSign Press.

Humphrey, J. H., & Alcorn, B. J. (1995). *So you want to be an interpreter: An introduction to sign language.* Amarillo, TX: H&H Publishers.

Lane, H. (1999). *The mask of benevolence: Disabling the Deaf community.* San Diego: DawnSign Press.

Lane, H., Hoffmeister, R., & Bahan, B. (1996). *A journey into the deaf-world.* San Diego: DawnSign Press.

Liddell, S. (2003). *Grammar, gesture, and meaning in American Sign Language.* Cambridge, MA: Cambridge University Press.

Moore, M. S., & Levitan, L. (2006). *For hearing people only* (3rd ed.). Rochester, NY: Deaf Life Press.

Moores, D. F. (2001). *Educating the Deaf: Psychology, principles, and practices* (5th ed.). Boston: Houghton Mifflin Company.

National Center for Health Statistics. (1994). *National Health Interview Survey, 10,* 188.

Padden, C. (1989). The Deaf community and the culture of Deaf people. In S. Wilcox (Ed.), *American Deaf culture* (pp. 1–16). Burtonsville, MD: Linstock Press, Inc.

Padden, C., & Humphries, T. (2005). *Inside Deaf culture.* Cambridge, MA: Harvard University Press.

Stokoe, W., Casterline, D., & Groneberg, C. (1976). *Dictionary of American Sign Language on linguistic principles.* Burtonsville, MD: Linstock Press, Inc.

Turner, J., Klein, H., & Kitson, N. (2000). Interpreters in mental health settings. In P. Hindley & N. Kitson (Eds.), *Mental health and deafness* (pp. 297–310). Philadelphia: Whurr Publishers.

CHAPTER 16

Assessment and Management of Posttraumatic Stress Disorder in Palliative Care Patients

Vyjeyanthi S. Periyakoil

W e live in traumatic times, and trauma is ubiquitous in our world. Studies show that large numbers of Americans have been exposed to some type of trauma during their lifetime (Breslau, Davis, Andreski, & Peterson, 1991; Norris, 1992; Vrana & Lauterbach, 1994). The fourth edition of the *Diagnostic and Statistical Manual of Mental Disorders (DSM IV TR)* (American Psychiatric Association, 2000) defines "trauma" as any event that a person experiences, witnesses, or is confronted with that threatens death or serious injury, or is a threat to the physical integrity of oneself or others. Not all persons exposed to trauma develop posttraumatic stress disorder (PTSD), but about 25% of those who have been exposed to trauma go on to develop PTSD during their lifetime (Breslau et al., 1991).

WHAT IS PTSD?

PTSD is an anxiety disorder that can develop when a person has experienced, witnessed, or been confronted with a traumatic event. The *DSM IV TR* classifies PTSD as an anxiety disorder characterized by a triggering trauma, followed by a series of intense negative emotional responses to the trauma as follows:

1. **Triggering trauma.** Exposure to an extreme traumatic stressor involving one of the following:
   a. Direct personal experience of an event that involves actual or threatened death or serious injury (natural or technological disaster, mass violence, war, illness, etc.).
   b. Other threat to one's physical integrity.
   c. Witnessing an event that involves death or injury.
   d. A threat to the physical integrity of another person.

    e. Learning about the unexpected or violent death, serious harm, threat of death, or injury experienced by a family member or other close associate. A large epidemiologic study has shown that PTSD in community dwellers is especially common in persons who have experienced the sudden and unexpected death of a loved one (Breslau et al., 1998).

2. **Response to trauma.** The person's response to the traumatic event must involve intense fear, helplessness, or horror.

3. **Three characteristic symptom clusters.**

    a. *Persistent reexperiencing* of the traumatic event, or "flashbacks." Recurrent and intrusive distressing recollections of the event—including images, thoughts, or perceptions—may occur. In young children, aspects of the trauma may be expressed during play. Recurrent distressing dreams may occur. Young children may experience frightening dreams without recognizable content. A person who is suffering from PTSD may act or feel as if the event is recurring repeatedly; he or she may relive the experience or have hallucinations or dissociative flashback episodes. Symbols of the traumatic event may trigger intense psychological distress as well as a physical and physiological response to the psychological distress.

    b. *Persistent avoidance* of stimuli associated with the trauma and numbing of general responsiveness, including efforts to avoid thoughts or feelings associated with the trauma; efforts to avoid activities, places, and people that recall the trauma; inability to recall important aspects of the trauma; feelings of detachment from others; restricted range of affect (e.g., inability to have loving feelings); a sense of a foreshortened future (e.g., inability to foresee a marriage, career, children, etc.).

    c. *Persistent hyperarousal,* including hypervigilance, difficulty falling asleep and staying asleep, irritability or outbursts, difficulty concentrating, or an exaggerated startle response.

4. **Duration.** The full symptom picture must be present for more than 1 month. (Note that the full symptom picture can occur either immediately after the trauma or at any time later in the person's life.)

5. **Functional impairment.** The disturbance must cause clinically significant distress or impairment in social, occupational, or other important areas of functioning.

Risk Factors

PTSD often coexists with anxiety, depression, and substance abuse. Risk factors for PTSD include a history of child abuse, chronic mental illnesses, female gender, and ethnic minority status. PTSD is more common in Hispanics and African Americans, because it is thought that people from these groups are more likely to have experienced trauma. PTSD is also more common in war veterans, with an estimated prevalence of about 30% in Vietnam veterans, 10% in Desert Storm veterans, 6%–11% in Enduring Freedom (Afghanistan) veterans, and 12%–20% in Iraqi Freedom veterans (Boscarino, 2008). PTSD can develop at any age, including during childhood. Symptoms of PTSD typically begin within 3 months of the triggering traumatic event, although occasionally they do not begin until years later.

Memory Impairment

PTSD patients report deficits in declarative memory (remembering facts or lists), fragmentation of memories (both autobiographical and trauma related), and dissociative amnesia (gaps in memory that can occur for anywhere from minutes to days and are not due to ordinary forgetting). Trauma-related memory can be triggered by somatosensory triggers; for example, a terminally ill patient with PTSD due to a history of sexual trauma may present with agitation and flashbacks when the hospice nurse helps her with bathing or toileting. Pain related to the terminal illness may trigger repeated flashbacks for a PTSD patient who was tortured as a prisoner of war.

Physical Health Status

PTSD is associated with poor physical health, and PTSD patients demonstrate high-risk health behaviors. An estimated 21% of adults in the United States currently smoke, but the figure is 45% for PTSD sufferers. Research indicates a direct link between severe stress exposure and a broad spectrum of diseases. Boscarino (2008), who studied the long-term health effects of PTSD on Vietnam veterans, demonstrated that PTSD significantly raises the risk of premature death from heart disease.

PTSD IN PALLIATIVE CARE PATIENTS

Virtually no research addresses the intersection of PTSD and terminal illness (Feldman & Periyakoil, 2006). Patients with cancer have a higher incidence of PTSD than the general population; however, it is unclear whether the terminal illness is the instigating trauma or is a trigger for preexisting PTSD.

PTSD has a strong impact on the trajectory and experience of terminal illness:

- PTSD is associated with premature mortality and morbidity.
- PTSD is co-morbid with depression and other chronic mental illnesses.
- The threat to life inherent in any terminal illness may mimic the original trigger trauma, leading to exacerbation of previously mild PTSD symptoms due to *chronic PTSD*. It may also precipitate new symptoms due to *delayed onset PTSD* symptoms and lead to significant distress for the patient and family.
- It is possible that the trauma related to the diagnosis and manifestations of cancer and other terminal illnesses could precipitate new onset acute stress disorder or acute PTSD, although further research is needed to gain a better understanding of this process.

PTSD Complicates the Dying Process

PTSD symptoms overlap with those of terminal illness. These common symptoms include pain, appetite or weight changes, fatigue and low energy, sleep disturbances, difficulty concentrating, diminished interest in usual activities, feelings of isolation, and a sense of a foreshortened future.

PTSD also skews the normal process of dying in the following ways:

- PTSD is associated with chronic pain syndromes. It is associated with poor coping skills and can thus amplify the distress or lead to refractory pain and nonpain symptoms. Many terminally ill patients suffer from pain, dyspnea, nausea, fatigue, and many other symptoms that could be exacerbated by PTSD.
- PTSD is co-morbid with smoking, substance abuse, depression, and suicidality, as well as other chronic mental illnesses that can significantly skew the dying process.
- Avoidance symptoms are central to the diagnosis (Amir et al., 1997; Bryant & Harvey, 1995; Bryant, Marosszeky, Crooks, Baguley, & Gurka, 2000; Payne & Massie, 2000). This can lead to poor medical adherence and may result in communication challenges (Shamesh et al., 2004).
- When key memories are trauma related, the normal process of life review (Butler, 1963) can lead to intense anxiety, sadness, guilt, or anger.
- Patients with PTSD tend to be socially isolated (see Table 1) and have poor support systems.

Table 1

PTSD Symptoms and Palliative Care Implications

PTSD SYMPTOMS	PRESENTATION AND IMPLICATIONS
Reexperiencing the traumatic event	• Intrusive, distressing recollections of the trigger trauma with or without intrusive recollections of the terminal diagnosis and persistent thoughts of death and dying. • Flashbacks: Feeling as if the traumatic event is recurring while awake. • Nightmares about the traumatic event or frightening images of death and dying that recur frequently in dreams. Patients may be wary of opioids and other soporific medications because they precipitate nightmares. • Exaggerated emotional and physical reactions to triggers that remind the person of the trauma. The terminal illness itself may serve as a constant reminder of the trigger trauma.
Avoidance	• Patients may avoid thoughts, feelings, or conversations related to the terminal illness, its implications, and necessary therapy. They may become noncompliant and noncooperative.
Emotional numbing	• Loss of interest, loss of pleasure: May be due to PTSD or co-morbid depression. • Feeling detached from others: Dissociation, common in PTSD, leads to social isolation and lack of caregiver support. • Restricted emotions related to the terminal illness process skews the process of life review commonly seen in a palliative care setting.

PTSD SYMPTOMS	PRESENTATION AND IMPLICATIONS
Increased arousal	• Irritability or outbursts of anger alienate healthcare teams as well as family and caregivers. • Hypervigilance in the setting of a terminal illness and associated fatigue and lack of energy lead to patient exhaustion. • Difficulty concentrating has negative consequences for PTSD patients who may have to adhere to the complex therapeutic regimens mandated by a terminal illness. • Difficulty sleeping is common in a palliative care setting; this can be exacerbated by insomnia and nightmares related to PTSD.

Source: Materials for the module on Posttraumatic Stress Syndrome created by V.S. Periyakoil, MD, for the CancerPEN Project (http://ecampus.stanford.edu).

For all these reasons, terminally ill patients with PTSD may be less likely to access and benefit from needed palliative care services on an ongoing basis.

Assessment of PTSD in a Palliative Care Setting

It has been well documented that, like many other chronic mental illnesses, PTSD is underdiagnosed and undertreated; this is especially true in the palliative care setting. Even when clinicians identify a patient's symptoms, they often fail to correctly diagnose PTSD, instead identifying related symptoms of depression and anxiety (Samson, Bensen, Beck, Price, & Nimmer, 1999). In addition, many healthcare providers hesitate to ask about sensitive issues such as sexual trauma or combat experiences, because they are concerned about potential negative consequences for the patient. However, research has demonstrated that while it may be painful for some patients to discuss traumatic life incidents, most feel supported by the opportunity to speak about their experiences (Zatzick et al., 2001). Exploratory questioning about past events as part of eliciting social and occupational history is quite effective. A brief and validated inventory such as Prins and colleagues' four-item questionnaire (2003) is a structured and very effective screening tool for PTSD in a primary care setting (see Table 2). The tool screens for intrusive thoughts, avoidance, hypervigilance, and numbness or detachment; it is considered positive for PTSD if the patient has two out of four symptoms. We have successfully used it in both inpatient and outpatient palliative care settings, and our clinical experience has shown that even one positive answer out of four warrants further investigation.

Table 2

PTSD SCREENING QUESTIONNAIRE
In your life, have you ever had any experience that was so frightening, horrible, or upsetting that *in the past month,* you… 1. Have had nightmares about it or thought about it when you did not want to? 2. Tried hard not to think about it or went out of your way to avoid situations that reminded you of it? 3. Were constantly on guard, watchful, or easily startled? 4. Felt numb or detached from others, activities, or your surroundings?
The screen is positive if patient answers "yes" to any two of the four questions. However, according to the author's clinical experience, it is important to keep a high index of suspicion even if the patient answers "yes" to one of the four questions.
Source: Prins et al., 2003.

Many terminally ill patients have fleeting thoughts of death and suicide; these thoughts are more pronounced in PTSD patients. Thus, in patients with depression and/or PTSD, the clinician should gently explore for the presence of suicidality (Oquendo et al., 2005). The presence of severe symptomatology or clear suicidality should always trigger referral to a mental health professional for further assessment and management.

MANAGEMENT OF PTSD IN A PALLIATIVE CARE SETTING

The key to management of PTSD is sensitive and thorough assessment and a patient-centered approach: making services available when they are needed, treating patients with dignity and respect, and allowing patients to share in decision making. Interweaving psychosocial support, pharmacological therapy, and high-quality palliative care can alleviate the distress of life-limiting illness

(Feldman & Periyakoil, 2006; Henbest & Stewart, 1989; Penk & Flannery, 2000; Williams, Weinman, & Dale, 1998). See Table 3.

Psychosocial Management of PTSD

High-quality psychosocial management of PTSD in a palliative care setting is challenging for the following reasons:

a. Lack of evidence-based guidelines on the appropriate psychosocial management of PTSD in patients with advanced illnesses.
b. Shortage of mental health professionals in the palliative care arena (Feldman & Periyakoil, 2006).
c. Inability of many palliative care patients to participate in and complete conventional psychosocial therapeutic interventions for PTSD. In addition, most psychosocial treatments require considerable time investment, which may not be feasible for vulnerable patients who have a limited prognosis and frequent medical appointments, and are struggling with treatment-related side effects.

Table 3

A FRAMEWORK FOR PROVIDING PSYCHOSOCIAL SUPPORT FOR PTSD PATIENTS	
Assess	• Use gentle exploratory questioning and screening tools to assess for type and intensity of symptoms. • Assess for specific somatosensory triggers that precipitate flashbacks. • Assess for history/presence of co-morbid mental illness, suicidality, and recreational drug use.
Align	• Take an egalitarian stance with the patient.
Affirm	• Assure the patient of your support. • Emphasize the patient's control over medical decisions.

A FRAMEWORK FOR PROVIDING PSYCHOSOCIAL SUPPORT FOR PTSD PATIENTS	
Act	• Educate the patient and family members. • Educate fellow healthcare team members. • Provide nonpharmacological therapeutic interventions (e.g., massage therapy, guided imagery, aromatherapy, counseling). • Identify mental health professionals with expertise in PTSD management so you can consult them should the need arise. • If you are a mental health professional, consider adapting your therapeutic interventions (cognitive behavioral therapy, psychotherapy) to the needs of the patient and the patient's prognosis.

Source: Materials for the module on Posttraumatic Stress Syndrome created by V.S. Periyakoil, MD, for the CancerPEN Project (http://ecampus.stanford.edu).

Thus, psychosocial management of PTSD in a palliative care setting may fall to the medical providers. Fortunately, physicians and nurses are in an excellent position to listen, provide emotional support, normalize patients' experiences, and encourage patients to enlist help from friends and family (Oquendo et al., 2005). Additionally, it is critically important that physicians and nurses caring for PTSD patients seek help from colleagues with mental health and counseling expertise and work collaboratively to augment patient outcomes (Periyakoil, 2008).

The following are some other key variables that may help structure care of PTSD patients in a palliative care setting:

Terminal illness per se as a triggering traumatic event. Cancer diagnosis can cause new incidence of PTSD. Many patients with advanced illness suffer from many distressing symptoms. The terminal illness diagnosis may be traumatic to the patient and may add to the cumulative lifetime trauma load, thereby precipitating or exacerbating PTSD symptoms. As the illness advances, most patients lose functionality and become dependent on others for their care needs. Such dependence may make the patient feel helpless and thus mimic the primary trauma—for example, a rape victim who receives help with bathing and toileting or a former prisoner of war who is bedbound and feels like a "prisoner" in his home. A painful medical procedure may flash a delirious patient back to a past traumatic experience.

Avoidance in PTSD patients. Avoidance is a very common coping strategy in PTSD that undermines patient-physician communication (Amir et al., 1997; Bryant & Harvey, 1995; Bryant et al., 2000; Payne & Massie, 2000; Shamesh et al., 2004). Most patients with terminal illness struggle with increased fatigue, distressing pain and nonpain symptoms, social isolation, fiscal challenges, and spiritual and existential questions. These symptoms may increase the avoidance behaviors, leading to alienation from clinicians and loved ones alike. PTSD patients often are distrustful of authority (especially if the clinicians are perceived to be very directive), which may lead to lack of adherence to therapeutic interventions. This causes the clinicians to view the patient as uncooperative and hostile, leading to issues related to transference and countertransference. Creating a therapeutic alliance with the patient, with a strong emphasis on egalitarianism (Feldman & Periyakoil, 2006), and fostering the patient's sense of self-determination and control can help circumvent suspicion and reduce avoidance. Using principles of patient-centered and collaborative care, and gentle persistence, the clinician can gain the patient's trust and thereby provide comfort and solace to the traumatized palliative care patient. Urgent mental health consultation should be sought if a patient exhibits dysfunctional behaviors such as hostile outbursts, or seems to threaten harm to self or others.

When to seek psychiatric consultation in palliative care patients with PTSD? Consider a psychiatric consultation for patients experiencing intense PTSD symptoms, including severe agitation, hyperarousal, and hostility.

All PTSD patients should be assessed for suicidality. Suicidality as a result of PTSD and clinical depression should be differentiated from the fleeting thoughts of death often seen in a palliative care setting. While preliminary assessment for suicidal ideation can be performed by the palliative care team, it is recommended that patients with persistent thoughts of death and suicide be referred to a mental health professional and placed under close and continuous observation until the crisis has passed.

Pharmacotherapy of PTSD patients

Selective serotonin reuptake inhibitors (SSRIs) are the drug of choice for PTSD. The U.S. Food and Drug Administration (FDA) has approved sertraline and paroxetine for PTSD. Other SSRIs—such as citalopram, escitalopram, fluoxetine, and fluvoxamine—are also effective and well tolerated. SSRIs help palliate all symptom groups (reexperiencing, avoidance, hyperarousal). Tricyclic antidepressants (TCAs) are the second line for treatment of PTSD. TCAs are thought to alleviate intrusive symptoms, anxiety, depression, and insomnia.

When using the narcotic analgesic class of drugs (morphine, oxycodone, methadone, etc.) to treat pain in PTSD patients, clinicians should remember that these patients are at more than a fourfold risk of drug misuse and dependence. Patients with even a remote history of recreational opioid use may need high doses of opioids to control their illness-related pain. These patients are also more prone to refractory pain syndromes and require skilled palliative care services. Also, research suggests that drug abuse or dependence in persons with PTSD might be caused by efforts to self-medicate.

Some terminally ill patients who are on narcotic analgesics or sedative hypnotics (benzodiazepines like lorazepam, diazepam, etc.) for palliation are unable to dissociate from their trauma-related memories. Opioids and benzodiazepines may precipitate distressing flashbacks and nightmares in these patients. These patients refuse to take the opioids as prescribed even in the face of severe pain.

Patient and Clinician Education

Ongoing patient, family, and clinician education is necessary for PTSD management. Psychoeducation is a key component of many psychotherapies for PTSD, and adapting psychoeducation to suit the needs of the terminally ill patient is likely to secure patient cooperation (Penk & Flannery, 2000). Clinical education is also a critical component of PTSD management.

CONCLUSION

Traumatic life events are very common. Currently, 7.8% of Americans have a diagnosis of PTSD (Kessler, Sonnega, Bromet, Hughes, & Nelson, 1995). About 1.2 million Americans die every year. Thus, an estimated 94,000 dying Americans will struggle with PTSD every year. PTSD symptoms are extremely distressing, underdiagnosed, and undertreated. Systematic assessment and appropriate management of PTSD will greatly diminish the suffering and improve the quality of life for palliative care patients and their families.

Vyjeyanthi (VJ) Periyakoil, MD, *is a nationally recognized leader in palliative care. She is a clinical assistant professor of medicine at Stanford University School of Medicine, and she directs the Stanford University Hospice and Palliative Medicine Fellowship Program and the U.S. Veterans Affairs Palo Alto Interprofessional Palliative Care Fellowship program. Her current projects focus on cross-cultural issues in aging and the end of life. In addition, she has a special interest in the pedagogy of virtual education. A free full-text palliative care online curriculum directed by Periyakoil can be obtained from http://endoflife.stanford.edu. The comprehensive Cancer Palliation Education Network curriculum directed by Periyakoil can be accessed at http://ecampus.stanford.edu.*

REFERENCES

American Psychiatric Association. (2000). *Diagnostic and statistical manual of mental disorders* (4th ed.). Washington, DC: American Psychiatric Association.

Amir, M., Kaplan, Z., Efroni, R., Levine, Y., Benjamin, J., & Kotler, M. (1997). Coping styles in posttraumatic stress disorder (PTSD) patients. *Personality and Individual Differences, 23,* 399–405.

Boscarino, J. A. (1997). Diseases among men 20 years after exposure to severe stress: Implications for clinical research and medical care. *Psychosomatic Medicine, 59*(6), 605–614.

Boscarino, J. A. (2006). Posttraumatic stress disorder and mortality among U.S. Army veterans 30 years after military service. *Annals of Epidemiology, 16*(4), 248–256.

Boscarino, J. A. (2008). A prospective study of PTSD and early-age heart disease mortality among Vietnam veterans: Implications for surveillance and prevention. *Psychosomatic Medicine, 70*(6), 668–676.

Boscarino, J. A., & Chang, J. (1999). Higher abnormal leukocyte and lymphocyte counts 20 years after exposure to severe stress: Research and clinical implications. *Psychosomatic Medicine, 61*(3), 378–386.

Breslau, N., Davis, G. C., Andreski, P., & Peterson, E. (1991). Traumatic events and posttraumatic stress disorder in an urban population of young adults. *Archives of General Psychiatry, 48,* 216–222.

Breslau, N., Kessler, R. C., Chilcoat, H. D., Schultz, L. R., Davis, G. C., & Andreski, P. (1998). Trauma and posttraumatic stress disorder in the community: The 1996 Detroit area survey of trauma. *Archives of General Psychiatry, 55*(7), 626–32.

Breslau, N., Roth, T., Burduvali, E., Kapke, A., Schultz, L., & Roehrs, T. (2004). Sleep in lifetime posttraumatic stress disorder: A community-based polysomnographic study. *Archives of General Psychiatry, 61,* 508–516.

Brett, E. A., & Ostroff, V. (1985). Imagery and posttraumatic stress disorder. *American Journal of Psychiatry, 142,* 417–424.

Bryant, R. A., & Harvey, A. G. (1995). Avoidant coping style and post-traumatic stress following motor vehicle accidents. *Behaviour Research and Therapy, 33,* 631–635.

Bryant, R. A., Marosszeky, J. E., Crooks, J., Baguley, I., & Gurka, J. (2000). Coping style and post-traumatic stress disorder following severe traumatic brain injury. *Brain Injury, 14,* 175–180.

Butler, R. N. (1963). The life review: An interpretation of reminiscence in the aged. *Psychiatry, 26,* 65–76.

Calhoun, P. S., Dennis, M. F., & Beckham, J. C. (2007). Emotional reactivity to trauma stimuli and duration of past smoking cessation attempts in smokers with posttraumatic stress disorder. *Experimental and Clinical Psychopharmacology, 15,* 256–263.

Centers for Disease Control and Prevention. (2006). Fact sheet: Adult cigarette smoking in the United States, current estimates. Washington, DC: U.S. Department of Health and Human Services.

Davidson, J., Baldwin, D., Stein, D. J., Kuper, E., Benattia, I., Ahmed, S., et al. (2006). Treatment of posttraumatic stress disorder with Venlafaxine Extended Release: A 6-month randomized controlled trial. *Archives of General Psychiatry, 63,* 1158–1165.

Davidson, J., Rothbaum, B. O., Van der Kolk, B. A., Sikes, C. R., & Farfel, G. M. (2001). Multicenter double-blind comparison of sertraline and placebo in the treatment of posttraumatic stress disorder. *Archives of General Psychiatry, 58,* 485–492.

Feldman, D. B., & Periyakoil, V. S. (2006). Posttraumatic stress disorder at the end of life. *Journal of Palliative Medicine, 9*(1), 213–218.

Feldner, M. T., Babson, K. A., & Zvolensky, M. J. (2007). Smoking, traumatic event exposure, and post-traumatic stress: A critical review of the empirical literature. *Clinical Psychology Review, 27*, 14–45.

Foa, E. B., Molnar, C., & Cashman, L. (1995). Change in rape narratives during exposure therapy for posttraumatic stress disorder. *Journal of Traumatic Stress, 8*, 675–690.

Geuze, E., Westenberg, H., Jochims, A., De Kloet, C. S., Bohus, M., Vermetten, E., et al. (2007). Altered pain processing in veterans with posttraumatic stress disorder. *Archives of General Psychiatry, 64*, 76–85.

Hamner, M. B., Robert, S., & Frueh, B. C. (2004). Treatment-resistant posttraumatic stress disorder: Strategies for intervention. *CNS Spectrums, 9*, 740–752.

Helzer, J. E., Robins, L. N., & McEvoy, L. (1987). Post-traumatic stress disorder in the general population. *New England Journal of Medicine, 317*, 1630–1643.

Henbest, R. J., & Stewart, M. E. (1989). Patient-centeredness in the consultation: A method for measurement. *Family Practice, 6*, 249–253.

Kessler, R. C., Sonnega, A., Bromet, E., Hughes, M., & Nelson, C. B. (1995). Posttraumatic stress disorder in the National Comorbidity Survey. *Archives of General Psychiatry, 52*, 1048–1060.

Koenen, K. C., Hitsman, B., Lyons, M. J., Niaura, R., McCafferty, J., Goldberg, J., et al. (2005). A twin registry study of the relationship between posttraumatic stress disorder and nicotine dependence in men. *Archives of General Psychiatry, 62*, 1258–1265.

Marshall, R. D., & Pierce, D. (2000). Implications of recent findings in posttraumatic stress disorder and the role of pharmacotherapy. *Harvard Review of Psychiatry, 7*, 247–256.

Marshall, R. D., Schneier, F. R., Fallon, B. A., Knight, C. B., Abbate, L. A., Goetz, D., et al. (1998). An open trial of paroxetine in patients with noncombat-related, chronic posttraumatic stress disorder. *Journal of Clinical Psychopharmacology, 18*, 10–18.

Morissette, S. B., Tull, M. T., Gulliver, S. B., Kamholz, B. W., & Zimering, R. T. (2007). Anxiety, anxiety disorders, tobacco use, and nicotine: A critical review of interrelationships. *Psychological Bulletin, 133*, 245–272.

Norris, F. H. (1992). Epidemiology of trauma: Frequency and impact of different potentially traumatic events on different demographic groups. *Journal of Consulting and Clinical Psychology, 60,* 409–418.

Oquendo, M., Brent, D. A., Birmaher, B., Greenhill, L., Kolko, D., Stanley, B., et al. (2005). Posttraumatic stress disorder co-morbid with major depression: Factors mediating the association with suicidal behavior. *American Journal of Psychiatry, 162,* 560–566.

Payne, D. K., & Massie, M. J. (2000). Anxiety in palliative care. In H. M. Chochinov & W. Breitbart (Eds.), *Handbook of psychiatry in palliative medicine* (pp. 63–74). New York: Oxford.

Pearlstein, T. (2000). Antidepressant treatment of posttraumatic stress disorder. *Journal of Clinical Psychiatry, 61,* 40–43.

Penk, W., & Flannery, R. B. (2000). Psychosocial rehabilitation. In E. B. Foa, T. M. Keane, & M. J. Friedman (Eds.), *Effective treatments for PTSD: Practice guidelines from the International Society for Traumatic Stress Studies* (pp. 224–246). New York: Guilford.

Periyakoil, V. S. (2008). Growing pains: Health care enters "team" age. *Journal of Palliative Medicine, 11*(2), 171–175.

Prins, A., Ouimette, P., Kimerling, R., Cameron, R. P., Hugelshofer, D. S., Shaw, H. J., et al. (2003). The primary care PTSD screen (PC-PTSD): Development and operating characteristics. *Primary Care Psychiatry, 9,* 9–14.

Samson, A. Y., Bensen, S., Beck, A., Price, D., & Nimmer, C. (1999). Posttraumatic stress disorder in primary care. *Journal of Family Practice, 48,* 222–227.

Saxon, A. J., Davis, T. M., Sloan, K. L., McKnight, K. M., McFall, M. E., & Kivlahan, D. R. (2001). Trauma, symptoms of posttraumatic stress disorder, and associated problems among incarcerated veterans. *Psychatric Services, 52*(7), 959–964.

Shamesh, E., Yehuda, R., Milo, O., Dinur, I., Rudnick, A., Vered. Z., et al. (2004). Posttraumatic stress, nonadherence, and adverse outcome in survivors of myocardial infarction. *Psychosomatic Medicine, 66,* 521–526.

U.S. Department of Health and Human Services. (2004). *The health consequences of smoking: A report of the Surgeon General.* Washington, DC: U.S. Department of Health and Human Services.

Van der Kolk, B. A. (1994). The body keeps the score: Memory and the evolving psychobiology of posttraumatic stress. *Harvard Review of Psychiatry, 1,* 253–265.

Van der Kolk, B. A., Burbridge, J., & Suzuki, J. (1997). The psychobiology of traumatic memory: Clinical implications of neuroimaging studies. *Annals of the New York Academy of Sciences, 821,* 99–113.

Van der Kolk, B. A., & Fisler, R. (1995). Dissociation and the fragmentary nature of traumatic memories: Overview and exploratory study. *Journal of Traumatic Stress, 8,* 505–525.

Van der Kolk, B. A., Hopper, J., & Osterman, J. (2001). Exploring the nature of traumatic memories: Combining clinical knowledge with laboratory methods. *Journal of Aggression, Maltreatment, and Trauma, 4*(2), 9–31.

Van der Kolk, B. A., & Van der Hart, O. (1991). The intrusive past: The flexibility of memory and the engraving of trauma. *American Imago, 48,* 425–454.

Vrana, S., & Lauterbach, D. (1994). Prevalence of traumatic events and post-traumatic psychological symptoms in a nonclinical sample of college students. *Journal of Traumatic Stress, 7,* 289–302.

Williams, S., Weinman, J., & Dale, J. (1998). Doctor-patient communication and patient satisfaction: A review. *Family Practice, 15,* 480–492.

Zatzick, D. F., Kang, S. M., Hinton, W. L., Kelly, R. H., Hilty, D. M., Franz, C. E., et al. (2001). Posttraumatic concerns: A patient-centered approach to outcome assessment after traumatic physical injury. *Medical Care, 39,* 327–339.

Men, Women, and Loss: Changing Perspectives on Gender and Grief

Kenneth J. Doka

Gender influences the way we experience, express, and adapt to grief. In years past, gender was thought to be a primary determinant in how we experience grief. Today, researchers and practitioners recognize that gender is only one of many factors that influence how we grieve.

Corr, Nabe, and Corr (2009) note three distinct perspectives regarding the relationship between grief and gender. The first perspective, labeled the *feminization of grief*, stressed that expressing emotion and seeking social support is critical to effectively cope with loss. This focus on affective expression was generic to the counseling field. Sue and Sue (2008) criticize this bias toward emotional disclosure and claim that it has inhibited work with cultural groups that value emotional control and restraint. Additionally, much of the early research on grief was based on widows—hence their modes of dealing with loss were often perceived as a normative standard. Staudacher (1991), for example, asserted that "there is only one way to grieve" that is, "only by experiencing the necessary emotional effects of your loved one's death" (p. 3). Using this perspective, men are seen to have difficulties in coping with grief. "This does not mean that men are not grieving; it does indicate that they may not accomplish the task as successfully as women" (LeGrand, 1986, p. 31).

A second perspective proposed that men have their own distinct patterns of grief. These patterns emphasize mental, active, and problem-solving approaches to grief. With this perspective, men might show more limited and muted emotional responses to loss, such as anger or guilt. Men were thought to value self-reliance and solitude in coping with loss. While men had a different experience of grief, their methods of coping were seen as no less effective than those of women. It was recognized, then, that counseling interventions should not challenge men's way of coping, but rather should find ways to deal with loss congruent with masculine inclinations. This perspective of men's grief often drew from anthropological sources that ritualized gender differences in grief as well as literature that emphasized biological differences between the genders (Golden, 1996; Lund, 2000).

Martin and Doka's early work (1996, 1998) began to transition to a perspective less focused on gender. They described a *masculine* and *feminine* pattern of grief. With the masculine pattern, individuals often exhibit more mental and active responses toward grief. In the feminine pattern, the experience and expression of grief was more emotive and expressive. By describing masculine and feminine patterns, Martin and Doka were beginning to move away from the idea that grief responses were inextricably linked to gender. From this perspective, while men were more likely to experience a masculine pattern of grief, gender was only one factor among others that determined grieving patterns.

Later work by Martin and Doka (2000) completed the transition to a third perspective that placed even less value on gender as a critical determinant for how people grieve. They proposed a continuum of grieving styles from an *intuitive* style, where grief is experienced and expressed in more affective ways, to an *instrumental* style, where grief is experienced in more physical and mental reactions and expressed in more active modes. This perspective posits a number of influences that affect the grieving style of individuals, including culture, gender, socialization experiences, birth order, and temperament, among other factors. The critical point is that gender influences, but does not *determine*, grieving styles. Both men and women may, based on their different experiences and cultural backgrounds, exhibit either style. With this model, gender-based terminology is no longer used to describe the different ways individuals grieve. This perspective fits well with current attitudes that move away from seeking universal reactions to a more nuanced understanding of the individual pathways of grief.

References

Corr, C., Nabe, C., & Corr, D. (2009). *Death and dying, life and living* (6th ed). Belmont, CA: Wadesworth.

Golden, T. (1996). *Swallowed by a snake: The gift of the masculine side of healing.* Kensington, MD: Golden Healing Publishing.

LeGrand, L. (1986). *Coping with separation and loss as a young adult.* Springfield, IL: Charles C. Thomas.

Lund, D. (Ed.). (2000). *Men coping with grief.* Amityville, NY: Baywood.

Martin, T., & Doka, K. J. (1996). Masculine grief. In K. Doka (Ed.), *Living with grief after sudden loss: Suicide, homicide, accident, heart attack, stroke* (pp. 161–171). Washington, DC: Hospice Foundation of America.

Martin, T., & Doka, K. J. (1998). Revisiting masculine grief. In K. Doka & J. Davidson (Eds.), *Living with grief: Who we are, how we grieve.* Washington, DC: Hospice Foundation of America.

Martin, T., & Doka, K. J. (2000). *Men don't cry, women do: Transcending gender stereotypes of grief.* Philadelphia: Brunner/Mazel.

Staudacher, C. (1991). *Men and grief.* Oakland, CA: New Harbinger Publications.

Sue, D. W., & Sue, D. (2008). *Counseling the culturally diverse: Theory and practice* (5th ed). New York: John Wiley & Sons.

Aspects of Death, Grief, and Loss in Lesbian, Gay, Bisexual, and Transgender Communities

Brian de Vries

INTRODUCTION

Gordon Allport was an influential trait theorist often identified as the father of personality theory; he studied some of the many ways in which a person might be described and considered. He has been credited with saying that it may be useful to think of a person along the lines of how he or she is like all other persons, like some other persons, and like no other person (Allport, 1961). This view provides a framework of levels ranging from the level at which all people are seen as alike in some fundamental manner to a level at which no two persons share common attributes. For example, in many ways (such as our basic needs) and in many contexts (which may include the final act of dying), people may be much more alike than different; at the same time, our histories and the social and personal experiences we bring to the circumstances and times of our lives may be unlike any that have gone before or will follow. In between might be the familiar social organizations of life (such as the roles of culture and gender, among others) that render us comparable to some and different from others. This is a practical framework for considering the diversity of people and experiences.

In many ways, lesbian, gay, bisexual, and transgender (LGBT) persons are like heterosexual persons in their ways of living and dying; in other ways, they differ because of the social context in which their lives (and deaths) unfold; in still other ways, each LGBT person—every person—is a unique individual unlike anyone else and not defined by a single label or term. An authentic encounter with any person, particularly at salient and meaningful life junctures, necessarily begins at this unique level. The appreciation of singularity and uniqueness is joined by an understanding of the social forces and shared basic needs that render a complete image of a person. This is the context for the description of LGBT persons in this chapter and the comments on how various characteristics and circumstances can manifest in end-of-life experiences.

PARAMETERS OF THE NORTH AMERICAN LGBT POPULATION

Numbers matter, as the census reliably demonstrates; a dependable count of LGBT persons can help frame issues and tailor discussions (Smith & Gates, 2001). Estimates of the prevalence of LGBT persons in North American society vary dramatically; the variance is attributable to many factors, including important historical, cultural, and social factors. The legacy of stigma and discrimination endured by many in the LGBT communities may be associated with an age-related self-protective reticence to publicly identify—to come out—as an LGBT person, which is a necessary prerequisite to being counted.

For example, the oldest cohort of LGBT persons may recall and still recoil from the systematic persecution and destruction of lesbians and gay men, along with Jews and others deemed unworthy, under the inhumane Nazi regime. The cohort slightly younger than these elders remember and still live with having been labeled "sick" by those from whom they sought medical treatment; "immoral" by those from whom they sought spiritual guidance; "unfit" by those whose orders they were expected to obey and for whom they were willing to sacrifice their lives; and a "menace" by those empowered to maintain peace and justice for all (Kochman, 1997). A cohort younger still will recall that their expressions of love were "diagnosed" as a psychiatric disorder until 1973. Even today, lesbians and gay men in committed relationships are denied the opportunity to marry (with a few exceptions) and regularly endure public discussion of the "naturalness" and validity of their intimate relationships, which are somehow seen to threaten the "sanctity" of marriage and are the subject of intense debate, and threats and acts of constitutional exclusion in the United States.

Competing with social stigma as a challenge in addressing the numbers and needs of this population is the mutability of sexuality and the contested distinction between sexual orientation and gender identity (de Vries, 2007). Increasingly, the LGBT acronym is joined by Q for queer and questioning and I for intersex; moreover, a finer conceptualization of those who identify as transgender is emerging in the literature. For example, transgender persons include heterosexual, homosexual, and bisexual persons. They include persons who present as male or female in varying situations; they include persons who may be postoperative, preoperative (i.e., transitioning), or nonoperative male-to-female (MTF) or female-to-male (FTM) (Cook-Daniels, 2006). As Brian de Vries (2007) has pointed out, these additions to the lexicon and the deeper appreciations are themselves motivated by a variety of social forces, including age and cohort (e.g., the term *queer* is more commonly endorsed by younger rather than older gay men and lesbians [Adelman, Gurevitch, de Vries, & Blando, 2006], perhaps in the service of empowerment or to neutralize or claim a pejorative label); an increased attention to process (e.g., *questioning* reflects a more fluid appreciation of sexual experiences and categories); and advances in theory and the body of knowledge (e.g., the reframing and deeper understanding of those born with genitalia that are neither exclusively male nor female, now identified as *intersex*). In this way, history and biography intersect in encounters with LGBT persons and our understanding of this population.

Within these many and varied constraints, several estimates of prevalence have been offered: Cahill, South, and Spade (2000) propose that there may be between 10 and 15 million LGBT persons in the United States, disproportionately in urban centers (Appelbaum, 2008). Smith and Gates (2001) report that 99.3% of U.S. counties report at least one same-gender partnership household. Based on the estimates of Cahill and colleagues (2000), there may be between 2 and 6 million LGBT baby boomers in the United States and perhaps as many as 3 million LGBT persons ages 65 and older. These are numbers that matter and merit our attention.

Emergent Trends in Studies of LGBT Adults

The baby boom and older cohorts of LGBT persons have recently garnered some empirical attention. They are the first cohort to age and achieve later life as relatively openly identified members of a sexual minority (Beeler, Rawls, Herdt, & Cohler, 1999). Interestingly, research into LGBT aging had its beginnings in the 1970s with some of the pioneering work of Doug Kimmel (1977) and others. When AIDS was identified in the early 1980s, however, the very notion of "gay" and "aging" was questioned and even ridiculed (de Vries & Herdt, in press). Research attention shifted away from LGBT aging and normative development and instead explored how the LGBT communities in general and gay men and lesbians in particular rose to the challenge of caring for those dying of AIDS—at a time when many families, medical facilities, and governments shamefully retreated from their responsibilities. A host of studies have commented on the almost incomprehensible losses endured by lesbians and especially gay men at this time and the enduring legacy of the trauma. Martin and Dean (1993) compare the AIDS experience to "previously studied stressors, such as the experiences of concentration camp survivors and soldiers in combat" (p. 323). Schwartzberg (1992) perceptively writes:

> The enormity of loss in the gay community has a secondary, cumulative effect that is greater than the sum total of the various deaths: It creates an unavoidable climate of loss to the community as a whole...survivors [grieve] not only for their most personal losses, but also for all the victims, for strangers and for the loss of community and culture (p. 424).

We can still use this context to consider the experiences of midlife and older LGBT persons and their approaches to their later and final years.

The vast majority of research has focused on gay men and, to a somewhat lesser extent, lesbians. Bisexuals are often named but rarely included in research studies (Dworkin, 2006); intersex and transgender persons have similarly been neglected in research and analyses. The body of empirical data in this developing literature derives largely from community-based studies. Few national studies exist, with some exceptions (e.g., AIDS-related research, the MetLife study mentioned below), owing to sampling and identification problems and the exclusion of LGBT as a minority category in federally funded research. In contrast, many urban communities have become cognizant of the issues affecting their elders (perhaps modeled on community responses to the AIDS pandemic), resulting in dozens of local surveys that attempt to describe some of the unique needs of aging LGBT individuals. The needs assessment studies suggest the particular resources and challenges of these people—a valuable compilation in the absence of comparable national data (de Vries, 2006).

Several consistent themes emerge from these reports and others that speak to the social context, needs, lives, and approaches to death of LGBT adults. For example, the LGBT samples as a whole tend to be more highly educated than the broader (presumably primarily heterosexual) community from which they were selected (often compared with census data). Black, Gates, Sanders, and Taylor (2000) have reported similar findings from larger and more representative samples. If education can be seen as a proxy for problem solving, solution seeking, and action taking, as Lopata (1993) has suggested, such data provide some optimism. These data can also be seen as supporting the concept of crisis competence introduced by Kimmel (1979). Kimmel proposed that, compared with heterosexual men and women, older gay men and lesbians may be better suited to cope with age-related changes, having survived years of being homosexual in a homophobic society. Those who survived adopted a stance along the lines of "that which doesn't kill or hurt us will ultimately make us stronger" (de Vries and Herdt, in press). It is worth noting that others have challenged this perspective. Lee (1991), for example, cautions that such proposals of "extraordinary aging" may be misleading in that they might lead researchers to overlook the realities of aging among persons who have remained hidden to social research. The MetLife study of 1,000 LGBT baby boomers (i.e., between the ages of 40 and 61), probably the first national sample of this cohort, asked if being LGBT helped prepare for later life in any way—probably one of the first and certainly one of the few surveys to explicitly examine the notion of crisis competence. In response, nearly 4 out of 10 respondents said they have developed positive character traits, greater resilience, or better support networks as a consequence of being LGBT (MetLife Mature Market Institute, 2006).

Surprisingly—and, again, as reported in larger surveys and reviews (Badgett, 1998)—the income levels of the LGBT persons surveyed at the community level are mostly quite comparable to those of the local census comparison residents, even with the higher levels of education. Such data challenge persistent myths proclaiming LGBT persons as members of an affluent North American elite: "Lesbian, gay, and bisexual people are spread throughout the range of household income distribution, just as heterosexual people are" (Badgett, 1998, p. 15).

The financial resources available to these lesbians and gay men may be further limited by the fact that many of them are without partners or living alone. Several surveys (reported in de Vries, 2006) found that, on average, as many as half of lesbian and gay respondents report their relationship status as single—often with very sizable gender differences. For example, in our San Francisco Bay Area study (Adelman et al., 2006), among those ages 65 and older, almost three-quarters of gay men and almost half of lesbians reported their relationship status as single. For gay men in particular, these data are almost a literal inverse of the proportion of married heterosexual men (which Tamborini [2007] reports as just under 74%). Additionally, 24% of gay men over the age of 65 and just over 19% of lesbians in the study live alone; these proportions are also much higher than those for comparable heterosexual persons, particularly for men. These comparisons neatly articulate distinctions that must be drawn, not only on the basis of sexual orientation and gender, but also between relationship status and living arrangement. The two are not synonymous, for either LGBT or heterosexual persons.

In addition to the economic issues of being single and living alone, there are significant social, health, and caregiving implications. These may be exacerbated by the higher incidence of childlessness in LGBT populations, although this childless (or child-free; see Seccombe, 1991) status is certainly not restricted to LGBT adults. From the surveys mentioned above, the majority of older (i.e., ages 65 and over) gay men and lesbians (roughly two-thirds of those surveyed) do *not* have children, compared with an estimated 10% of older presumably heterosexual Americans. Gay men are less likely than lesbians to have children (an estimated 25% of gay men and 55% of lesbians reported that they have at least one child). The gerontological literature has proposed the principle of substitution (Shanas, 1979) in its heteronormative consideration of caregiving: Those in need of care first turn to their spouse and adult children; only when these options do not exist or have been exhausted are more distant family and then friends considered. But in the absence of a spouse or children, to whom do people turn?

This question was frequently posed in the surveys, and many respondents said they would turn to friends. For example, in our Bay Area study we found that more than 20% of gay men and just under 10% of lesbians would turn exclusively to their friends in times of need. An additional 25% of gay men and over 40% of lesbians would include friends in combination with others. Comparable proportions were noted in other community-based samples. These large numbers suggest important connections that are infrequently considered in caregiving literature and policy. Sadly, several studies noted sizable numbers of respondents who were unable to identify someone on whom they might call; these estimates ranged from 10% to almost 25%.

Social services were sometimes mentioned; however, many respondents commented on previous negative interactions with social services and the medical community, attributable to sexual orientation insensitivity on the part of service providers (18% in one study); additionally, as many as 25% of respondents reported not being "out" to their providers or rarely discussing sexual orientation with their providers (de Vries, 2006)—justifiably, in some instances. For example, the Gay and Lesbian Medical Association (GLMA) (n.d.) cited a study in which more than 40% of nursing students thought that lesbian, gay, and bisexual persons should keep their sexuality private; between 5% and 12% of these nursing students found LGB persons "disgusting." In the MetLife study (2006), 19% of the respondents said they have little or no confidence that medical personnel will treat them with dignity and respect as LGBT people in old age.

The negative experiences of LGBT adults in North American healthcare settings (Brotman, Ryan, & Cormier, 2003) have made many of them hesitant to seek out healthcare services (Harrison & Silenzio, 1996); discriminatory experiences have also led to a negative evaluation of the delivery of such services (Kaufman & Raphael, 1996). Also, owing to the lack of recognition of same-sex relationships and the inability to marry in most states and federally, LGBT persons—especially lesbians and transgender persons—tend to be overrepresented among the medically uninsured—further limiting access and delaying care (GLMA, n.d.). When LGBT support and services are available— still rare, and certainly an urban phenomenon—they tend to be well used (Quam & Whitford, 1992) and evaluated more positively (Jacobs, Rasmussen, & Hohman, 1999).

The MetLife study (2006) also inquired about end-of-life issues. Just over half of these 1,000 LGBT boomers have not prepared living wills or advance healthcare directives, documents spelling out the healthcare decisions they would want made for them should they become incapacitated. Only about two in five (43%) have assigned decision-making authority to someone else through a legal document such as a durable power of attorney or a healthcare proxy. For LGBT persons, these legal and financial preparations for the end of life take on particular importance in a culture that does not acknowledge the vital role of chosen, nontraditional families (e.g., friends) and largely does not offer same-sex couples the rights enjoyed by traditional families and married couples. These surveys and data characterize an understudied population and suggest some of the particular needs and issues that call for attention at life's end. What follows is an exploration of these issues and implications for those whose work will bring them into contact with LGBT persons who are dying or grieving and seeking support.

Providing Sensitive Care

It is worth noting at the outset that the LGBT boomer and older populations comprise women and men who have had significant experience with death, directly or indirectly. In our focus group research in San Francisco, for example, late-middle-aged gay men recalled attending almost weekly funerals for friends and loved ones who died from AIDS. One gay man poignantly noted that he stopped counting the funerals he attended and the friends who had died after the number reached 50. Martin and Dean (1993) commented that two important aspects of the epidemiology of AIDS-related bereavement are the experience of multiple losses and the occurrence of chronic bereavement. They found that almost 30% of their sample of bereaved gay men had experienced two or more deaths (of lovers, former lovers, or close friends) within a 12-month period in 1987, and nearly half of the sample had experienced three or more deaths (not including deaths of social network members, acquaintances, or friends of friends). The extent to which these cultural and historical death experiences will present themselves when these women and men face their own deaths remains to be seen.

Later life may bring with it some unique physical and mental health issues for LGBT persons. Herdt and Kertzner (2006) reported evidence of higher levels of depression and psychological distress among midlife and older lesbians and gay men, which they attributed to the accumulation of a lifetime of stigma. Barker (2004) comments that older lesbian and bisexual women may suffer an exacerbation of prevalence, earlier onset, and manifestation of common disorders. Health issues for some transgender persons are complicated by the interaction of the aging body with the introduction of hormones for those who have transitioned from one gender to another. Many persons who have undergone surgery or other procedures to bring their physical bodies in line with the gender they identify with have had long-term introduction of hormones; the outcomes of the interaction of these hormones with the aging body (and with some chronic conditions that might accompany aging) are as yet undetermined and undocumented.

Several recent publications aim to help healthcare providers and others offer a safer and more welcoming environment for LGBT clients (e.g., "Guidelines for the Care of Lesbian, Gay, Bisexual and Transgender Patients" [GLMA, n.d.]). Acquaviva (2006) began a similar effort with respect to hospice care and LGBT persons as part of the American Society on Aging's constituent group, LGBT Aging Issues Network, and its quarterly newsletter *Outword*. The efforts share many features, including the overall goal of informing professionals about the issues involved in working sensitively with dying and grieving LGBT clients, and designing programs and interventions that are welcoming, accepting, and appropriate.

A program can signal its welcoming environment in the media and through participation in LGBT events, such as LGBT Pride festivals, which are typically held in June. An inclusive environment shows sexual and racial diversity in the images it presents (e.g., same-sex couples pictured in brochures or on posters), displays brochures and posters from LGBT organizations at its office, and includes LGBT-friendly symbols (such as the rainbow flag) on its website (GLMA, n.d.). Attention should be paid to expressions of faith and spiritual beliefs, as some of these expressions may not affirm the identity of the LGBT person.

Acquaviva (2006) writes that since hospice services are predominantly provided at home "and include the family as the unit of care, hospice may be an intimidating type of care for LGBT elders who are not fully open about their sexual orientation or gender identity" (p. 1). Even among the generally "out" respondents to the MetLife survey (most were invited to participate on the basis of prior disclosure of sexual orientation), only 34% said they are out to everyone. The overwhelming majority (87%) are out to their closest friends, but one-third or more have not disclosed their sexual orientation to other significant people in their lives, including family members, coworkers, and neighbors. More than one-third of participants have not revealed their sexual orientation to their healthcare providers—the medical personnel on whom they are likely to rely increasingly as they age. These are significant and important proportions to consider; the act of disclosure is an act of trust, and it is neither immediate nor necessarily predictable.

The lack of disclosure compromises the authenticity of the setting; the norms and presumptions of heterosexuality and the "family-centrism" that pervades societal institutions can exclude (or at least not invite) the LGBT elder (Cahill, 2002). A fear of potential rejection or disrespect by staff may lead some LGBT persons to avoid hospice and related services (Acquaviva, 2006). On the other hand, older LGBT persons who have struggled to come out and live openly in a frequently hostile environment "often find themselves having to go back into hiding when they begin to require healthcare services" (Brotman et al., 2003, p. 193). Suspicion and fear of discrimination are real and strong, and a culturally competent staff will be sensitive to these issues. Intake and informational forms should be inclusive, using terms such as "relationship status" rather than "marital status" and "partner" in lieu of or in addition to "spouse." In general, care should be taken to avoid assumptions about sexual partnerships and sexual behaviors.

It is also important to recognize the nontraditional systems of support constructed by LGBT persons in their communities. The families that LGBT persons create, either in lieu of or in addition to their biological families (Weston, 1991)—what Maupin (2007) refers to as "logical kin"—are often not recognized and honored by those outside these intimate circles (de Vries & Hoctel, 2007). Friends figure prominently in these creative social arrangements. "Family" should not be assumed; patients and those who seek the services of hospice and other programs should be asked to identify those with whom a "family-like" relationship has been established or maintained. As with any admission into hospice or palliative care, care must be taken to determine the person(s) with authority to make decisions in the event that the patient is unable to communicate or make such a decision him- or herself. As Acquaviva (2006) notes, this process is more complicated for persons in a same-sex partnership, because in most instances the patient's partner is not automatically afforded the legal authority guaranteed to partners in heterosexual marriages.

Agencies should work vigorously to encourage members of the LGBT community to complete advance directive, care planning, and associated legal documents. In the absence of such documents, conflicts may arise between biological and chosen kin, especially if the patient has been estranged from his or her family of origin (a situation that may be rooted in the family's beliefs and perspectives on homosexuality).

These issues are most dramatically illustrated among transgender persons, as Witten (2006) comments. Gender changes can disrupt families and create estrangement; marital couples have to redefine their relationship if they want to remain together, and this redefinition may not be public or accepted by others in their environment. Perhaps more than LGB persons, transgender persons may rely on significant others, friends, and allies for support near the end of life. Transgender persons may feel particularly mournful for the life experiences they missed during the years they lived in their natal gender; and issues of disclosure, isolation, and healthcare needs may be especially salient given an apparent mismatch between genital anatomy and gender of presentation (Witten, 2006). After the death of a transgender person, those grieving and carrying out final wishes may encounter additional challenges, ranging from the gender listed on the death certificate (which may not match the gender lived by the deceased) to the presentation of the body in a funeral (occasioning conflict with those for whom the transition from one gender to the other remains unresolved).

CONCLUSION

In some ways, LGBT end-of-life issues and concerns about the services needed and delivered do not differ from those of other groups: All persons deserve comfort, care, and compassion at the end of life. In other ways, many of the issues discussed in this chapter are shared by people outside the LGBT community—those who are restricted by a particular relationship status (i.e., unmarried or domestic partnerships); parental status (e.g., childless or child-free); or some other social construct. But in yet other ways, the cumulative effects of stigmatization and the legacy of discrimination endured by people who live outside heterosexual and traditional family norms and ideals create unique issues throughout and at the end of life for LGBT persons. Studying these particular contexts and experiences, as well as the source and type of care LGBT persons need and receive, is a necessary prerequisite to the development of appropriately tailored services. Such efforts may ultimately benefit all (de Vries & Blando, 2004). The consideration of LGBT lives and end-of-life experiences may have much to contribute to our understanding of dying, death, grief, and bereavement in general by encouraging us to question our assumptions and reframe our ideas—ultimately fostering a more holistic and inclusive environment for the care and support of all persons at the end of life.

Brian de Vries, PhD, is professor of gerontology at San Francisco State University. He received his doctorate in life span developmental psychology from the University of British Columbia in 1988 and was a postdoctoral fellow at Simon Fraser University in Vancouver and the University of Southern California. He is a fellow of the Gerontological Society of America, member of the leadership council of the American Society on Aging, and cochair of the LGBT Aging Issues Network. Recently, he became a policy advisor for AARP California. He is editor of the journal Sexuality Research and Social Policy *and former associate editor of the* International Journal of Aging and Human Development *(2000–2006). He has edited four books:* Kinship Bereavement in Later Life, End of Life Issues, Narrative Gerontology, *and* Gay and Lesbian Aging; *authored or co-authored more than 75 journal articles and book chapters; and given more than 100 presentations to professional audiences on a variety of topics.*

References

Acquaviva, K. D. (2006). Providing hospice care to LGBT elders. *Outword, 13*(1), 1–6.

Adelman, M., Gurevitch, J., de Vries, B., & Blando, J. (2006). Openhouse: Community building and research in the LGBT aging population. In D. Kimmel, T. Rose, & S. David (Eds.), *Lesbian, gay, bisexual, and transgender aging: Research and clinical perspectives* (pp. 247–264). New York: Columbia University Press.

Allport, G. (1961). *Pattern and growth in personality.* New York: Holt, Rinehart, & Winston.

Appelbaum, J. S. (2008). Late adulthood and aging: Clinical approaches. In H. J. Makadon, K. H. Mayer, J. Potter, & H. Goldhammer (Eds.), *Fenway guide to lesbian, gay, bisexual and transgender health* (pp. 135–156). Washington, DC: American College of Physicians.

Badgett, L. (1998). *Income inflation: The myth of affluence among gay, lesbian, and bisexual Americans.* Washington, DC: Policy Institute, National Gay and Lesbian Task Force, and the Institute for Gay and Lesbian Strategic Studies. Retrieved January 10, 2008, from http://thetaskforce.org/downloads/reports/reports/IncomeInflationMyth.pdf

Barker, J. C. (2004). Lesbian aging: An agenda for social research. In G. Herdt & B. de Vries (Eds.), *Gay and lesbian aging: Research and future directions* (pp. 29–72). New York: Springer.

Beeler, J. A., Rawls, T. D., Herdt, G., & Cohler, B. J. (1999). The needs of older lesbians and gay men in Chicago. *Journal of Gay and Lesbian Social Services, 9*(1), 31–49.

Black, D., Gates, G., Sanders, S., & Taylor, L. (2000). Demographics of the gay and lesbian population in the United States: Evidence from available systematic data sources. *Demography, 37,* 139–154.

Brotman, S., Ryan, B., & Cormier, R. (2003). The health and social service needs of gay and lesbian elders and their families in Canada. *The Gerontologist, 43,* 192–202.

Cahill, S. (2002). Long-term care issues affecting gay, lesbian, bisexual and transgender elders. *Geriatric Care Management Journal, 12,* 4–8.

Cahill, S., South, K., & Spade, J. (2000). *Outing age: Public policy issues affecting gay, lesbian, bisexual, and transgender elders.* Washington, DC: Policy Institute, National Gay and Lesbian Task Force.

Cook-Daniels, L. (2006). Trans aging. In D. Kimmel, T. Rose, & S. David (Eds.), *Lesbian, gay, bisexual, and transgender aging: Research and clinical perspectives.* New York: Columbia University Press.

de Vries, B. (2006). Home at the end of the rainbow: Supportive housing for LGBT elders. *Generations, 29*(4), 65–70.

de Vries, B. (2007). LGBT couples in later life: A study in diversity. *Generations, 31*(3), 18–23.

de Vries, B., & Blando, J. A. (2004). The study of gay and lesbian lives: Lessons for social gerontology. In G. Herdt & B. de Vries (Eds.), *Gay and lesbian aging: Research and future directions* (pp. 3–28). New York: Springer.

de Vries, B., & Herdt, G. (in press). Gay men and aging. In T. M. Witten, (Ed.), *Handbook of GLBTI aging.* Baltimore: Johns Hopkins Press.

de Vries, B., & Hoctel, P. (2007). The family friends of older gay men and lesbians. In N. Teunis & G. Herdt (Eds.), *Sexual inequalities: Case studies from the field* (pp. 213–232). Berkeley: University of California Press.

Dworkin, S. H. (2006). The aging bisexual: The invisible of the invisible minority. In D. Kimmel, T. Rose, & S. David (Eds.), *Lesbian, gay, bisexual, and transgender aging: Research and clinical perspectives* (pp. 37–52). New York: Columbia University Press.

Gay and Lesbian Medical Association. (n.d.). *Guidelines for the care of lesbian, gay, bisexual and transgender patients.* Available from http://ce54.citysoft.com/_data/n_0001/resources/live/GLMA%20guidelines%202006%20FINAL.pdf

Harrison, A. E., & Silenzio, V. M. (1996). Comprehensive care of lesbian and gay patients and families. *Primary Care: Models of Ambulatory Care, 23,* 31–46.

Herdt, G., & Kertzner, R. (2006). I do, but I can't: The impact of marriage denial on the mental health and sexual citizenship of lesbians and gay men in the United States. *Sexuality Research and Social Policy, 3*(1), 33–49.

Jacobs, R., Rasmussen, L., & Hohman, M. (1999). The social support needs of older lesbians, gay men, and bisexuals. *Journal of Gay and Lesbian Social Services, 9*(1), 1–30.

Kaufman, G., & Raphael, L. (1996). *Coming out of shame: Transforming gay and lesbian lives.* New York: Doubleday.

Kimmel, D. C. (1977). Psychotherapy and the older gay man. *Psychotherapy: Theory, Research, and Practice, 14,* 386–393.

Kimmel, D. C. (1979). Life history interviews of aging gay men. *International Journal of Aging and Human Development, 10*(3), 239–248.

Kochman, A. (1997). Gay and lesbian elderly: Historical overview and implications for social work practice. In J. Quam (Ed.), *Social services for senior gay men and lesbians* (pp. 1–25). New York: Haworth Press.

Lee, J. A. (1991). Foreword. In J. A. Lee (Ed.), *Gay midlife and maturity.* New York: Haworth Press.

Lopata, H. Z. (1993). The support system of American urban widows. In M. S. Stroebe, W. Stroebe, and R. O. Hansson (Eds.), *Handbook of bereavement: Theory, research, and intervention* (pp. 381–396). New York: Cambridge University Press.

Martin, J. L., & Dean, L. (1993). Bereavement following death from AIDS: Unique problems, reactions, and special needs. In M. S. Stroebe, W. Stroebe, & R. O. Hansson (Eds.), *Handbook of bereavement: Theory, research, and intervention* (pp. 315–330). New York: Cambridge University Press.

Maupin, A. (2007). *Michael Tolliver lives.* San Francisco, CA: HarperCollins.

MetLife Mature Market Institute. (2006). *Out and aging: The MetLife study of lesbian and gay baby boomers.* New York: MetLife Mature Market Institute.

Quam, J. K., & Whitford, G. S. (1992). Adaptation and age-related expectations of older gay and lesbian adults. *The Gerontologist, 32,* 367–374.

Schwartzberg, S. (1992). AIDS-related bereavement among gay men: The inadequacy of current theories of grief. *Psychotherapy, 29,* 422–429.

Seccombe, K. (1991). Assessing the costs and benefits of children: Gender comparisons among childfree husbands and wives. *Journal of Marriage and the Family, 53*(1), 191–202.

Shanas, E. (1979). The family as a social support system in old age. *The Gerontologist, 9*(2), 169–174.

Smith, D. M., & Gates, G. J. (2001). Gay and lesbian families in the United States: Same-sex unmarried partner households: A preliminary analysis of 2000 United States Census data: A Human Rights Campaign report. Retrieved from http://www.urban.org/UploadedPDF/1000491_gl_partner_households.pdf

Tamborini, C. R. (2007). The never-married in old age: Projections and concerns for the future. Washington, DC: U.S. Social Security Administration, Office of Policy. Retrieved from http://ssa.gov/policy/docs/ssb/v67n2/v67n2p25.html

Weston, K. (1991). *Families we choose: Lesbians, gays, kinship*. New York: Columbia University Press.

Witten, T. M. (2006). Transgender elders and their caregivers face unique issues regarding the end of life. *Outword, 13*(1), 3–7.

Index

M

N

Y

Z